Developing
poverty

Developing poverty

The State,
Labor Market Deregulation,
and the Informal Economy
in Costa Rica and
the Dominican Republic

José Itzigsohn

The Pennsylvania State University Press
University Park, Pennsylvania

Library of Congress Cataloging-in-Publication Data

Itzigsohn, José, 1960–
　　Developing poverty : the state, labor market deregulation, and the informal economy in Costa Rica and the Dominican Republic / José Itzigsohn.
　　　p.　　cm.
　　Includes bibliographical references and index.
　　ISBN 0-271-02027-X (cloth : alk. paper)
　　ISBN 0-271-02028-8 (pbk. : alk. paper)
　　1. Informal sector (Economics)—Costa Rica.　1. Informal sector (Economics)—Dominican Republic.　3. Labor market—Costa Rica.　4. Labor market—Dominican Republic.　I. Title.

HD2346.C8 I89 2000
338.98—dc21

　　　　　　　　　　　　　　　　　　　　　　　　　　　　　　　　　　99-05443

Copyright © 2000 The Pennsylvania State University
All rights reserved
Printed in the United States of America
Published by The Pennsylvania State University Press,
University Park, PA 16802-1003

It is the policy of The Pennsylvania State University Press to use acid-free paper for the first printing of all clothbound books. Publications on uncoated stock satisfy the minimum requirements of American National Standard for Information Sciences—Permanence of Paper for Printed Library Materials, ANSI Z39.48–1992.

To my parents

Contents

	Figure and Tables	ix
	Preface and Acknowledgments	xi
1	The Limits of Development and the Informal Economy	1
2	Comparing Development Histories	29
3	Industrialization, Regulatory Regimes, and Labor Absorption	61
4	Labor Market Regulation and Labor Market Segmentation	87
5	The Organization of Informal Production	125
6	The Informal Economy, Poverty, and Social Policy	153
7	Toward an Informal Future?	169
	Bibliography	181
	Index	193

Figure and Tables

Figure
1.1 Dimensions of Regulatory Regimes   22

Tables
2.1 Some Indicators of Socioeconomic Development in
     Costa Rica and the Dominican Republic   31
2.2 Two Leading Exports as Percentage of Total Export Value
     for Costa Rica and the Dominican Republic, 1955–1985   32
2.3 Real GDP per Capita in Costa Rica and the Dominican
     Republic, 1950–1988   33
2.4 GDP and GDP per Capita Rates of Growth for Costa Rica
     and the Dominican Republic, 1960–1988   34
2.5 Agriculture and Manufacturing Shares of GDP in Costa Rica
     and the Dominican Republic, 1950–1990   35
2.6 Sectoral Distribution of the Labor Force, 1950–1980   36
3.1 Labor Absorption in Costa Rica and the Dominican Republic
     During the Import-Substitution Period   67
3.2 Trends in Urban Labor Absorption in Costa Rica and the
     Dominican Republic During the ISI Period   69
3.3 Evolution of Urban Employment by Occupational Categories
     in the Dominican Republic and Costa Rica During the 1980s   71
3.4 Evolution of the Labor Market in Santo Domingo in the 1980s   72
3.5 Evolution of the Labor Market in San José in the 1980s   74
3.6 Summary of the Labor Market Trends in Costa Rica and the
     Dominican Republic Under Two Development Models   84

Figure and Tables

4.1 Basic Demographic Characteristics of the Sample 93
4.2 Distribution of Employment by Occupational Categories and Mean Income of Occupational Categories 95
4.3 Structure of the Labor Market in San José and Santo Domingo 115
4.4 Independent Variables Included in Multivariate Analyses 117
4.5 OLS Regression of the Logarithm of Personal Income on Personal, Family, and Occupational Variables 119
4.6 Multinomial Logit Regressions of Occupational Categories 122
5.1 Typology of Forms of Commodity Chains of Informal Firms 129
5.2 Semistructured Interviews by Trade and City 130

Preface and Acknowledgments

This book is an attempt to deal with some issues that have puzzled me in the study of development: issues about the origin and presence of large informal economies, the capacity of the state to affect the development process, and the limits imposed on the state by its position in the world economy and the interstate system. First, I try to address one of the key paradoxes of the process of peripheral industrialization. Modernization and economic growth do not lead to the universalization of wage employment but rather are accompanied by the emergence of a large informal economy. In Latin America, decades of fast growth and industrialization were not enough to absorb the entire urban labor force into formal employment. This process was made worse by two decades of structural adjustment that brought with it a downgrading of employment for the labor markets of the region. In this book, I link different theoretical approaches to the study of informal economic activities—approaches that focus on labor market regulations, state institutions, and peripheral industrialization—and I attempt to present new elements in the analysis of the structure and dynamics of the informal economy.

A second puzzle has to do with the role of the state in the development process and in regulating labor markets. The postwar developmentalist project placed its hopes on the state as the guide of the industrialization process, hopes that soon proved false. During the last two decades, the hegemony of neoliberalism and the acknowledgment of "globalization" processes have transformed the state into either a villain or an irrelevant institution. I think that the demise of the state is, for now, greatly exaggerated; yet the question is still open as to what results the state institutional intervention in the economy can accomplish. In this book, I try to appraise the possibilities and limits for the

Preface and Acknowledgments

state's institutional agency. I focus on how development policies and labor market regulations structure labor markets and the informal economy.

I have found theoretical guidance to address the role of the state in institutional approaches that attempt to "bring the state back in." However, my own "upbringing" in the broad field of world-system analysis made me feel uneasy with purely institutional answers that do not account for world-systemic constraints. On the other hand, world-system analysis did not give me the tools necessary to deal with middle-range processes and local institutional histories and developments, which were the focus of my interest. This book attempts to bring these two approaches to bear on the analysis of the informal economy; the goal is to establish the scope of and limits to state agency in structuring labor markets in the constraints of the world economy and the interstate system.

Many people and institutions helped to make this book possible. In Costa Rica and the Dominican Republic, I had the invaluable institutional support of Facultad Latinoamericana de Ciencias Sociales (FLACSO) and the researchers and staff, and I owe them a debt of gratitude. In particular, without the help and support of Juan Pablo Pérez Sáinz and Rafael Menjívar Larín in San José and Wilfredo Lozano and Rafael Durán in Santo Domingo, this study would not have been possible. Several microenterprise development agencies opened their doors to me, shared their experiences and ideas, and helped me with my initial contacts. In Santo Domingo, I benefited from the assistance of Asociación para Desarrollo de la Microempresa (ADEMI), Fundación Dominicana de Desarrollo, FONDOMICRO, and Instituto Dominicano de Desarrollo Integral. In San José, AVANCE, Fundación Acción Ya, and Sector Social Productivo (an agency that does not exist anymore) helped me with my research. Although they may not agree with my conclusions, their help was invaluable in completing this project.

Several colleagues and friends helped me in completing this book. Carlos Dore introduced me to the details and complexities of Dominican society and history. I listened fascinated to his "oral history" of the Dominican Republic during many hours and over countless cups of coffee. He was also kind enough to listen to and comment on my ideas. Alejandro Portes taught me most of what I know about sociological research and supported this project from the beginning. Mario Lungo, Mariam Pérez, and Rick Tardanico provided valuable help for the completion of my research. Calvin Goldscheider, Paget Henry, Jim Mahoney, Suzanne Oboler, María Elena García, and Richard Schauffler read several drafts of the chapters and provided valuable comments. They have contributed greatly to improving the manuscript. The responsibility for the content—and the mistakes—is, of course, solely mine. Richard Schauffler and María Elena García provided invaluable help in putting this manuscript into "standard English." I also want to acknowledge those who made this research materially possible. The survey presented in this book was financed by grants from the Ford and Mellon Foundations. My fieldwork was financed by a doctoral research grant from the Program in Comparative International Development at the Department of Sociology of the Johns Hopkins University.

More than anyone else, I owe a debt of gratitude to the informal microentrepreneurs and workers who talked to me about their experiences, answered my questions, and allowed me to look at their daily lives. This book would not have been possible without their collaboration, and I hope that I can give back to them, through this discussion, a bit of what they gave me. Many times during my interviews and observations, people wanted to know what benefits they could gain from this project. Sometimes they told me that they hoped my work could help them get access to credit or that it could help them sell their products. I was always clear that this was an academic study and that there was really nothing I could offer in terms of credit or markets. After a short while, I began all interviews with this line. I hope, however, that I was, at least to a small extent, wrong. I hope that this book contributes to our understanding of the dynamics of the informal economy and perhaps in that way, to the development of better policies toward the informal economy and informal microenterprises.

1

The Limits of Development and the Informal Economy

Picture in your mind the workshop of a jewelry craftsman in Santo Domingo. A cramped, small room holds a few tools and some working materials. Three workers are engaged in different stages of jewelry production. All are skilled craftsmen who work there temporarily, when the owner has orders for jewelry. Each is paid by the piece. Asked if they would rather work in a large factory for a regular wage, they answer that they can make more money by working in a number of casual jobs than in a regular job. Moreover, at the jeweler's, they work at their own pace. In a yard in front of the workshop are some scattered auto parts. This workshop not only makes jewelry: In times of slack demand, the owner transforms it into an auto body shop. This snapshot of the world of work in Latin American cities provides a window through which we can begin to approach this world, a world very different from that imagined by the promoters of development and industrialization policies.

This book deals with a well-known paradox of the development process in the periphery of the world system: Modernization, industrialization, and high rates of economic growth do not translate into universal formal employment. Despite rapid industrial growth, a large number of people in Latin American and Caribbean cities make their living in the informal economy. This book looks at how the people involved in the informal economy subsist and thrive and how state policies affect their economic life chances. It examines the effects of state labor regulations on the organization of the informal economy and the structure of labor markets.

As far as labor is concerned, the history of modern capitalism is the history of the proletarianization of the labor force. Capitalism brought an epochal change in the ways production is organized and the labor force is used. The history of work under capitalism is a gradual but constant shift from production organized through the use of coerced labor, household labor, and petty commodity production toward the expansion of production organized around the use of wage labor, labor "bought and sold" in labor markets. The expansion of modern industry and services was a key stepping stone in this process. This process of universalizing proletarianization, however, was always offset by the pervasiveness and constant re-creation of other forms of using labor, such as household labor and petty commodity production. The informal economy is an expression of the historical process of partial proletarianization (Smith and Wallerstein 1992; Tilly and Tilly 1998).

The issue of labor absorption into wage employment in developing countries figured prominently in the development debates between scholars and policymakers in the post–World War II period. Development theories and policies predicted that industrialization would lead to the gradual absorption of the labor force into formal wage employment (Lewis 1954; Ranis 1989). This prediction was soon proved wrong. In spite of impressive rates of growth in the modern manufacturing and service sectors, large segments of the urban population became part of informal economies. Moreover, under the current neoliberal model of development, the boundaries that differentiate formal from informal employment are increasingly blurred.

This book analyzes the effects of state policies on the structure of labor markets and informal economies in Latin America. It focuses on four areas that are key to understanding the functioning of Latin American informal economies: (1) the historical evolution of formal and informal employment under peripheral industrialization; (2) the linkages between formal and informal economic activities; (3) labor market segmentation and mobility; and (4) informal microentrepreneurs' strategies for subsistence or accumulation. These four areas provide a multilayered view of the informal economy, a view that encompasses three levels of analysis: a macro-level look at the broad trends in labor absorption, a middle-level view of labor market segmentation and the linkages of informal and formal firms, and a micro-level analysis of the growth potential of informal microenterprises and the logic of action of informal economic actors. The following chapters investigate how different state policies affect the structure and dynamics of each of these areas.

To analyze the effects of different state policies and institutions, I compare the above-mentioned processes in two countries, Costa Rica and the Dominican Republic, by exploring the informal economies of their capitals—San José and Santo Domingo. Comparisons pose multiple problems about the appropriateness of the comparative designs and the generalization of their results (problems addressed in Chapter 2). It is in fact difficult to speak about a generalized Latin American experience in any area of social research. Each country has its peculiar characteristics, and there are a large number of differences among the various Latin American countries. Still, comparisons and generalizations are possible and indispensable for the advancement of knowledge on social processes. It is necessary, however, to specify the theoretical and conceptual parameters that give meaning and specificity to the comparative enterprise.

What allows the comparison of Costa Rica and the Dominican Republic—and a cautious generalization of our results to other Latin American countries—is the fact that they are part of the periphery of the world system. Both countries share a similar insertion in the world economy, and both countries followed parallel development paths, yet they differ in the ways in which the respective states intervened in the development process, particularly in the areas of social policy and labor market regulation. The systematic comparison of these two cases allows us to reach some general conclusions about the evolution of informal economies and about the effects that state policies and institutions can have in the context of peripheral capitalism.

The institutional capacity of the state is at the center of this analysis. Yet, states as institutional actors are constrained by their position in the world economy and interstate system. This study combines institutional and world systems in the exploration of the possibilities of and limits to the institutional action of peripheral states in the world system. The remainder of this chapter develops the analytical tools necessary for this task. First, I present the different paradigms of thinking about the informal economy. Second, I discuss the question of state regulation of the labor market and introduce the concept of regulatory regimes. Finally, I address some methodological problems in the empirical study of the informal economy.

The Meandering Evolution of an Elusive Concept

Much has been written about the informal economy. Many scholars from different theoretical persuasions have analyzed this pervasive phenomenon and have created many definitions of the informal economy and many explanations of its origin. Therefore, to say something meaningful about the informal economy, it is necessary first to define it precisely. Moreover, to say something new about informal economies, it is necessary to locate the definition of the concept in the existing field of studies on informal economies and show that a new study can advance our understanding of such a debated topic. For this reason, it is necessary to trace the meandering history of this concept.

The concept of the informal economy has gone through several transformations. When first confronted with the results of peripheral industrialization, Latin American sociologists elaborated the concept of *marginality*, attempting to capture the reality of peripheral cities, where large masses of people subsisted outside the circuits of formal employment (Kay 1989; Quijano 1974). The concept of marginality presented a dualistic image of Third World cities, with a privileged segment of the population participating in the modern economy and large masses engaged in "traditional" subsistence activities, detached from the modern sector. This conceptualization, however, failed to capture the multiple linkages of the "marginal" people to the rest of the urban economy. Research on Third World cities proved that so-called marginal people in fact participated in the urban economy in multiple ways (Lomnitz 1975; Perlman 1976; Portes 1983; Roberts 1995).

The concept of marginality was superseded by the concept of the *informal economy*. Keith Hart (1973) coined the term in his study of the urban economy of Accra, Ghana. For Hart, the informal economy consisted of all the economic activities that provided a subsistence living for the urban poor who made a living outside formal wage labor relations. His seminal study conceptualized the formal and informal sectors as separated segments of the urban economy, engaged in trade relations with each other. Hart's introduction of the concept and the ensuing debate about labor absorption in Third World cities raised important questions as to characteristics of the informal economy: How can we account for the pervasiveness of the informal economy? Are informal activities marginal or functional to capital? What is the internal structure of the informal economy? Does the informal economy behave in a countercyclical or in a cyclical way? Does the informal economy exhibit a potential for growth, or is it merely a subsistence sector? These questions are still debated today (Pérez Sáinz 1991).

Dependent Industrialization and the Informal Sector

One of the most widely accepted approaches to the study of the Latin American informal economy links its origins to the existence of a large surplus labor force that cannot be absorbed into the formal sector. This structural surplus of the labor force originates in the particular form of industrialization in Latin America, an industrialization process characterized by the import of capital-intensive technologies in a context of rapid growth of the urban population. In this historical context, creating new jobs was very costly, and in spite of impressive rates of economic growth, large segments of the urban population could not gain access to modern wage employment. To subsist, the people excluded from modern employment had to "invent" their own jobs in the informal sector. This point of view has been developed in numerous works by researchers linked to the International Labor Office (ILO) and its former Latin American program Programa Regional de Empleo para América Latina y el Caribe (PREALC), and it was rooted in the analysis of Latin American industrialization made by Raúl Prebisch and his associates at the Economic Commission for Latin America and the Caribbean (ECLAC) (Mezzera 1987, 1992; Tokman 1985, 1989a).

Tokman and the PREALC/ILO researchers described the Latin American urban economies as composed of a modern/formal sector and an informal sector subordinated to the former.[1] The informal sector was defined as a segment of the urban economy composed of small firms characterized by ease of access, simple technologies, and a low capital-to-labor ratio. This sector was seen as heterogeneous, made up of segments with differential access to capital and income. Informal microenterprises, for example, have access to small amounts of capital and generate incomes for their owners that are often better than the incomes of wageworkers in the modern sector. Nevertheless, informal firms usually insert themselves in very competitive markets, which makes it difficult for them to thrive. Self-employed people generally have no access to capital, and their income is among the lowest in the urban labor market. In times of economic downturn, this sector behaves in a countercyclical way, as a cushion for people expelled from the formal sector. These people are usually absorbed as self-employed in the worst segments of the informal sector (Mezzera 1992; Tokman 1989a, 1989b).

This approach focused on informal firms as the units of analysis and linked informality with the use of simple technologies and the small size of the establishments. This line of argument was developed during the period of industrialization through import substitution. Pérez Sáinz (1998a, 1994) argues that this approach must be updated to address present Latin American conditions. More specifically, he claims that the neoliberal model of development has broken the association between small firms and low productivity and simple technologies. Moreover, he states, structural adjustment and the rise of nontraditional agroexports, tourism, and assembly manufacturing have blurred the differences between working conditions in the modern and the informal

---

1. The difference between the terms *informal sector* and *informal economy* becomes clear as this discussion develops.

sectors. Pérez Sáinz coins the term *neoinformality* to refer to this new situation and posits three main scenarios of neoinformality: (1) economies of poverty, characterized by contexts of exclusion and activities of subsistence conducted with very limited resources; (2) subcontracting for the tradable sector, which amounts to a subordinated incorporation into the global economy; and (3) agglomeration of small dynamic business, which implies a dynamic incorporation into the global economy based on cooperation among small firms and solidarity based on local identities.[2]

The strength of the work of Tokman, Mezzera, Pérez Sáinz, and other researchers working in this theoretical paradigm is that it roots the analysis of the informal economy in the particular characteristics of dependent industrialization in Latin America—a process of industrialization characterized by the limited absorption of labor into the modern sector of the economy. The weakness of this approach is that there is no particular place in this analysis for the role of the state and labor regulations. These scholars have conducted several comparative studies and are aware of the differences in the size and shape of the informal economies of the different countries, but they have not developed a systematic explanation for those differences (Funkhauser 1996; Menjívar Larín and Pérez Sáinz 1993; Tokman 1982).

To be sure, the state is not completely absent from the work of these researchers. Tokman (1985, 1989a) argues that the state in Latin America has played a key role in the industrialization process because of the weakness of the local bourgeoisies. Yet, he also argues that if there is a correlation between informality and operating beyond established state regulations, this is not the result of state regulations or a defining characteristic of informal activities, but a consequence of operating in a context characterized by a structural labor surplus (Tokman 1991, 1992). Pérez Sáinz (1998b) discounts the importance of the state under the new economic model and argues that, as far as the extension of social rights is concerned, the main actors are the rising entrepreneurial elites. Pérez Sáinz is undoubtedly right in arguing that the position of the state vis-à-vis the entrepreneurial elites has weakened under the neoliberal model of growth. However, the dismissal of the role of the state in the process of capital accumulation may be exaggerated.[3]

---

2. This scenario parallels that of the industrial district (see Capechi 1989, and Pyke, Becattini, and Sengenberger 1990). Pérez Sáinz (1997) analyzes cases of these types of scenarios in a number of local economies in Central America (for another view of the question of the informal economies of growth, see Portes and Itzigsohn [1997] and Itzigsohn [1998]).

3. The state has played a key role in the process of switching to export-oriented development and privatization. Indeed, the successful adoption of the neoliberal model of industrialization

State Regulation and the Informal Economy

A central tenet of this book's argument is that the state plays a key role in structuring markets. States have had a key role in the rise of modern markets and in promoting industrial development (Evans 1995; Gerschenkron 1962; Polanyi 1957). States have a key role in regulating labor markets. Tilly and Tilly (1998) point to the numerous ways in which state actions regulate the process of proletarianization. For example, states regulate the labor demand through fiscal and monetary policies, they influence the labor supply through immigration or welfare laws or the provision of training or child care. States can also affect labor relations through labor legislation and its implementation (or lack of it). This partial list emphasizes the importance of looking at the ways in which state institutions structure the labor market and labor relations. Tilly and Tilly (1998) provide insightful guidelines for the analysis of labor markets and the various roles of the state in their regulation. Their analysis, however, focuses on labor markets at the core of the capitalist world system. I plan to examine the role of the state in the structuring of labor markets and the informal economy in the periphery of the world system in the historical context of dependent development.

The issue of the relations between the state and the informal economy in Latin America was addressed by Hernando De Soto (1989) in a book that was influential in the late 1980s and by Alejandro Portes and several associates in a large body of academic work focused on developing the implications of state regulation in the emergence and shape of informal economies in the periphery and core of the world economy (Portes 1994b; Portes, Castells, and Benton 1989; Portes and Sassen Koob 1987; Portes and Schauffler 1993). De Soto and Portes both link the rise of informal economies to the presence of state regulations, although they differ in their explanations of how state regulations lead to the rise of informal economies.

For De Soto (1989), the informal sector is created by the burdens imposed by state regulation on the entrepreneurial activities of poor people. The reason for the pervasiveness of these regulations is the presence of a "mercantilist state" dominated by elites who use their political power to ensure their economic positions. These elites use the regulation of economic activities to avoid the entry into profitable economic activities of migrants who arrive from the

---

is associated with strong states. Moreover, the international financial institutions (IFIs) seem to have rediscovered a role for the state in addressing the worst consequences of this model of development (World Bank 1995, 1997).

rural hinterlands to the city in search of a better economic future. These immigrants see their possibilities of upward economic mobility blocked by encumbering state regulations that preclude them from engaging in profitable economic endeavors. De Soto's book is a long and lively description of how the institutions of the Peruvian state are set to make it almost impossible for poor people to operate within the boundaries of the law. The informal economy is the response of those excluded from the modern sector by state regulation. De Soto's work is best understood as reflecting the wide popularity of neo-utilitarian arguments during the 1980s, arguments about how state bureaucracies act to maximize their utilities by enacting rents and engaging in rackets and other forms of profit extraction. The neo-utilitarian solution to this problem is to embrace the market (Alt and Shepsle 1990; Bromley 1994; Buchanan, Tollison, and Tullock 1980; Evans 1995).[4]

The informal sector, according to De Soto, represents the true market forces inherent in the entrepreneurial character of the urban poor who rebel against the coercion of the state. Lift state regulations and the market economy, represented by the informal microentrepreneurs, thrives. For De Soto, the informal sector encompasses all the production, trading, and subsistence activities carried out on the margins of state regulation. In spite of this heterogeneous portrayal, he equates every informal-sector worker with a potential entrepreneur. Thus, the entire informal sector is seen as formed by entrepreneurs, or would-be entrepreneurs, coerced by state regulation.[5]

Portes's analysis developed from neo-Marxist debates about the articulation of modes of production and the pervasiveness of petty commodity production under capitalism (Portes and Walton 1981). Portes's innovation was to link those debates to the analysis of the incentives created by state regulation of labor markets. He defines the informal economy as income-earning activities that are not regulated by the state in contexts where similar activities

---

4. De Soto is an economist, but he is more concerned with political action than academic analysis. His work is important because of its theoretical linkage to the neo-utilitarian critique of state intervention in the economy and the wide influence that it had and still has over policymakers. De Soto articulated many of the assumptions that underlie the policies of promotion of microenterprises as a solution to the employment and poverty problems caused by structural adjustment.

5. In fact, De Soto's own descriptions of informal activities belie his argument that they constitute an unregulated market economy. De Soto shows in a compelling way that informal economic activities are embedded in social networks and alternative social institutions that make possible the emergence of trust and that guarantee the fulfillment of agreements. Unfortunately, this part of De Soto's work has not been analyzed, because it is shadowed by his argument about the mercantilist state and the informal economy as the true market economy.

are regulated. He sees informal economic activities as an integral part of urban economies in peripheral and core capitalism. Formal and informal economic activities are part of the same economic system and are articulated by networks that link formal and informal enterprises. This approach focuses on the structure of the linkages between formal and informal firms and hence is known as the *structuralist* approach to the study of the informal economy. Because formal and informal firms are linked through networks of subcontracting and supply chains, Portes argues that we cannot really distinguish between two separate sectors; hence he prefers to talk about an informal economy rather than an informal sector. Moreover, informality is present in the modern sector of the economy, as many workers in modern firms do not receive the protections prescribed by the law.

According to this approach, the shape of the informal economy is determined by the type of state regulation of economic activities and labor relations and the extent of the enforcement of those regulations. For Portes, the relations between state regulation and the informal economy are characterized by a paradox: The more the state attempts to regulate labor relations, the more formal firms attempt to evade those regulations. Formal firms evade labor regulations by subcontracting parts of their production or marketing processes or by hiring workers off the book (Portes 1994b). The informal economy is functional to the process of capital accumulation in two main ways. On the one hand, the informal economy contributes to the process of capital accumulation by providing cheap goods and services that lower the cost of reproducing the labor force. This provision of cheap goods and services reduces the cost of subsistence for workers and allows formal firms to pay lower salaries. The informal economy also contributes to the process of capital accumulation by directly lowering labor costs through subcontracting production or marketing activities and through off-the-books hiring of informal workers. This functional relation is present in both peripheral and core capitalism (Portes 1995; Portes, Castells, and Benton 1989; Portes and Sassen-Koob 1987; Portes and Schauffler 1993).[6]

Portes incorporates the analysis of labor regulations into the analysis of the class structure of urban Latin America. Using control of the means of

---

6. The question of the functionality of informal activities in the process of capital accumulation was developed in the 1970s by several authors. Most, but not all, worked within a Marxist paradigm and were concerned with the permanence of petty commodity production and the articulation of modes of production under capitalism (see Moser 1978, 1994, and Pérez Sáinz 1991, for a review of this literature). Portes's innovation was to link this literature with the role of the state in regulating labor markets and to develop the concept of the informal proletariat.

production, control of labor power, and form of remuneration (i.e., whether the worker is paid according to existing labor regulations) as classification criteria, Portes (1985) distinguishes five main classes in Latin America. These are the dominant class, the bureaucratic-technical class, the formal proletariat, the informal petty bourgeoisie, and the informal working class. The last two strata constitute the core of the informal economy. Portes sees the informal petty bourgeoisie as heterogeneous and engaged in different types of economic activities. He distinguishes three types of informal economic activities, according to their articulation with the formal economy: direct subsistence activities; informal production and trade subordinated to formal firms; and autonomous clusters of small, informal enterprises with the capacity for capital accumulation. In Latin America, the first two types are predominant, with only a handful of examples of the third type (Portes and Itzigsohn 1997; Portes and Schauffler 1993).[7]

The work of Portes and De Soto helps to "bring the state back in" to the analysis of informal economies. De Soto's work underscores the importance of looking at the institutional organization of the state. Portes's work establishes the relation between state regulation of the labor market and the structure of the informal economy. Moreover, Portes's work moves the study of informal activities from a focus on small firms and microenterprises to the analysis of the linkages that connect different economic units at the national and global levels. Where the work of Tokman or De Soto sees a dualist field of modern and informal firms—and in that sense they speak about an informal sector—Portes points us to the various uses of labor and to the linkages that connect different types of firms in the urban economy: hence his understanding of the informal economy as crossing the boundaries of different sectors. His conceptualization of the informal proletariat as located in the modern sector of the economy as well as in the informal sector is of central relevance to this study.

De Soto and Portes make an important contribution to the analysis of the informal economy by bringing the state into the central stage. However, both analyses leave some unanswered questions in their assessment of the role of the state and its relation to the informal economy. De Soto's exclusive focus on the state as rent seeker dismisses the state's role in promoting development and expanding social welfare. Moreover, his analysis is limited to only one case, the Peruvian state, which raises the question of the extent to which the Peruvian experience can be generalized to represent other Latin American states. Portes's

---

7. This classification of the economic activities of the informal petty bourgeoisie parallels Pérez Sáinz's scenarios of neoinformality.

emphasis on the similarities between the informal economies in the core and the periphery and the generality of the formal-informal linkages in the world economy does not acknowledge the particularities of peripheral capitalist development. His analysis of the paradoxes of labor regulation is insightful but raises a question that is at the core of our research: Does more regulation always lead to more informality? This notion is taken for granted when in fact it is a hypothesis waiting for empirical confirmation or rejection. Moreover, his exclusive focus on labor market regulations dismisses other ways in which state actions shape the urban labor market, particularly the state's role in promoting particular models of capital accumulation.

In this work, I argue that it is possible and necessary to bring together the insights of institutional and world-system analysis to the analysis of informal economies. The book shows how the institutional action of the state affects the structure of the labor markets and informal economies in the particular historical context of peripheral industrialization. In other words, I explore the scope of action open to state institutions and the limits imposed on the state by a peripheral insertion in the world economy. Combining institutional and world-system analyses involves an exercise of theoretical synthesis. In terms of the theoretical approaches discussed above, it means bringing together the institutional concerns expressed in De Soto's work—although leaving out his particular conceptualization of the state—and the analysis of peripheral industrialization proposed by Tokman and other researchers working in the PREALC/ILO framework to apply to Portes's pioneering analysis of the structure of the informal economy.

Given my focus on the effects of state actions and institutions on informal economies, I adopt Portes's definition of the informal economy, defining it as activities that avoid state regulation. This definition places the state and its policies at the core of the analysis. However, defining the informal economy as economic activities that avoid state regulation poses the problem of equating different forms of avoidance of regulations, such as lack of business registration and permits, tax evasion, and noncompliance with labor regulations. For the purposes of this study, it is necessary to delineate more clearly the boundaries of the informal economy. To do this, I distinguish between two main types of avoidance of regulations. The first type refers to the avoidance of regulations about registration and taxation. The second type concerns the evasion of labor market regulations such as regulations governing the minimum salary, social security, and hiring and firing or regulations about working conditions such as health and safety regulations. I focus on the latter type of regulation in defining and operationalizing the informal economy. I make this distinction for analytical purposes, because in reality firms cannot be so neatly distinguished (Tokman 1992). Nevertheless, this analytical distinction focuses the analysis on the question of compliance or avoidance of labor regulations, which is the central element in the definition of the informal economy used in this book.[8]

The goal of the book is to look at how different forms of state regulation of the labor market and the economy affect the shape and structure of the informal economy in a peripheral region, Latin America.[9] The institutional capacity of the state to design and implement policies is at the center of the analysis pursued in this book. The capacity of action of the peripheral state, however, is limited by the systemic constraints of the world economy. I expect a particular position in the world economy and a particular historical path of industrialization to impose boundaries on the scope and effectiveness of state action: hence the emphasis on the effects of the common experience of peripheral industrialization. Still, a common historical path of industrialization does not necessarily produce the same sociopolitical configuration in each country. It is impossible to deduce every social trait of national units from general world-systemic characteristics, and it is impossible to discount the action of social institutions—in this case the state—and its effects on social structures: thus the emphasis on institutional analysis. Finally, I cannot accept the premise that state actions always have the same results, regardless of the historical-institutional configuration of different states: hence the need to develop a comparative typology of state apparatuses. The synthesis of historical-institutional and world-system perspectives in the analysis of the structure and dynamics of informal economies in Latin America constitutes one of the distinctive characteristics of this book.

States as Institutional Actors

For the purpose of this analysis, I define the state as a territorial organization that claims a monopoly in the legitimate use of authority and coercion of the

---

8. Much of the discussion about the relations between state regulations and informality has suffered from a lack of conceptual clarity arising from a failure to separate these different dimensions of regulation. As a result, scholars compare different phenomena (see the otherwise very interesting volume edited by Tokman [1992] for an example of the problems caused by the failure to establish an analytical distinction between different areas of regulation).

9. Because different regions of the periphery have different histories of relations with core areas and different institutional histories, we cannot assume that the institutional dynamics are the same in all the regions of the periphery.

people included in its geographic boundaries. This definition centers the analysis on the institutional ability of the state to develop and implement policies. States' apparatuses are composed of a number of different bureaucratic agencies charged with administrating policies, maintaining order, enforcing the law, securing political legitimacy, and collecting the revenues necessary for the functioning of the state apparatus and the implementation of state policies. The bureaucratic organizations that compose the state apparatus sometimes work coherently together and sometimes work at cross-purposes. Therefore, to understand the administrative and political capacities of a state apparatus, it is imperative to look at its institutional structure (Skocpol 1985). Different political regimes develop different organizational characteristics and institutional capacities. In his analysis of national labor administrations in the Southern Cone, Buchanan (1995), for example, shows the importance of analyzing the institutional structures through which the state attempts to deal with the incorporation of labor into the capitalist system.

The peripheral state is located at the intersection of local class and other social actors and the global economic and political system. This location is a source of opportunities for autonomous actions and at the same time constitutes the limits of state action. In Latin America, the weakness and divisions of the local classes have pushed the state to the center of the stage of economic development and have provided a fertile field for the emergence of "Bonapartist" regimes. At the same time, Latin American states have been notorious for their lack of institutional capacity and their lack of ability to break the boundaries of dependent development and move up in the world-system hierarchy (Anglade and Fortín 1985; Betances 1995; Borón 1995; Evans 1995; Tokman 1989a). For the purpose of this analysis, we must develop a conceptual typology that captures the variations in state institutional apparatuses and compares how different institutional apparatuses distinctly affect the structures of the labor market and the informal economy. At the same time, we cannot lose sight of the peripheral character of the Latin American states and the systemic constraints imposed on them by their position in the world economy.

The State and the Informal Economy

The state and its actions are at the center of Portes's structuralist analysis. Portes (1994a) makes a general argument about the diffusion of values and the legislation of labor laws, arguing that Latin American states have copied their labor legislation from developed countries and as a result they are unable, unwilling, or both, to enforce that legislation. This argument implies, in fact, that there are no significant institutional differences between the different Latin American countries. Portes backs his hypothesis with extensive evidence about the presence of subcontracting chains that connect formal and informal firms. He has not produced, however, a systematic empirical and comparative research on state institutions, labor legislation, and their relations to the informal economy.

For a historical analysis of the institutions of an actual state, we have to look at De Soto's (1989) work. De Soto argues that the Peruvian state has been a mercantilist state since colonial times. By this, he means that the institutions of the Peruvian state are controlled by elites, who use the instruments of power for the benefit of themselves and their class allies. From this point of view, state regulations are no more than barriers of entry to gainful economic activities, put in place to protect economic monopolies. I do not quarrel here with De Soto's description of the workings of the Peruvian state. I argue, however, that his description of the Peruvian state corresponds to a particular form of state apparatus that Evans (1995) calls "predatory states."

In his analysis of different types of states, Evans introduces two ideal types of state apparatuses, extremes in a continuum of empirical cases. At one extreme are predatory states, where central control and bureaucratic norms have disintegrated and corruption rules. Different groups in the state bureaucracy attempt to maximize their own profit by selling their services in the market. In fact, everything, from contracts to justice is up for grabs, subject to the logic of the market. Those with means to buy state services or privileges get them, while the rest of the population has no choice but to exit the state institutional system. Evans (1995) uses Zaire as the example of a predatory state, and his description coincides with Davidson's (1992) characterization of the "Mobutist paradigm." The Peruvian state described by De Soto does not reach the levels of disintegration and corruption that characterized Mobutu's Zaire, but it is close to that end of the continuum.

At the other end of Evans's continuum are developmental states. Developmental states are characterized by the presence of well-functioning and centrally coordinated state bureaucratic agencies working along Weberian lines. Unlike the Weberian model, however, those bureaucracies are not isolated from society, but are connected to the main economic actors through different organizational and career networks. These linkages ensure the flow of information, ideas, and people between state bureaucracies and the main economic actors, guaranteeing a feedback system for their needs. These networks, however, do not affect the autonomous work of the state bureaucracies. Evans calls this situation of autonomous yet socially connected bureaucracies "embedded

The Limits of Development

autonomy." In the comparison pursued in this book, I find Evans's work useful, especially because it focuses on the role of the state in economic growth and introduces variation in the types of state apparatuses. Evans's typology of state apparatuses provides an initial set of tools to begin my analysis of the effects of state institutional actions on informal economies.

Evans's typology, however, poses some problems for the purposes of this study. First, his work focuses on economic growth performance, but does not look at labor regulations, social policies, or labor market structures.[10] Second, Evans's example for the developmental state type is Korea. No Latin American or Caribbean state approaches the institutional and economic performance of the East Asian Tigers. The Latin American states are found at different points between the developmental and predatory poles. Evans uses the example of Brazil, perhaps the Latin American case closest to the developmental state pole, and describes its state apparatus as an intermediate case, combining a mix of developmental and predatory institutions. Moreover, in a departure from his earlier work on Brazil, Evans (1979) does not locate his typology in the historical context of peripheral capitalism. His comparative institutional analysis helps overcome the bias of some of the world-system literature that often ignores the importance of local and institutional factors in understanding social change. Yet, it is not clear from his account whether there is any relation between what state institutions can achieve and the systemic constraints of the world system.

The transformation of Evans's typology into a set of concepts appropriate for the purposes of this study presents us with two tasks. First, it is necessary to expand it with conceptual tools that allow us to address the topic of this study, that is, the structure of labor markets and informal economies. I address this task in the next section. Second, it is necessary to locate our typology in the historical context of peripheral capitalism, that is, to conceptualize the historical context and the systemic constraints in which the Latin American states act. This task is addressed in the next chapter.

The State and the Reproduction of the Labor Force

Because of the commodity exchanged in them—labor power—labor markets are a special type of market. Their commodity is characterized by the fact that it

---

10. In the final chapter of *Embedded Autonomy*, Evans discusses the cases of Kerala and Austria as developmental states that have addressed social and labor issues, but he does not develop his analysis of these cases. For an illuminating analysis of how state policies have affected labor market structures in Korea, Taiwan, and Singapore, see Deyo (1989).

is embodied in the bodies and minds of workers; thus, it needs to be reproduced daily—that is, workers need to replenish their physical and mental capacities to work every day and also need to raise a new generation of workers (Marx 1976; Peck 1996). Who should bear the costs of the reproduction of the labor force: individuals and their families, firms, or the state (Folbre 1994; Smith and Wallerstein 1992)? States intervene in the reproduction of the labor force through the regulation of labor relations and the provision of a series of benefits and services that constitute an indirect salary—such as pensions, health care, and education. The regulations governing labor relations include laws about minimum salary, hiring and firing of workers, workplace conditions, labor representation and contract negotiations, social security, and the like. The state also intervenes in the reproduction of the labor force as an employer, creating public employment, and as an agent of development, promoting the creation of jobs.[11] States differ in the extent and way in which they regulate the labor market. In some cases, state regulation guarantees the reproduction of the labor force. In others, social protections are not present or are present but not enforced. In still other cases, even when enforced, social legislation and public social expenditures cannot guarantee the reproduction of the labor force.

The form and extent of labor market regulation are the result of the balance of forces between different social actors. Portes (1994a) argues that in Latin America, labor market regulations did not arise out of the strength of working-class organizations, but were enacted as a result of a process of diffusion of certain values about modern labor relations. Latin American states copied their labor regulations from core countries. Although the labor codes look good on paper, the problematic result has been that Latin American states are either unwilling or unable to enforce those regulations (Portes 1994a). The protections afforded by labor regulations are enjoyed only by a small segment of wageworkers. According to this argument, the unintended consequence of a well-intentioned action—enacting labor laws—is to create a segmented labor market with a small labor aristocracy and a large informal sector. This is due to the fact that labor market regulations increase the cost of labor, but the lack of enforcement creates opportunities for employers to bypass regulations and reduce their labor costs. Large employers achieve this goal by subcontracting production to small firms that operate informally or by having only part of their workforce covered by the existing regulations (Portes 1994a; Portes and

---

11. This is also related to the question of citizenship. In Latin America, access to social citizenship, that is, those rights and obligations that guarantee every member of the community participation in socially accepted standards of living, has been historically linked to state social protections accessed through formal employment (Roberts 1998).

Schauffler 1993). According to this argument, labor regulation creates both the incentive and the opportunity to operate informally.

Portes (1994a) differentiates between four different types of labor standards: basic rights (rights against the use of child labor, physical coercion, and involuntary servitude); civic rights (rights to free association and collective representation); survival rights (rights to a living wage, accident compensation, and a limited work week); and security rights (right protecting against arbitrary dismissal, right to retirement compensation, right to survivors' compensation). The first two types of rights, he suggests, should be international standards; the last two should be applied flexibly according to local conditions. In particular, the indiscriminate legislation of security rights, that is, rights that limit the flexible use of the labor force, is a powerful incentive for the dominant class and the informal petty bourgeoisie to informalize their operations. The issue of the effectiveness and consequences of labor regulation is one of the central questions in this book.

There is an increasing body of empirical research on the effects of labor market regulation on the functioning of the labor market in Latin America (Edwards and Lustig 1997; Marquez 1995; Marshall 1994; World Bank 1997). The empirical results of this literature illustrate a great variety of national situations in reference to labor legislation, in terms of both the implementation of labor legislation and labor market outcomes. In spite of this empirical heterogeneity of national situations, the policy conclusions tend to be rather homogeneous in support of deregulation of labor relations. These studies' recommendations tend to support Portes's argument about the need for a limited regulation of the labor market.

This literature represents an important contribution to the study of labor markets and the state in Latin America because it takes the empirical analysis of state regulation seriously. Nevertheless, it suffers from a number of limitations. First, the intellectual agenda of much—although not all—of this literature is to promote the reform of labor market regulations in the direction of reducing labor costs and eliminating restrictions to the functioning of the labor market. The empirical results in this literature, however, present a complex variety of outcomes and national situations that do not necessarily support many of the conclusions and policy recommendations emerging from these studies.[12] Second, this literature focuses on labor laws but does not look at the

12. For example, a study by Lustig and McLeod (1997) on the effects of minimum wage on poverty finds that minimum wages consistently reduce poverty. Nevertheless, the authors go a long way to argue against endorsing the increase of minimum wages as an antipoverty policy. For a dissenting voice on the deregulation of labor markets, see Marshall (1994).

institutional capacity of the states in which these laws are legislated, so that one does not necessarily know if and how the laws are being implemented.[13] Finally, this literature is usually based on detailed case study analyses. This is a welcome feature because it allows us to see the diversity of national situations. Yet, these studies are not really comparative because they do not establish clear parameters to compare the cases; readers do not know what the effects of labor regulations are across the different national situations.

Analysts of Latin American labor markets agree that during the last two decades the region has experienced a process of de facto deregulation, a process that was not reflected in institutional changes. Until the early 1980s, the Latin American and Caribbean states attempted, with generally modest success, to introduce labor and social welfare legislation. Since then, the states of the region have retreated from their intervention in the reproduction of the labor force, leading to a reduction of social protections and the downgrading of employment of the region's labor markets (Geller 1991; Itzigsohn 1996; Lagos 1994; Mesa-Lago 1994; Tardanico and Menjívar Larín 1997). Although researchers agree that the region's institutions must address these changes in the labor market, there is no consensus about how to go about doing this. For example, Tokman (1989b) agrees with Portes's argument that existing labor laws in Latin America are impossible to enforce. If enforced, they would wipe out the informal petty bourgeoisie, which operates with very small margins of profit and can subsist only through noncompliance with existing regulations. Enforcing labor laws would create a larger problem than the one the laws attempt to solve, because enforcement would leave a large number of currently employed people without a job. Tokman, however, does not propose eliminating the legislation of survival and security rights. He suggests that the cost of some of the survival and security rights, such as accident compensation and pensions, should be passed on from the employers to the state. In other words, the costs should be financed from general taxes rather than payroll taxes. This leads us back to the analysis of the state's institutional capacity to develop and implement labor regulations and social policies.

To analyze and compare how state capacity and institutional action structure the labor market and the informal economy, we need to develop conceptual tools capable of expanding the scope of Evans's (1995) typology. We can find such a complement in Standing's (1991) typology of state labor market regulations. Standing presents a complex view of labor regulations, one that

---

13. For example, an analysis of the Brazilian labor market shows that the existing labor laws do not constrain the flexibility of the labor market (Amadeo and Camargo 1997).

allows us to develop a typology of state apparatuses suitable for the analysis at hand. He argues that the state intervenes in the labor market not only to guarantee the reproduction of labor, but also to guarantee the smooth accumulation of capital, and posits a distinction among protective, paternalistic, and repressive regulations. Protective regulations are those achieved by workers negotiating with employers and the state as a result of the strength of workers' organizations. Paternalistic regulations are those legislated by the state either as an attempt to co-opt certain segments of the working class or as a result of values about these issues held by the elites in office. In this case, these regulations do not necessarily reflect the relative class balance of power in society. Repressive regulations are designed to limit collective action on the part of workers. What is generally called deregulation does not necessarily mean the absence of regulations. Many of the examples of labor market *deregulation*, such as occurred in Chile or Korea, are in fact examples of the predominance of repressive regulations (Deyo 1989; Díaz 1997; Standing 1991).

Moreover, Standing argues that the presence of protective or paternalistic labor market regulations, even when not universally applied, may raise the living standard of workers in all segments of the labor market. He maintains that although guidelines established by labor regulations are not followed everywhere, they nevertheless do set general minimum levels that help improve the situation of the workers in the lower ends of the labor market. According to this argument, labor regulations may indeed lead to increasing subcontracting, but their overall effect is to improve the working conditions of all segments of the labor market (Standing 1991). Hence, in spite of their limitations, labor regulations contribute to a reduction in overall labor market segmentation.

A look at the labor laws in my two case studies, Costa Rica and the Dominican Republic, shows that they are similar. One of the main concerns about the relations between labor laws and job creation is the flexibility—or lack of it—in firing workers. In Costa Rica and the Dominican Republic, employers can fire workers with relative ease, but they do have to give workers severance payments that increase in relation to time of service.[14] Another main concern in the discussion of labor laws is the cost of fringe benefits and payroll taxes.

14. Article 29 of the Costa Rican labor code stipulates the right of employers—and employees—to end the labor contract without justification. The party making this decision must let the other know in advance within a certain period established in the law. If the employer takes the decision, he or she must pay an indemnification in an amount that is related to the time of service (Vincenzi 1991). Articles 68 and 69 of the Dominican labor code establish the same legal procedure, termed *desahucio* in the Dominican legal parlance. This decision should be communicated to the relevant authorities within forty-eight hours (Hernández Rueda 1989). Employers make use of this provision in the labor code to reduce their personnel as they see fit. *Desahucio* allows

Both countries stipulate that employers should make payroll contributions to social security. However, in the Dominican Republic, few workers are insured. Costa Rica has a more effective enforcement of the existing labor laws and generalized social security; in fact, the Costa Rican state is probably the closest to a welfare state in Latin America (Huber 1996). In both countries, the pension and social security system, however, experiences continual financial problems for which the state is partly responsible. By law, the state should complement the payroll taxes with its own contributions to the social security fund, but, in fact, it is perennially in arrears. Both countries have legislated a set of minimum wages for different occupations, yet only in Costa Rica is this legislation applied consistently. Moreover, only in Costa Rica does the minimum wage allow workers to fulfill their subsistence needs.

Following Portes's (1994a) classification of workers' rights, the labor laws in the two countries cover basic and civic rights. In both countries, legislation addresses survival rights, although it is enforced only in Costa Rica. With respect to security rights, both countries allow for the flexible use of the labor force. Both countries have a pension system, although it is weak in Costa Rica and almost nonexistent in the Dominican Republic. In both countries, labor legislation was the result of the actions of the elites that controlled the state. These elites responded to situations of labor unrest, but they did not incorporate labor into the policymaking process. Still, labor in Costa Rica did have more of a voice in the political process than in the Dominican Republic (Betances 1995; Bulmer-Thomas 1987, 1994). Using Standing's (1991) typology of labor market regulations, we can characterize the labor regulation system in Costa Rica as paternalistic-protective and that in the Dominican Republic as paternalistic-repressive.

Defining Regulatory Regimes

State intervention in the development process and state regulation of the labor market are two aspects of a set of state policies and institutions designed to

---

for the flexible management of the labor force. Hernández Rueda (1989), a professor of labor law, argues that this practice is an abuse of the labor code, because there are legal dispositions for the reduction of personnel. In this case, the firm should let workers go in a certain order determined first by nationality and second by seniority. In the event that the reduction of personnel is permanent, the firm should obtain the approval of the Department of Labor. The administrative authorities in charge of enforcing the labor laws, however, have argued that the law does not allow them to take action in these cases. Moreover, unions often demand in collective contracts the *desahucio* of a certain number of workers each year. The reason for this is that, as I show in Chapter 4, this practice is perceived as a form of accessing savings.

intervene in and regulate the process of capital accumulation. Both also affect labor markets and the reproduction of the labor force. Using Evans's (1995) classification of state apparatuses and Standing's (1991) typology of forms of labor market regulation, we can think about two intersecting axes defining a two-dimensional space in which we can position different types of state interventions. The position of a state along these two dimensions characterizes its particular regulatory regime. This conceptualization has the advantage of incorporating the dimensions of labor regulation and social policy, which are not included in Evans's developmental-predatory typology, into our analysis of state apparatuses.

I prefer to think about a two-dimensional plane rather than a two-by-two table because states can move along the axes in the plane without leaving the quadrant in which they are located. Placing a state close to the y axis indicates that its labor regulation regime is not purely protective or repressive, but combines a strong element of paternalism with protection/repression. Placing a state close to the x axis indicates that its state apparatus corresponds to what Evans calls intermediate states apparatuses. Thus, a plane allows us to capture historical and cross-sectional variation in the different typological categories.

Figure 1.1 locates the two states in the space of regulatory regimes. My two cases are found at very different points in this space. I locate Costa Rica in the developmental-protective quadrant and the Dominican Republic in the predatory-repressive one.[15] Neither of the two countries, however, is very far from the intersection point. Their states are not close to the ideal types of developmental and predatory apparatuses, and their labor regulations are not clearly protective or repressive. In Costa Rica, for example, unions are weak and do not have a central role in negotiating labor conditions. In the Dominican Republic, the law formally protects workers and there is no repression of union activities, but the law is not implemented and unions are very weak. In both countries, the labor regulation regime has a strong component of paternalism. Yet, the fact that the two countries are distant from the ideal types that define our typology does not erase the fact that their regulatory regimes are located in different quadrants of our plane and that they are qualitatively different.

The concept of regulatory regimes allows us to capture variation in state apparatuses and their relation to the labor market and the informal economy.

---

15. My two cases occupy two quadrants of the plane. It is not difficult to think of cases of developmental-repressive regulatory regimes—the Korean developmental state immediately comes to mind. On the other hand, it is more difficult to think of examples of predatory-protective regimes. I consider this an empty category.

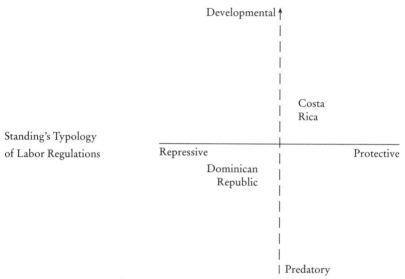

Fig. 1.1 Dimensions of regulatory regimes

I argue that what matters is not the "amount" of regulation—both countries have rather similar labor and welfare laws—but the overall character of the state apparatus. We expect different regulatory regimes to lead to differences in the structures of the labor markets and the informal economies, in spite of the fact that the labor laws are similar and that both countries followed similar industrialization policies.[16]

As the following chapters show, there are important differences between the labor markets and informal economies of Costa Rica and the Dominican Republic. In Santo Domingo, the informal economy is proportionally larger and labor market segmentation is more pronounced, whereas in San José the

---

16. There are, indeed, additional actors that shape the structure of the labor market in addition to the state: class organizations, such as unions or employers' associations, and social movements. The labor market is also structured around accepted cultural notions about the gender and ethnoracial division of labor and their institutionalization. Some of these elements are addressed in parts of this book, but they are admittedly not at the center of my analysis, not because I ignore their importance, but because my intention is to focus the analytical attention on the crossroads of state institutional capacity and world-systemic constraints.

general standard of living is higher. These differences are particularly noticeable when one compares the more marginal sectors of the labor market. Overall, a stricter regulation of the labor market in a developmental-protective regulatory regime can lead to a larger proportion of people working in the formal economy with a better standard of living than does a less strict regulation in a predatory-repressive regulatory regime.

My argument places the state, its institutions, and its policies at the core of my analysis. This choice may be questioned in a period in which the theme of globalization seems to dominate all debates. The concept of globalization, however, is rather vague and refers to different social, cultural, and economic processes. In Latin America and the Caribbean, the debt crisis of the 1980s ended the attempts to "catch up" in the world economy through inward-oriented industrialization. Since then, the region has attempted to reinsert itself into the world division of labor through exports based on its static comparative advantages (availability of raw materials and cheap labor). In spite of the emphasis on exports, this model of growth depends on the constant influx of capital from the core of the world economy. This has limited the state's scope of action, as it is compelled to adopt policies that guarantee capital flows. The states of the region, however, are not powerless. On the one hand, they have played an active role in promoting the current socioeconomic model, and they still have degrees of freedom to act within its boundaries. On the other hand, they retain powers they can use in case of a political or economic crisis of the current model of insertion in the world economy.

I reject, therefore, "globalization" arguments that deny the state its political capacities in the context of the current global political-economic conditions. Indeed, the need for state intervention and regulation seems to be staging a comeback in mainstream discourse (World Bank 1997). On the other hand, I also reject state-centered arguments that ignore the position of different countries in the political and economic orders of the world system. In spite of differences in regulatory regimes, Costa Rica and the Dominican Republic show similar general trends in labor absorption and in the structure of the linkages between formal and informal activities. This pattern of differences and similarities is explainable in terms of the interaction between state capacity and insertion in the world economy and interstate system, the tense relations between national regulatory regimes and world-system constraints. I contend that the form of insertion of countries in the global economy, as well as their position in the geopolitical order, imposes limits on the scope of state action. Both countries share a similar insertion in the world economy, and that insertion conditions many of their internal political-economical processes.

The intersection of institutional capacity and world-system position determines the opportunities and constraints confronted by states.

Indeed, one of the main theoretical-methodological arguments of my study is the importance of combining different theoretical tools and levels of analysis to capture the complexity of social phenomena. The units at a lower—that is, more "micro"—level of analysis have a relative autonomy vis-à-vis the units at a higher level. Yet, units at a lower level of analysis are constrained by the structural limits of the higher-level units of analysis. Thus, the world system constrains the possibilities of action at the state level, but does not erase spaces of social action. Similarly, structural and institutional constraints limit the action of individuals, but the latter can use elements of those social structures to develop strategies of mobility.[17]

Studying the Informal Economy

Having established the conceptual tools for this study, it is necessary to address the question of how to research such an elusive phenomenon as the informal economy. Most studies of the informal economy in Latin America use household surveys to measure the size of the informal sector and its evolution. Those studies usually use PREALC's operationalization of the informal sector as composed by firms with less than four employees, the self-employed, and, sometimes, domestic service (Funkhauser 1996; Infante and Klein 1991). These studies are useful to capture general trends in labor absorption, but they do not help us measure the informal economy as defined in this work, that is, work performed outside existing labor regulations.

Some studies focus on particular case studies and describe in detail the practices and linkages of a particular group of informal actors (Benería and Roldán 1991; Birkbeck 1978; Bromley 1978; Murphy 1990; Pérez Sáinz 1997). These are useful for understanding the internal structure of the informal economy and the logic of its actors, but they tell us little about general trends in labor absorption and about the broad effects of state regulations on the informal economy. Finally, some studies use surveys conducted for the purpose of clarifying a particular aspect of informal economic activities (Menjívar Larín and Pérez Sáinz 1993; Pérez Sáinz 1989). These types of studies are obviously

---

17. This "relative autonomy-cum-constraints" model holds for periods of social stability or of orderly systemic change, not for periods of system collapse.

helpful to analyze the particular aspect of informal activities that they are designed to capture, but again, obtaining from them a general picture of the structure and dynamics of the informal economy is difficult.

This brief methodological review shows the complexity of the task that I attempt to complete, that is, to achieve a general understanding about the ways in which regulatory regimes affect the structure of labor markets and informal economies. Still, I found methodological clues about how to proceed in the writings of institutional analysts of labor markets. In a survey of old and new approaches to the study of labor markets, John Dunlop (1988) argued that the researcher should go beyond the world of mathematical modeling or statistical analysis and become acquainted with the ways in which labor market institutions, labor organizations, and enterprises work. Tilly and Tilly (1998) provided a superb example of how to combine historical analysis with interviews and secondary data analysis to interpret the different forms of organization of work under capitalism.

In this study, I follow those methodological guidelines by combining several sources of data and methodologies of analysis. The first source is a comparative survey conducted in low-income neighborhoods in Santo Domingo and San José; the second source is a series of semistructured interviews conducted with informal microentrepreneurs and workers in these two cities. I participated in the design of the survey and conducted all the semistructured interviews.[18] The survey and the semistructured interviews are described in detail in the chapters in which the data are presented and analyzed. Additional data come from studies conducted by other researchers in these countries and official sources such as household surveys. In addition, I use historical secondary sources to describe the evolution of the state apparatuses and to establish the institutional and world-systemic context for my analysis.

Each of these data sources has limitations similar to those mentioned above. I hope that combining them provides a general view of the informal economy and its relations to the state regulatory regime. The survey allows us to analyze the general trends in labor market segmentation in San José and Santo Domingo. The semistructured interviews provide an in-depth look at the organization of informal firms, their linkages, and the logic of their actors. They also offer a direct acquaintance, of the type Dunlop recommended, with the institutional and organizational reality that constitutes the subject of the study. Moreover, they allow us to grasp the logic of action of the actors involved

---

18. The survey was conducted in the winter of 1991–92, and the semistructured interviews were conducted in the summers of 1992 and 1993.

in the informal economy. Research by other scholars lets us contrast my results and refine my conclusions. Official data provide a broad view of the general trends in labor absorption. Secondary historical sources help me to establish my argument about the differences in state apparatuses and the commonalties in the development paths between the two countries.

Each of these methodologies and sources of data complements one another and provides a reliable general view of the effects of regulatory regimes on the informal economy. Moreover, these different sources of data provide a multilayered view that is seldom found in studies of the informal economy. This view ranges from the macrotrends in labor absorption through the segmentation of the labor market and the structure of linkages of formal and informal firms to the microview of the logic of individual actors. This multilayered view, the systematic and in-depth comparison of two cases, and the combination of institutional and world-system approaches constitute the elements that make this work unique in the field of studies on the informal economy.

All that remains before embarking on my study is to describe its organization. The next chapter introduces the comparative method used in my analysis and compares the historical formation of the modern state apparatuses in Costa Rica and the Dominican Republic. In the first part of the chapter, I describe the comparative logic used in this work, the "most similar systems" design. The second part presents the historical background of my research, describing the development history of Costa Rica and the Dominican Republic since the 1940s. Chapters 3, 4, and 5 present the key empirical findings of my research. Chapter 3 addresses the macrodimensions of the empirical analysis. The chapter analyzes the labor market changes that accompanied the industrialization process in the two countries. It examines the process of labor absorption under import-substitution industrialization and under structural adjustment and shows that the differences in regulatory regimes lead to differences in the rates of absorption of labor into formal employment, in the rates of unemployment, and in the size of the informal economy. Chapter 4 compares the labor market segmentation and patterns of occupational mobility in San José and Santo Domingo and examines how they are shaped by the different regulatory regimes. The chapter shows that a developmental-protective regulatory regime leads to the improvement of the working conditions of the less protected sectors in the labor market. A key point of this chapter is the centrality of gender in the structuring of labor-market segmentation. Chapter 5 focuses on the economic and social articulations of informal economic actors. The chapter looks at the forms of articulation of informal microenterprises in the urban economy and the social networks of informal microentrepreneurs and their strategies for subsistence or growth. The chapter shows that state policies affect the linkages between the informal and the formal economies and the position of informal microenterprises in the prevalent model of development in the region. Overall, these chapters demonstrate that a developmental-protective regulatory regime can lead to a smaller informal economy, less unemployment, less poverty, less segmentation in the labor market, and less inequality.

Chapter 6 asks whether the informal economy can help in reducing the increasing poverty and unemployment found in Latin American cities. Programs for the development and support of microenterprises are at the core of current labor market and antipoverty policies. The chapter analyzes microenterprise development policies and the role the state can play in promoting informal firms. The chapter argues that policies toward the informal economy can alleviate some forms of social exclusion, but they cannot be the basis on which extended social citizenship is built. Chapter 7 presents the main conclusions of this study, addresses the question of whether labor market deregulation is a solution to the problems of employment in the region, and finishes with some reflections on the challenges of institutional change confronted by Latin American societies.

2

Comparing Development Histories

Comparative research is at the heart of the social science enterprise and is the source of some of its most valuable insights. Comparative work, however, raises thorny questions about the purposes of the comparison, the comparability of units of analysis, and the appropriateness of the comparative research design. Because a large and rich literature addresses the methodological problems of comparative research (Mahoney 1999; Rueschemeyer, Huber Stephens, and Stephens 1992; Skocpol and Somers 1980), I do not here discuss the multiple questions posed by comparative research. However, it is certainly necessary to detail the rationale of the comparative approach that guides this work. My basic approach to comparative studies is that research should be based on theoretical concerns and should be conducted by paying close attention to context and history. My research emphasizes theoretically informed and historically based empirical comparative research. My goal is to produce contextually based answers to questions, answers that inform theoretical debates and point to avenues for further research.

The comparative strategy followed in this book is designed to investigate the claim of a relation between different types of regulatory regimes and the structure of labor markets and informal economies. Different regulatory regimes produce different results in labor absorption and the organization of work and production. This relation is contextualized by a particular history of insertion in the world economy and by development attempts characteristic of a particular region in the periphery of the world system. I adopt what Przeworski and Teune (1970) call the "most similar systems" comparative research design. Przeworski and Teune argue that comparative social research should look for causal patterns between variables in social processes. They are aware, however, of the importance of the context in which social processes take place and argue that contextual, historical, and institutional factors always affect causal relations between variables. Their solution to the problem posed by contextual effects is to replace the proper names of the contexts in which processes are investigated by measurable variables. For example, if there is a difference in the relation between two variables in two different countries, this difference should be attributed to some theoretically relevant difference between the countries—such as the level of development or the political system—rather than to the particularities of the countries. In this case, I replace the proper names of the countries being researched with different categories in a typology of regulatory regimes.

The "most similar" comparative design is used to compare cases that share a large number of characteristics in common and differ in a small number of traits considered important to the phenomena under study. The common characteristics are considered control variables and the different traits explanatory variables. Differences in the dependent variable between cases are attributed to the differences in the explanatory variables—that is, to the differences in the contextual characteristics between the cases. The conclusions reached are generalizable only to other cases that share the same characteristics as those being compared. The conclusions, however, can be examined in cases with different characteristics to test whether and how they are relevant in different contexts. This comparative design is useful to search for causal patterns; at the same time, it is sensitive to history and context.

The countries, Costa Rica and the Dominican Republic, constitute the contextual level in this study. Costa Rica and the Dominican Republic share a series of common characteristics in terms of social structure and insertion in the world economy: Both are in the periphery of the world system, both were latecomers to industrialization, and in both cases serious industrialization efforts were not attempted until the 1960s. At that point, both countries had small economies dependent on the export of a few commodities for growth: sugar in the Dominican case, coffee and bananas in the Costa Rican case. Both countries applied an import-substitution industrialization (ISI) model during the 1960–80 period, and both switched back to an export-oriented development (EOD) model during the 1980s (Bulmer-Thomas 1987, 1994; Jacobstein 1987; Lozano 1985). The two countries differ, however, in two aspects that are theoretically important: (1) level of socioeconomic development, and (2) type and degree of state regulation of economic activities and labor relations. As shown in Table 2.1, Costa Rica has a better-educated population, a higher life expectancy, and a lower infant mortality rate. Costa Rica also practices a more extensive regulation of economic activities and labor relations than the Dominican Republic. Moreover, in Costa Rica, the existing regulations are more consistently applied than in the Dominican Republic (Lozano and Duarte 1992; Mesa-Lago 1994; Wilson 1998).

Table 2.1 Some indicators of socioeconomic development in Costa Rica and the Dominican Republic.

	Costa Rica	Dominican Republic
Public expenditure in education (percentage of GDP in 1985)	5.1	1.5
Adult illiteracy (percentage in 1990)	7.0	17.0
Infant mortality rate (per 1,000 live births in 1993)	14	40
Life expectancy at birth (1993)		
Male	74	68
Female	79	72

SOURCES: ECLAC (1991) Table 29; World Bank (1995).

The independent effects of these two elements—level of socioeconomic development and type of state regulation of economic activities—on the structure of the labor market are hard to disentangle. It is obvious that a higher level of economic development can enhance the state's enforcement capacity. Intervention in the development process and intervention in the reproduction of the labor force are two aspects of an overall set of institutions through which states intervene and regulate the process of capital accumulation; I refer to these institutional settings as regulatory regimes. My claim is that the differences in labor market regulation and in the level of development in Costa Rica and the Dominican Republic are the result of the differences in the state apparatuses and the policies followed by each country during the process of industrialization.

Comparing Apples and . . . ?

Are Costa Rica and the Dominican Republic comparable cases according to the "most similar" research design? Remember that this strategy is used to

Table 2.2 Two leading exports as percentage of total export value for Costa Rica and the Dominican Republic, 1955–1985 (percentages).

	Costa Rica		Dominican Republic	
1955	Coffee	48.6	Sugar	58.6
	Bananas	38.7	Coffee	16.6
	Combined	87.3	Combined	75.2
1965	Coffee	37.9	Sugar	55.8
	Bananas	24.0	Coffee	15.3
	Combined	61.9	Combined	71.1
1975	Bananas	27.1	Sugar	64.5
	Coffee	18.8	Coffee	4.8
	Combined	45.9	Combined	69.3
1985	Coffee	32.2	Sugar	32.2
	Bananas	22.1	Ferronickel	16.4
	Combined	54.3	Combined	48.6

SOURCE: Wilkie, Contreras, and Komisarik (1995), Part II, Table 2404.

compare systems that resemble each other in a large number of features and vary in key dimensions considered to be explanatory variables. For most people, Costa Rica appears much more developed than the Dominican Republic, and as shown above, its socioeconomic indicators are better than those of the Dominican Republic. The economic structures of the two countries, however, are more similar than they appear. Table 2.2 highlights the basic similarities between the two economies during the last four decades; as peripheral countries, their insertion in the world economy has been based on the exports of a few primary commodities: coffee and bananas in Costa Rica and sugar in the Dominican Republic. This dependence on a couple of commodities changed during the last decade, as both countries attempted to develop new exports and tourism to compensate for the decline in value of their main exports; but the new sources of foreign currency, such as tourism and export assembly industries, are similar in both countries. Characteristic of peripheral economies, the new export sectors are based on low skills and low pay.[1]

The World Bank classifies both countries as middle-income economies. In 1993, the price purchasing power (PPP) of Costa Rica's gross national product (GNP) per capita was 22.3, and that of the Dominican Republic was 14.7. The United States, the benchmark for this type of comparison, equals 100 (World Bank 1995). These numbers indicate that Costa Rica's standard of living is

---

1. One important difference, however, is the relevance of migrant remittances in the economy of the Dominican Republic (Itzigsohn 1995). The Dominican Republic is a country of emigration, whereas Costa Rica is a country that receives immigrants from the rest of Central America.

Table 2.3 Real GDP per capita in Costa Rica and the Dominican Republic, 1950–1988 (1975 international prices for the period 1950–1980 and 1985 international prices for 1988).

	Costa Rica	Dominican Republic
1950	819	719
1960	1,180	926
1970	1,601	1,113
1980	2,170	1,564
1988	3,800	2,570

SOURCE: Summers, Roberts, and Allan Heston (1984, 1991); Penn World Tables, Mark 3 for 1950–1980, Mark 5 for 1988.

about one-third higher than the Dominican standard of living, but the standard of living in both countries is low when compared with that of developed countries. Moreover, Table 2.3 shows that at the onset of industrialization the two countries had a similar level of development, whereas significant and consistent differences in GDP per capita developed during the years in which both countries embarked on industrialization projects.[2] Table 2.4 shows that from the 1960s to the 1980s both countries enjoyed quite high average rates of growth of gross domestic product (GDP) and GDP per capita. During the 1960s, the Dominican Republic had slightly higher rates of growth of GDP and GDP per capita, whereas during the 1970s Costa Rica's mean rate of growth was about one point higher. The table also shows that both countries experienced a brutal halt in their economic growth during the 1980s.

In both countries, at the onset of industrialization, the sectoral composition of the GDP was very similar. Table 2.5 shows that until 1970, the contribution of manufacturing to the GDP was higher in the Dominican Republic than in Costa Rica. During the 1970s, the proportions change: Although the importance of manufacturing in the GDP in Costa Rica grew, in the Dominican Republic it began a slow decline. This picture corresponds to the situation portrayed in Table 2.4, which shows that during the 1970s economic growth in

---

2. Tables 2.3 and 2.4 are based on the Penn World Tables (Summers and Heston 1984, 1991). The Penn World Tables try to develop a system of real national accounts that can be compared through time and between countries. The measures of these tables are constructed by taking into consideration the different levels of internal prices. The different measures are expressed in one constructed currency, which the authors label $International. Real gross domestic product (RGDP) is GDP per capita based on price purchasing parities (PPPs) and measured in constant international prices. These measures are very useful because they allow a more accurate comparison between the two countries. These numbers should not be compared to measures of GDP based on exchange rates.

Table 2.4 GDP and GDP per capita rates of growth for Costa Rica and the Dominican Republic, 1960–1988 (percentages).

	GDP		GDP/C	
	Costa Rica	Dominican Republic	Costa Rica	Dominican Republic
1960–1973	6.6	6.8	3.4	3.9
1973–1980	5.1	4.3	2.6	1.7
1980–1988	1.7	2.0	−0.6	−0.3

SOURCE: Summers, Roberts, and Alan Heston (1991); World Penn Tables, Mark 5.

Costa Rica surpassed that of the Dominican Republic. Table 2.6 shows that both countries experienced a large reduction in the proportion of people engaged in agriculture, a mild rise in the proportion of people engaged in manufacturing, and a rapid rise in the proportion of people engaged in service employment. The table also highlights differences between the two countries; in Costa Rica, the proportion of people involved in agriculture was smaller by the 1950s, and the proportion of people engaged in industry and services was higher during the whole period the table covers.[3]

To sum up, Costa Rica and the Dominican Republic have a similar position in the world economy; both countries have small economies based on the exports of a few commodities and services. Both countries are within the World Bank's "middle-income economies" range. In 1950, at the onset of industrialization, both countries had a similar standard of living. Forty years later, the PPP of the GNP per capita is about one-third higher in Costa Rica than in the Dominican Republic (World Bank 1995). The explanation for the difference in the level of development achieved by each country, I argue, lies in the different ways in which each state intervened in the process of industrialization and in the reproduction of the labor force.

The Development of the State Apparatuses

After the 1930 depression and in particular after World War II, the Latin American states occupied a central position in guiding capital accumulation. The state

---

3. The process of expansion of public employment had already begun during the 1940s, a period in which the Dominican state was under the personal control of Rafael Trujillo, who held a tight control over internal migrations, forcing people to remain in the countryside. This fact can explain the larger proportion of people engaged in service work in Costa Rica from the beginning of industrialization.

Table 2.5 Agriculture and manufacturing shares of GDP in Costa Rica and the Dominican Republic, 1950–1990 (percentages).

	Agriculture		Manufacturing	
	Costa Rica	Dominican Republic	Costa Rica	Dominican Republic
1950	38.3	34.5	11.5	12.5
1960	29.4	33.9	12.5	14.6
1970	17.8	20.2	18.6	15.7
1980	19.6	18.5	17.6	13.1

SOURCE: Wilkie, Contreras, and Komisarik (1995), Part II, Tables 3431, 3433.

had a central role in the industrialization process in the region. Tokman (1985) argues that this role is the result of the weakness of the local class actors. Borón (1995) argues that peripheral capitalism seems to give rise to Bonapartist regimes, that is, regimes in which the state enjoys a high degree of autonomy vis-à-vis the local classes. The character of the state apparatus is the key explanatory variable in this study. The previous section showed the multiple similarities in the social structure and development paths between Costa Rica and the Dominican Republic, similarities that emerge from their common peripheral condition. The two countries differ, however, in their respective regulatory regimes.

Institutional Continuity and Change

I characterized the Costa Rican state apparatus as developmental protective and the Dominican one as predatory repressive and argued that this difference should affect the structure of the informal economy in each country. At this point, I need to justify this characterization in greater detail and account for the emergence of the differences between the two countries. One problem in accounting for the differences in the history of regulatory regimes is the time that should be chosen to begin the account. At what point did the political-institutional trajectories of these two countries diverge? One could trace the differences back to colonial times and argue that the two countries have always been different. That conclusion, of course, would be true, but not very helpful because it would be equivalent to arguing that it is possible to derive the present institutional structure of the two countries from the institutional structure of colonial times and that is a questionable assertion. Although it might be possible to argue that some institutional traits are present since colonial times, the present institutional context is the result of more recent events. Moreover, to the extent that the colonial structures do have an effect on later institutional developments, there are a number of important similarities between

Table 2.6 Sectoral distribution of the labor force, 1950–1980 (percentages).

	Agriculture		Industry		Services	
	Costa Rica	Dominican Republic	Costa Rica	Dominican Republic	Costa Rica	Dominican Republic
1950	57.6	72.8	16.7	11.2	25.8	16.0
1960	51.2	63.3	18.4	12.8	30.5	23.6
1970	42.6	54.8	20.0	14.2	37.5	31.1
1980	30.8	45.7	23.2	15.5	46.1	38.9

SOURCE: Wilkie, Contreras, and Komisarik (1995), Part I, Table 1303.

these two cases. As Hartlyn (1998) notes, during the colonial period both countries were backwaters, both were poor and scarcely populated, and both had weak economic elites and relatively low levels of inequality.

I do not intend to repeat the "small farmers without inequality" myth, debunked by Gudmunson (1986), about Costa Rica. Yet, it is still true that in the general context of the social order in Latin America, Costa Rica was a backwater with lower levels of inequality than the centers of the Spanish colonial order, such as Mexico and Guatemala. An important difference between the core and the periphery of the colonial order was the relatively low use of coerced labor in backwater areas. Another important difference was peasant access to land; in Costa Rica there was an open rural frontier well into the middle of the twentieth century. Both statements are also true of the Dominican Republic, another backwater region, although the rural frontier was probably closed earlier in this country.

One could also trace the differences to the process of independence and the formation of the new nations. In this case, there are indeed important differences between the two countries. The process of state formation in the Dominican Republic took place in a context of external aggression from Haiti, protracted conflict between local elites that were separated along regional and economic lines, and external intervention by the United States. Hartlyn (1998) argues that the presence of major wars, economic devastation, and external intervention that help establish strong military institutions are the key determinants of the rise of what he calls neopatrimonial regimes in Latin America.[4] These elements were present in the Dominican Republic and absent in Costa Rica.

---

4. Hartlyn's (1998) definition of neopatrimonialism follows Weber's definition of patrimonialism and sultanism. Neopatrimonial regimes have two key characteristics: the centralization of power through patron-client relationships and the blurring of boundaries between the state's public interest and the ruler's private interests. Neopatrimonial regimes are a form of predatory state apparatus.

The Dominican state emerged from a struggle against its neighbor to the west, Haiti, rather than against the Spanish colonizer. Haiti occupied the Dominican territory from 1821 until 1844, and the threat of a Haitian invasion was present until the late 1850s. The external threat, however, did not lead to internal cohesion. The Dominican elites fought bitterly among themselves for the first four decades of independent existence and even annexed the country to Spain in the 1860s.[5] The time that the Dominican state began to function as a unified and coherent apparatus is a topic of debate among scholars. Betances (1995) argues that the formation of the Dominican state apparatus and the consolidation of its position of control over the national territory are protracted processes that began with the dictatorship of Ulises Hereaux (1886–89), continued under the regime of Ramón Cáceres (1906–11), and were consolidated during the first American occupation (1916–24). The consolidation of state institutions in the Dominican Republic took place under neopatrimonial regimes (Hartlyn 1998).

In comparison, the process of state formation in Costa Rica was much less conflictual. The battle of Ochomongo, in 1823, solved the question of the centralization of authority by establishing the city of San José as the country's capital. The Costa Rican elites were geographically concentrated in the central valley, and from the beginning of the state's independent life they specialized in the production of coffee. The history of Costa Rica is not, however, devoid of conflict. Forging a mythical image of the political evolution of the country, an image in which elite agreements and democracy prevail, is dangerous because the mythical image of a peaceful democracy is inaccurate. Costa Rica had its share of political instability and intra-elite conflict. There was a brief civil war in 1835, and during one-third of the period between 1824 and 1905 the country was under military rule. Yet, in a comparative perspective, the process of state formation in Costa Rica was faster and less conflictual than in the Dominican Republic (and in much of the rest of Latin America). Moreover, since the second half of the nineteenth century, the state was involved in the promotion of the coffee economy and, since the last quarter of the past century, the Costa Rican state was engaged in supporting the expansion of education (Booth 1998; Bulmer-Thomas 1987; Wilson 1998).

---

5. In 1869, the Dominican president Buenaventura Báez, one of the main caudillos in the internal struggles of the postindependence period, signed an agreement with the U.S. president Ulysses S. Grant for the annexation of the Dominican Republic to the United States. The American senate rejected the agreement. The United States was not yet ready for Caribbean expansion.

There were, then, important differences in the process of state formation in the two countries, and those differences affected the formation of state institutions. Yet, one cannot extrapolate the present state institutions from the past. The Costa Rican and Dominican state apparatuses of the second half of the twentieth century are different from those of the first half. Moreover, in the previous section, I showed that in terms of differences in economic development the divergence in the developmental trajectories between the two countries became pronounced only after the 1950s.

History has a key role in accounting for the divergences between the two countries, but an approach to history that can account for both institutional continuity and change is necessary. One can envision the history of the state apparatus as a trajectory characterized by long periods of institutional stability or slow change and punctuated by critical junctures of fast institutional change. During those junctures, different social groups struggle for the constitution of a new social and institutional order. The new institutional order is affected by the past social and institutional structures that constitute wide limits to the possibility of change, but it also depends on the outcome of the struggle between the different social forces (Collier and Collier 1991). The critical juncture in the formation of the modern state apparatus in Costa Rica is the period of social and political change that begins in the early 1940s and ends with the consolidation of the regime that emerged after the 1948 civil war. The critical juncture in the Dominican Republic is the period that begins with the death of Trujillo in 1961 and ends with the emergence of the Balaguer regime after the 1965 American invasion.

In Costa Rica during the 1940s, the government of a reform-minded member of the elite, Rafael Angel Calderón Guardia, unexpectedly launched the country on a path of social reform. The Calderón administration (1940–44) enacted a labor code and a progressive income tax and created the Social Security Institute (Caja Costarricense de Seguro Social—CCSS). To pursue this reform, Calderón forged an unusual alliance with the Communist Party—called the Popular Vanguard Party (PVP), and the Catholic Church. Calderón's reformist orientation continued under his hand-picked successor Teodoro Picado Michalski (1944–48). In 1948, a two-month civil war erupted over a dispute about the election outcomes of that year, elections in which Calderón attempted to win re-election for a new term in office. Contesting the results of the election was the spark that ignited an already tense situation, in which strong confrontations occurred over corruption in the political system, the communists' influence on the government, and the future direction of the country's development policies. Two peculiar coalitions opposed each other in the

1948 war. On one side stood Calderón, sectors of the elite who supported his reforms, and the Communist Party and its unions. On the other side were conservative sectors of the elite opposed to Calderón's reformist policies, allied with a group of young social democrat politicians who represented the emerging middle classes of Costa Rica and were organized under the leadership of José (Don Pepe) Figueres. The latter coalition emerged as the winners of the war.

After the war, Figueres, who controlled the military forces of the winners, made a pact with Otilio Ulate Blanco, the conservative winner of the 1948 elections, to rule for eighteen months as head of a revolutionary junta. During this period, the junta engaged in repression against the losers of the war, the Calderonistas and the communists and their unions. These attacks considerably weakened an already weak labor movement. At the same time, the junta continued and deepened the reforms initiated by the side that lost the war, creating the foundation for the reformist democratic system that has characterized Costa Rica since then. During this eighteen-month rule, Figueres laid down the cornerstones of the policies that characterized this period: the abolition of the army, the nationalization of the banking and insurance systems, and active participation in the economy by an interventionist state that promoted development. These measures stripped from conservative sectors of the elite the weapons they could use against the reformist state, established an environment of social consensus, and placed the resources of the state at the disposal of the growing middle classes. After the eighteen months, Figueres resigned and turned the government over to Ulate. During Ulate's government, Figueres and his supporters organized the National Liberation Party (Partido Liberación Nacional—PLN) that became the leading party in Costa Rica from the early 1950s to the 1980s, and its program was the base of the Costa Rican developmentalist policies (Booth 1998; Rojas Bolaños 1979; Rovira Más 1985; Wilson 1998).

The Costa Rican developmental state was not based on the same kind of autonomy by the main societal groups as was the case in the Korean developmental state. Rather, it was based on a broad social consensus about the reforms instituted by Figueres and his party—after all, both sides in the 1948 war had supported a path of social reforms—and the defeat of the more recalcitrant sectors of the elite. The result was a democratic reformist developmental state that combined democratic alternation in government and social concerns. The institutions of the Costa Rican state suffered from a measure of clientelism, as public employment became the reward for party loyalty; nevertheless, state institutions enjoyed a relatively high degree of bureaucratic autonomy that allowed them to function effectively.

Despite the fact that the PLN reforms were quite progressive in the Latin American and Caribbean contexts, Costa Rica did not suffer from the destabilizing external intervention that ended other reformist attempts in the region—such as the Guatemalan reformist government under Arbenz. Two elements help explain the lack of external intervention. First, Figueres and the PLN aligned themselves strongly with the United States in the framework of the Cold War. The Vanguardia Popular Party—the Communist Party—was outlawed for several years, despite its moderate character and despite the fact that its leaders were respected political figures even during the period of illegality. Second, the reforms in Costa Rica did not affect major U.S. economic interests. Moreover, as progressive as the Costa Rican reforms were, the state did not challenge the oligarchic sectors as a whole. Although it nationalized the financial sector, it left the structures of coffee processing and commerce unchanged. As Yashar (1997) notes, the post–civil war political order was based on the opening of political and economic spaces for the middle classes while maintaining the economic position of important sectors of the old elites.

Consolidation of the Dominican state as the holder of the monopoly of legitimate authority and the means of coercion in the Dominican territory was achieved under the American occupation of 1916–24. The legacy of the occupation, however, was not a democratic and legitimate political system, but a strong and unified military capable of imposing the authority of the state on the whole territory and over the different elite factions. Before long, the head of this new centralized military force, Rafael Leonidas Trujillo, occupied the presidency of the country. For the next three decades, until his death in 1961, Trujillo was the Dominican state. As a result, the consolidation of the Dominican state's authority occurred under an authoritarian, neopatrimonial regime; a regime that spoke the language of national development but that in fact subordinated national goals to the welfare of Trujillo and his family.

After Trujillo's death at the hands of opposition members, a complicated transition process led to elections in 1962. Emergent victor of these elections was Juan Bosch, the leader of the Dominican Revolutionary Party (Partido Revolucionario Dominicano—PRD), a reformist social-democratic politician with a vision not much different from that of Figueres. Bosch turned around the terms of political discourse by arguing that the key division in the country was not between trujillistas and antitrujillistas, but between rich and poor. The possibility suddenly opened for the Dominican Republic to embark on a reformist path similar to the Costa Rican one. The Dominican business and military elites, however, were unwilling to accept that course of action. They feared that Bosch's reformist orientation might threaten their interests and privileges. Moreover, they did not have a commitment to democracy, and although they had been beaten in elections, they controlled the main mechanisms of power.

Soon the military, the business elites, and the church began campaigning against the government, claiming that it was infiltrated by communists. In fact, Bosch was clearly a noncommunist, but he was committed to democracy and allowed the Communist Party and other groups of the left to operate legally. To compound problems, although a brilliant intellectual, a superb writer, and an accomplished orator, Bosch lacked the political acumen of Figueres (or Balaguer for that matter). Whereas Figueres was a pragmatist with a moderate discourse who guided significant social reforms in Costa Rica, Bosch was an unyielding leader more adept with words and ideas than with actions.

In September 1963, the military deposed Bosch's government and installed in power a civilian junta led by Donald Reid Cabral, a member of the Santo Domingo business elite. Although the U.S. government had been instrumental in guaranteeing the transition from the Trujillo regime and in insuring elections in 1962, it was by this time put off by Bosch's reformist discourse and friendliness toward the left. The U.S. reaction to the coup was to stand by and not rush to defend the democratic government, in fact accepting the legitimacy of the Reid Cabral government.

The junta did not bring political stability to the country and soon became highly unpopular. In April 1965, a civil-military coup led by the PRD and pro-Bosch factions in the army—who called themselves *constitucionalistas* (constitutionalists)—attempted to return Bosch to power. The coup met with resistance from conservative factions in the army, and soon the situation developed into a civil war and popular uprising. The reaction of the American embassy was to denounce the coup as communist. The *constitucionalistas* were by no means communists, but at that point, after the Cuban revolution and the Bay of Pigs fiasco, the United States was unwilling to accept any nationalist-reformist political experiment that remotely reminded American decision makers of Cuba. Four days after the coup, when it became clear that the conservative factions could not defeat the *constitucionalistas*, U.S. troops invaded the Dominican Republic. At the end of August, under pressure from the U.S. occupation forces, conservatives and *constitucionalistas* signed an agreement that established a provisional government and called for new elections.

The elections took place in 1966 with the country still under American occupation. Conservative Joaquín Balaguer, one of the prominent political figures of the Trujillo regime, won the election. Bosch, the campaigner who captured the imagination of the Dominican people in 1962, participated in the elections but did not campaign,[6] and the PRD activists suffered violent repression at the hands of the police and the army. Although Balaguer benefited from the harassment and violence suffered by the PRD, he had a real political support base in sectors of the elites and the peasantry and went on to become the dominant political figure in the Dominican Republic during the next three decades (Hartlyn 1998; Lozano 1985; Wiarda and Kryzanek 1982).

As Hartlyn (1998) points out, the post-Trujillo attempts to democratize the political system and to institute social reforms were carried out in very difficult conditions: without established democratic institutions, with a military that has been at the service of the dictator, with elites that were politically weak and insecure in the face of the landslide of a left-reformist party, and with American foreign policy concerned more with thwarting any independent radical reform in the region than with promoting democracy. These contextual conditions did not bode well for the consolidation of a democratic reformist regime Costa Rican style. The outcome of the process, however, was not preordained. A massive external military intervention was necessary to close the critical juncture. As happened three decades earlier, the legacy of American intervention was a neopatrimonial regime.

Balaguer's first twelve years (1966–78) were an example of Bonapartist rule (Lozano 1985). After the coup that deposed Bosch, the business and military elites showed themselves too divided to impose their rule effectively. Balaguer's regime was based on a compromise among the traditional agrarian and commercial elites, the rising urban middle classes, and the military, as well as the support of the United States, which guaranteed the regime's stability. Although the regime was formally a democracy, it was a rather authoritarian one. On the one hand, the PRD (Dominican Revolutionary Party), the main opposition party, did not participate in elections until 1978 because of the absence of minimal conditions for opposition activities. On the other hand, the left opposition was heavily repressed. The Balaguer regime led the country on a path of economic growth and social change that transformed the Dominican Republic into an urban society and gave rise to urban middle and working classes. However, it also promoted capital accumulation through the provision of cheap labor and the repression of the working class, thus lacking the social-democratic reformist orientation that characterized the Costa Rican political system (Lozano 1985).

---

6. The reasons for Bosch's passive attitude in 1966 are unclear. Some Dominicans argue that he considered that there were no guarantees for his safety. Others argue that he believed that his victory would lead to more political unrest and the permanence of the occupation troops, and as a result he conceded the elections to Balaguer.

Balaguer developed to a fine art the use of patron-client politics. He used the spoils of the state to buy the support of the traditional elites as well as parts of the popular sectors. State institutions were apportioned to the different supporters of the president, with the understanding that access to state office also meant access to the economic resources controlled by the office. At the same time, the president controlled a discretionary budget used to reward the political support of the popular sectors. The result was a predatory state apparatus and a political system that saw in the state a medium to achieve economic wealth. This system did not change during the eight years of PRD rule, between 1978 and 1984, or during the second period of Balaguer rule, from 1984 to 1996.

To summarize, the political systems in the two countries have historically suffered from clientelism. In both countries, public expenditures and government bills are used to guarantee and mobilize political support. In Costa Rica, however, clientelism is not the main form of mobilizing political loyalties. During the last five decades, the political system has functioned in a democratic way, and the state bureaucracy has been effective in carrying out reformist development policies. In the Dominican Republic, on the other hand, the neopatrimonial regime of Joaquín Balaguer introduced corruption and the "farming out" of state agencies to different interest groups as the ways to operate government activities.[7]

The State and Industrialization

Beginning in the 1930s and in particular after the end of World War II, the countries of Latin America attempted to emerge from their peripheral condition by pursuing policies of industrialization through import substitution (ISI). These policies were based on the protection of certain local industries and the expansion of internal markets, thus inducing state intervention in the economy through the creation of barriers to protect local products and the provision of an indirect salary to guarantee the reproduction of the labor force. The expansion in the state's role also led to the creation of a large number of jobs in the public sector. Costa Rica and the Dominican Republic were not oblivious to this trend, although both were latecomers to the industrialization process. During the 1960–80 period, both countries attempted to industrialize by substituting imports.

---

7. Beginning in 1996, under the administration of Leonel Fernández, the state apparatus started to change, albeit slowly and with great difficulty. Whether this will bring a fundamental change in the work of the state apparatus is too early to tell at the time of this writing.

In Costa Rica, ISI received major impulses in 1959, with the enactment of an industrial development law (Ley de Protección y Desarrollo Industrial—the Manufacturing Protection and Development Law), and in 1963, when the country joined the Central American Common Market. The import-substitution industrialization process in the Dominican Republic went through two phases. The first one began in the 1940s and lasted until the end of the Trujillo period. The second ISI period began with the establishment of the Balaguer government; its main instrument was a law enacted in 1968 for the protection and promotion of industries (Ley No. 299 de Protección e Incentivo Industrial—Law No. 299 for the Protection and Incentive of Manufacturing). In both countries, the main sources of hard currency used to finance industrialization policies came from the revenues of agricultural exports—sugar cane in the Dominican Republic; coffee and bananas in Costa Rica (Jacobstein 1987; Moya Pons 1992). Bulmer-Thomas (1987) characterizes the industrialization model in Costa Rica (in Central America in general) as a hybrid model because it was superimposed and coexistent with a policy of promoting export agriculture including the traditional products, coffee and bananas, and nontraditional products that experienced growth during the 1950s, particularly beef, cotton, and sugar. A similar process took place in the Dominican Republic where the state continued to support (and be supported by) the export of sugar during the years of import substitution.

Both countries thus applied a similar development model, but in Costa Rica the import-substitution process left a stronger social imprint, particularly in the areas of social policy and regulation of labor relations. The development process in Costa Rica was accompanied by the creation of an extended welfare state and a regulated labor market. The labor code, legislated in 1943, was seriously enforced, as were the minimum salary laws. After the 1948 war and the establishment of the hegemony of the PLN, the social security system was expanded. Coverage by the social security system increased from 7.4 percent of the total population in 1950 to 17.7 percent in 1961—when congress legislated the universalization of social security coverage—to 83.4 percent of the population in 1991.[8] In addition, salaries and social public expenditures were higher in Costa Rica than in the rest of the Caribbean Basin—despite the fact that trade unionism in Costa Rica has been weak, because of fragmentation and legal dispositions that rendered trade union activity difficult. These

---

8. Although obligatory, social security is linked to employment and not to citizenship. Employers and employees must pay a deduction from payroll to social security. Self-employed people must pay social security for employees in case they hire them. They can, but are not obligated, to pay social security taxes for themselves.

improved social conditions were the result of the conceptions of the hegemonic PLN, which promoted a class consensus through the state, by means of expanding social welfare while discouraging trade union organizations (Rovira Más 1985; Torres Rivas 1992).[9]

The development policies of the Dominican state promoted the expansion of industry, education, and public employment, all of which created opportunities for upward social mobility and the rise of urban middle classes. Balaguer's policy of modernization, however, was based on granting cheap labor to capital. The means to achieve this were, on one hand, freezing nominal salaries, resulting in the corresponding decline of real income; since 1970 real salaries have constantly declined. On the other hand, the Dominican state guaranteed cheap labor by failing to provide an indirect salary, in other words, by the absence of a welfare safety net and the absence of subsidies for collective consumption goods. In this way, the Dominican state protected firms from the costs of guaranteeing the reproduction of the labor force (Duarte 1986). The urban working class received a "subsidy" in the form of frozen prices for agricultural products, which was an important cause of the decline of the small peasantry and of rural-urban migration. At the same time, to guarantee its subsistence, the urban working class had to turn to the informal sector, whose numbers grew because of internal migration flows toward Santo Domingo. During the 1960–70 period, the Dominican Republic witnessed the rise of a large middle class and an even larger informal economy.

The labor code in the Dominican Republic was legislated under the dictatorship of Rafael Trujillo in 1951 and was replaced as recently as 1992 by a new labor code that is very similar to the previous one. In 1948, the social security law was legislated and, with modifications, is still in use. The labor laws legislated under Trujillo were the product of the concerns and initiatives of groups of intellectuals linked to the regime, who attempted to "modernize" the country by adopting accepted international standards. These reforms were seldom translated into actual practices because the Dominican working class at the time was very small and unorganized. In practice, workers were granted few protections in terms of job security and working conditions, and those protections were seldom effectively enforced (Hernández Rueda 1989; Lozano 1985; Murphy 1990).

---

9. This tendency was greatly enhanced since 1984, when a law promoting the formation of *solidarista* associations was legislated. *Solidarista* associations are a form of worker-employee organization at the firm level. Management and labor contribute to a firm savings fund whose purpose is to finance housing, health, and educational benefits for workers. *Solidarista* associations compete with and displace trade unions.

The Costa Rican state went further with the ISI process because it took control of the financial assets of the country and used them for social development and for the development of areas in which private capital was not interested. The Dominican state never performed the role of leader in the development process. Both countries witnessed a rise in the standard of living and a transformation of their occupational structure. Nevertheless, the policies followed by the Costa Rican state brought about a higher level of development, as well as higher standards of living for the working population.

Crisis and Restructuring

Toward the end of the 1970s, the easy phase of import substitution—the substitution of consumer goods—had been exhausted. The structural weaknesses of ISI are well known: constant trade imbalances caused by the growth of imports of capital and intermediate goods as the import-substitution process advanced and the fast saturation of limited internal markets in societies characterized by high levels of inequality. The 1979 increase in oil prices exacerbated the constant deficits in the current account balance. Combined with a worldwide recession and a decline in the prices of Latin American export commodities, the debt crisis brought about the deepest social and economic crisis in the area since the 1930s. The crisis led to a switch in development policies and a restructuring of the productive activities of Latin American and Caribbean countries. The new policies involved an emphasis on the growth of export industries (export-oriented development—EOD), an opening of the economy to foreign trade, and an adjustment of the size and scope of state intervention in the economy (García 1991; Gereffi 1990; Schoepfle and Pérez-López 1989).

The 1980s can be characterized as another critical juncture, not so much in regard to changes in the state apparatus, but in the structure of the economy and the relations between the state and the main economic sectors. The new model of development implies a change in the state's relations to the economy and society, affecting in that way the regulatory regimes. Neoliberal policies, with their emphasis on deregulation and the removal of the state from the economic sphere, are bound to affect the state's participation in the reproduction of the labor force. Both countries adopted the new economic model based on a reinsertion in the world economy through primary exports, low skilled services, low wage manufacturing, and in the case of the Dominican Republic, the export of labor force through migration. There are, however, significant differences between the two countries in the implementation of the new policies, differences that result from the character of each state.

The following account sketches the major economic and social changes that took place in the Dominican Republic and Costa Rica during the 1980s, the lost decade, and the ways that these affected the respective regulatory regimes. The survey and the semistructured interviews took place between 1991 and 1993, and for that reason I focus on the socioeconomic changes up to the beginning of the decade. I also briefly sketch the main trends of the 1990s to put my research in a broader perspective.

The Dominican Republic: Neoliberal Neopatrimonialism

The exhaustion of import substitution and the debt crisis prompted a transformation of the Dominican Republic into a service and labor export economy. The goal was to reduce imports and to achieve positive numbers in the current account that would allow payment of debt obligations. Tourism and export manufacturing—mainly assembly manufacturing—became the new growth sectors. To these one should add migrant remittances, which became one of the main sources of foreign exchange. Revenues from tourism represented 8.6 percent of exports of goods and services in 1977 and 30.4 percent in 1986. During the same period, remittances grew from 12.6 percent to 14.5 percent of hard currency revenues, and income from export-processing zones grew from 2.5 percent to 5.3 percent. By contrast, revenues from traditional exports decreased from 51.9 percent of hard currency revenues in 1977 to 22.8 percent in 1986. In 1990, sugar exports provided only 8 percent of export revenues, while tourism provided 40 percent (Ceara 1990, 1991; Fundación Economía y Desarrollo 1989).

This change in policies was the result of actions that the Dominican state took in response to the debt crisis. The change was aided by additional changes in the regional context, changes that were the result of U.S. policies during the presidency of Ronald Reagan. State policies gave great impetus to the development of the tourism industry, which by the mid-1980s had become the main source of foreign exchange. The legal and institutional framework for the development of export-free zones (EPZs) had been in place since the 1960s, but only in the 1980s did EPZs witness an enormous growth in terms of their participation in export income and as a source of employment. There were two main reasons for the fast growth of export assembly manufacturing. The first was a devaluation of the Dominican currency conducted in 1983 as part of the stabilization policy agreement signed with the International Monetary Fund

(IMF) (Abreu et al. 1989). With that devaluation, the Dominican government abandoned the parity with the dollar that had been the mainstay of its monetary policy. The second was the launching of the Caribbean Basin Initiative (CBI) by the Reagan administration, which promoted imports to the United States from the Caribbean Basin countries. The Reagan administration had been concerned about potential political destabilization in the region and developed the CBI as an instrument of economic growth in the region. The devaluation of the currency and the CBI provided strong incentives for the expansion of EPZs and assembly manufacturing.[10] At the same time, a rapid increase in migration occurred—mainly but not exclusively to the United States—as households' spontaneous response to the economic crisis, a response that was facilitated by the existence of a large Dominican community in New York City. The increase in the number of immigrants led to the rapid growth of migrant remittances.[11]

The various Dominican governments did not follow consistent structural adjustment policies. According to Miguel Ceara (1991, 1993), it is possible to distinguish four periods of economic policy during the 1980s, which coincide with four different administrations. During the first and second periods, from 1978 to 1986, the Dominican Revolutionary Party (PRD), a social-democratic party, governed the country. During its first administration under the presidency of Antonio Guzmán (1978–82), the PRD followed "demand side" policies, promoting the growth of aggregated demand through the expansion of current public expenditures. One result of these policies was the growth of real salaries, financed in part with external debt. In 1982, the second administration of the PRD took office under Salvador Jorge Blanco, confronting the

---

10. In 1980, the export zones employed 16,440 people; in 1985, employment in the EPZs was 30,902 persons; and in 1991, it was 134,998. This represents an average annual rate of growth of 9 percent (BID-FUNDAPEC 1992). The rate of employment growth in assembly manufacturing declined in the 1990s, particularly since the establishment of NAFTA has affected the textile imports from the Caribbean Basin (textiles constitute about 61 percent of the EPZs' employment). Nevertheless, EPZs continue to be an important source of employment and exports, and at the end of 1998, EPZ employment was estimated at 196,000. Moreover, since the enactment of the trade agreement, Caribbean countries have lobbied the U.S. Congress for parity with NAFTA, and at the time of this writing the U.S. Congress is considering legislative proposals in that direction.

11. During the 1980s, the United States turned a blind eye toward the rising Dominican migration because of its geopolitical goal of maintaining stability in the Caribbean Basin. In the 1990s, however, with the end of the Cold War, the growing number of Dominican immigrants, and the increase of anti-immigration sentiments, the American state hardened its attitude. Already at the end of the 1980s, it had become difficult for Dominicans to obtain American visas, and it has become increasingly so during the decade. Also, Dominicans were excluded from the "greencard lottery."

exhaustion of the ISI model and the explosion of the debt crisis. This administration signed an agreement with the IMF, committing itself to orthodox stabilization policies including the devaluation of the currency and restrictions in public expenditures. During this administration, services—tourism and assembly manufacturing—replaced sugar and other traditional exports as the main growth sectors.

The third period in economic policy began in 1986. In that year, popular discontent with the stabilization policies prescribed by the IMF brought Joaquín Balaguer back to power. Balaguer's fourth term in office, from 1986 to 1990, was characterized by a large growth in public investments in the construction sector. The goal of this administration's building program was to reactivate the economy and to create employment. As Hartlyn (1998) remarks, Balaguer pursued clientelist policies, but he was not a populist ruler. His attempts to consolidate political loyalties did not take the form of higher salaries and benefits for public employees and unionized workers, the two sectors usually favored by populist policies. Balaguer's policies kept salaries and benefits low. His clientelist policies took the form of particular projects usually related to construction (housing, roads, dams, and monuments), which provided jobs or benefited his supporters. These projects were financed from parts of the national budget that were kept under the discretionary control of the president.

Concomitant with the expansion of public construction projects, the country continued its emphasis on the expansion of production for export. These policies were contradictory, because the construction sector investments were based on an emphasis on the domestic market, whereas the export-oriented policies were based on the neglect of that internal market. These conflicting rationales caused high inflation and macroeconomic imbalances. In his fifth administration, Balaguer (1990–94) was forced to seek a new agreement with the IMF, initiating the fourth period in economic policy mentioned by Ceara (1991, 1993). This agreement was conditional on the implementation of stabilization policies, an opening of the economy, and a series of reforms of the public sector (Ceara 1993; CIECA 1992). These policies and reforms led to a reduction of inflation and a recuperation of growth, but in a context of increasing social inequality, unemployment, and poverty.

As for the social consequences of the economic changes, despite the meandering of Balaguer's policies and their departures from economic orthodoxy in the implementation of structural adjustments, the result of the policy changes of the 1980s and 1990s was a continuous reduction in the role of the state in the provision of social services and an indirect salary, particularly in the areas of health and education. Public expenditures in education decreased from 14.3 percent of total public expenditures in the 1979–82 period to 9.5 percent in the 1987–90 period. Real per capita public expenditures in education in 1990 equaled 45 percent of those in 1980. During the same periods, public expenditures in health grew from 7.3 percent to 7.9 percent of total public expenditures. This growth was the result not of an improvement in services, but rather of a spin-off from the Balaguer administration's construction policies. In essence, hospitals were built but not provided with the means to offer health services for the whole population. Moreover, the real per capita public expenditures in health in 1990 equaled 81 percent of those in 1980. Increasingly, larger segments of the population covered their health needs in the private sector; even the low-income sectors spent only half of their health expenditures in the public sector (CIECA 1992).

A look at the social security system of the country offers a similar view. At the beginning of the 1990s, the Instituto Dominicano de Seguro Social (Dominican Institute for Social Security—IDSS) found itself in near bankruptcy; in fact, the financial balance of the institute in May 1992 showed negative reserves for 54 million Dominican pesos (RD$) (at that time, the equivalent of approximately $4.3 million) (CNHE 1992). Dominican law (Ley 1896) establishes that the state must pay 2.5 percent of the social security contribution for each insured, along with the 7 percent paid by employers and the 2.5 percent paid by insured workers. The state thus must contribute close to 21 percent of the IDSS revenues. In fact, the IDSS budget comes almost exclusively from the contributions of employers and employees. During the 1979–89 period, the Dominican state, contrary to its own law, contributed only 2.9 percent of IDSS revenues. During the years 1986–92, the state actually paid RD$32.4 million of a stipulated payment of RD$467.3 million (CNHE 1992; Duarte 1986; Duarte and Tejada 1991). The amount of subsidies paid by the institute to the insured decreased, in constant 1988 Dominican pesos, from 7.2 million in 1979 to 2.8 million in 1989. Moreover, the number of medical services per insured worker was also reduced during the decade (CNHE 1992; Duarte and Tejada 1991). In Santo Domingo during 1987, more than half of the visits to physicians were conducted in the private sector (Gómez, Bitrán, and Zschock 1988).

The economic crisis and resulting change in the development model brought about an increasing social polarization. The real minimum salary in 1992 equaled only 77 percent of the real minimum salary in 1980 and 58 percent of that in 1970. The public-sector real minimum salary in 1992 represented only 32 percent of that in 1970. Public-sector salaries deteriorated consistently at a faster pace than did those in the private sector. In 1992, a public-sector employee needed 4.6 minimum salaries to be above the poverty line, whereas a private-sector employee needed only 2.4 minimum salaries. The percentage of the population under the poverty line grew to 47 percent in 1984 and to 70 percent in 1991 (CIECA 1993a, 1993b, 1993c). No serious compensation policies were put in practice to alleviate the social consequences of the switch in development models. Thus, by the mid-1990s, the participation of the Dominican state in the reproduction of the labor force was even lower than at the end of the ISI period.

By the beginning of the 1990s, when the survey and the semistructured interviews took place, the policies of the Dominican state had changed the composition of Dominican exports and employment. The regulatory regime, however, continued to be predatory repressive. Moreover, the economic restructuring took place in a context of low growth and increasing social polarization. The ISI years witnessed the growth of a massive informal economy, but they were experienced as years of general upward mobility. The 1980s were years of increasing poverty and increasing migration.

The Fernández administration (1996–2000) has made the reform of the state apparatus a priority and has tried to achieve this by a combination of institutional and economic reforms. On the institutional side, the Dominican government has attempted to rein in the worst forms of rent appropriation, such as border customs; has tried to strengthen the independence of the judiciary; and has developed innovative ways of consulting the population through a national dialogue. On the economic side, the Fernández administration has privatized parts of the national electricity company, probably the worst managed among the public enterprises, responsible for constant shortages in energy production; it has opened other public companies to private investment and has facilitated and promoted investment by foreign companies and Dominican immigrants abroad. The result was a three-year period during which the Dominican economy was among the fastest-growing economies in the world, a period that saw a reduction in the unemployment rate from 16.5 percent in 1996 to 14.3 percent in 1998. The institutional reforms are a clear step away from neopatrimonialism, and the economic performance of the country has been remarkable. Nevertheless, the structural problems of Dominican society are staggering, and, at the time of this writing, the extent to which Fernández has managed to rein in the predatory state apparatus is not clear; whether his administration represents the beginning of a real break with the predatory or the paternalistic-repressive practices of the past cannot yet be determined.

Costa Rica: Gradual Adjustment

An economic crisis of unprecedented proportions hit Costa Rica between 1980 and 1982. The political crisis of Central America during the 1980s, which eliminated the Central American market as a destination for Costa Rican products, only exacerbated the situation. In July 1981, one year before Mexico's announcement of its inability to pay its external debt inaugurated the 1980s Latin American debt crisis, Costa Rica declared a moratorium on debt payments.

The particular political conjuncture of Costa Rica at the end of the 1970s helped to compound the effects of the economic crisis. This emerged during an administration without a solid political base. Rodrigo Carazo (1978–82), a former social democrat elected as the leader of a shaky alliance of conservative parties, lacked the political strength to confront this situation. Two attempts to reach an agreement with the IMF to implement stabilization policies collapsed in the face of public opposition. As a result of public pressure, public expenditures grew, and the government lost its control over the exchange rate and inflation. At the end of the Carazo administration, the local currency, the colon, had been devalued by 500 percent; inflation passed the 100 percent mark; open unemployment reached 9.4 percent; and real salaries plunged to their 1975 level (ILO 1992; PREALC 1991).

The successive administrations that have governed the country since 1982 implemented structural adjustment policies and restructured the economy toward the production of exportable goods and services. The various Costa Rican governments signed two structural adjustment loan (SAL) agreements with the World Bank. The goal of the loans was to induce Costa Rica to restructure its economy, lower the protection for local industries, reduce subsidies for agricultural products, and promote exports beyond the Central American market. The World Bank also pressured for a redefinition of the role of the state, emphasizing the privatization of public enterprises and a retreat from the guiding role in the economy that the Costa Rican state held during the ISI years.

As in the case of the Dominican Republic, the model of development followed since 1982 pursued a new insertion in the world economy, based on the promotion of nontraditional exports of goods and services to markets beyond Central America—mainly the United States. The new sectors of growth are nontraditional agricultural exports, tourism, and assembly manufacturing—either in *maquilas*[12] or export-free zones (EPZs). During the 1980s, Costa

---

12. *Maquilas* refer here to firms that, although not located in EPZs, enjoy the same tax and customs advantages.

Rica successfully diversified both the structure of its export industries and the destination of its exports.

The Costa Rican state played a major role in the promotion of nontraditional exports. Already during the 1970s, Costa Rica had started promoting exports to markets other than the Central American Common Market, but after the crisis of 1980–82 export promotion became the centerpiece of state policy. The main policy instruments for these purposes were support for the development of *maquilas* and EPZs and tax credit for exports. These policy instruments had been introduced during the 1970s, but only after 1984 was their importance enhanced. That year, the government instituted a series of reforms of export incentives, which gave a strong push to nontraditional exports to markets outside Central America. The intervention of the Costa Rican state was limited, however, to facilitating the activities of the private sector and did not extend to designating strategic sectors and guiding the private sector toward those activities, as was the case of the export drives in Korea or Japan (Edelman and Monge Oviedo 1993; Franco and Sojo 1992; Ulate 1992).

In spite of the agreements with the World Bank and IMF, a gradual rather than a shock approach characterized the policies of the Costa Rican governments. The stabilization years were not accompanied by a recession and staggering social costs. Furthermore, when confronted with opposition, the Costa Rican administration backed away from unpopular measures, such as a steep increase in the price of electricity under Monge (1982–86) or the compulsory reduction of public employment under Calderón (1990–94).[13] The different administrations also implemented policies to protect the most vulnerable sectors. Thus, the Monge administration instituted a food distribution program that reached about 40,000 poor families; the Arias administration, confronted with housing shortages and land invasions, launched a program to build 80,000 new houses (the estimated number of actually built houses is 20,000); and the Calderón administration introduced a "food bond" for needy families and programs to promote self-employment and microenterprises (CEPAS 1992; Edelman and Monge Oviedo 1993).

This type of gradualism was the result of the character of the Costa Rican political system built under the PLN. The Costa Rican state had a social welfare

---

13. The administration of Rafael Angel Calderón Fournier enacted policies to drastically reduce the size of the public sector. As these policies turned out to be unpopular, he reduced the goals of the policies but did not completely abandon them. It is interesting to note also the closed character of the Costa Rican political elite. Calderón Fournier is the son of Calderón Guardia; his successor, José María Figueres Olsen (1994–98), is the son of Don Pepe Figueres. In the 1940s, the fathers fought each other but also agreed with each other in pursuing social reforms. In the 1990s, the sons succeeded each other in the task of dismantling the heritage of their fathers.

agenda that did not vanish with the crisis, and its political system dealt with protest and opposition by co-optation and a search for consensus. Nevertheless, what allowed the Costa Rican state to pursue its welfare and co-optation policies were massive amounts of foreign aid. Between 1983 and 1985, Costa Rica received $592 million in U.S. economic aid, and in 1985, the country was the second highest per capita recipient after Israel (Edelman and Monge Oviedo 1993; Torres Rivas 1992). The large amount of foreign aid was a form of geopolitical rent. Costa Rica benefited from its location as Nicaragua's neighbor. During the 1980s, when the Reagan administration was engaged in a war against the Sandinistas in Nicaragua, Costa Rica played a role as a "development showcase" in the American strategy against the Sandinistas. Therefore, it was important to spare it the worst consequences of structural adjustment.

Until 1990, the amount of annual aid continued to be more than $100 million. This foreign aid came mostly from the U.S. Agency for International Development (U.S. AID) and was subject to a number of conditions, foremost among them the privatization of public companies, the deregulation of the banking system, and the creation of institutions that parallel state functions, such as the Corporation for Development Initiatives (Corporación de Iniciativas para el Desarrollo—CINDE), whose purpose is to promote nontraditional exports. In other words, the large amounts of U.S. aid were conditional on the dismantling of the interventionist state, the same state that allowed Costa Rica to become a showcase for development (Edelman and Monge Oviedo 1993; Sojo 1991, 1992). Moreover, after the defeat of the Sandinistas, this source of aid dried up, compounding Costa Rica's difficulties in pursuing neoliberal policies without dismantling the welfare state.

The country achieved a major restructuring of its productive system, boosting the growth of nontraditional exports and tourism. This growth, however, did not appear to translate into an improvement in the welfare of the population. The trends in poverty show conflicting numbers and divergent interpretations. One study shows a rise in poverty from 21.1 percent in 1987 to 27.9 percent in 1991 (CEPAS 1992). Another shows a consistent decline from 17.1 percent in 1983 to 9.1 percent in 1992 (Cordero and Mora 1998). Researchers seem to agree that the process of adjustment alleviated the poverty caused by the economic crisis of the beginning of the 1980s. This alleviation was achieved mainly through the support of minimum wages, which were the only wages that did not deteriorate during the decade (Lungo, Pérez, and Piedra 1992). However, the poverty trends of the last years indicate that the new model of development led to an expansion of poverty. One study shows the level of poverty in 1996 to have reached 21.6 percent (Cordero and

Mora 1998). This high rate of poverty seems to be the result of the continuous implementation of structural adjustment policies in a context in which the country does not any longer enjoy a geopolitical rent.

During the 1980s, the Costa Rican state was subject to contradictory pressures over its social welfare policies. The state was confronted by the protests of different social groups affected by the adjustment, demanding the reversal of certain policies. From the outside, international agencies (i.e., the World Bank, IMF, and U.S. AID) insisted on the reduction of the public deficit, the withdrawal of the state from the economy, and the switch from universalist to focalized social policies. Social expenditures as a percentage of the GDP were reduced during the decade, but they were still kept at a high level, about one-fifth of the GDP. The largest deterioration was in health and education—the universalist components of public social policy (CEPAS 1992; Garnier 1991). At the same time, the social welfare institutions and services, such as the Costa Rican Institute for Social Security (Caja Costarricense de Seguro Social—CCSS), were forced to provide services to a larger population with less means. The CCSS has attempted to confront this situation through organizational reforms directed to decentralize the provision of services and to contract out the provision of health services with private and cooperative groups (Huber 1996; Mesa-Lago 1994).[14]

Perhaps the clearest effect of structural adjustment on the Costa Rican regulatory regime is a decline in the state's regulation enforcement capacities. The number of workers receiving below-minimum salaries in 1991 was well above the 1980 level, and a large number of complaints in this regard came from women working in the garment-assembly plants (Edelman and Monge Oviedo 1993). Invisible underemployment—that is, the proportion of workers who while working a normal work week are paid less than the legal minimum salary—was 9.4 percent of the labor force in 1991; this percentage was lower than in most years during the 1980s, but still higher than in 1980 (CEPAS 1992). A large number of employers, both small and large, also attempted to avoid social security payments. Moreover, between 1984 and 1990 the state did not pay about 1,900 million colones (the equivalent of $21 million at the 1990 exchange rate) in required contributions to the pension system of the CCSS (Ramírez, Lobo, and Acuña 1991).

The structural adjustment policies thus caused a deterioration, although not a dismantling, of the Costa Rican welfare state. Public-sector employment, while reduced, is still an important source of relatively well paid and stable

---

14. For a detailed description of the reforms, see Mesa-Lago 1994.

jobs. The Costa Rican state responded to the pressures of particular groups with ad hoc policies, such as the housing program of the Arias administration. Although there has been a small shift toward the targeting of social expenditures, at the beginning of the 1990s the bulk of the budget was still spent on universalist institutions and programs. The welfare institutions were kept in place, but forced to attend to the demands of an increasing population with reduced means.

Although the policy-making and regulation-enforcement capacities of the Costa Rican state have been reduced, they are still superior to the Dominican state and to the rest of the countries of the region. It remains to be seen whether the Costa Rican state will succeed in maintaining the welfare system under the present model of development based on cheap labor. The PLN Figueres administration (1994–98) continued the neoliberal orientation begun in 1982 by the Monge administration and signed a third structural adjustment loan with the World Bank (Figueres signed it in spite of the fact that during the campaign he had promised not to sign it). The result was a general disenchantment of the population with the state's capacity to address the social problems caused by two decades of structural adjustment.

On Similarities and Differences

This chapter has established the parameters for my comparative endeavor. First, I described the "most similar system" research design and showed the structural similarities between Costa Rica and the Dominican Republic, similarities that emerge from their common position in the periphery of the world system. During the 1960–80 period, Costa Rica and the Dominican Republic attempted to move up from their position in the periphery of the world economy through import-substitution industrialization (ISI) policies. In both countries, this attempt failed because of the countries' continued dependence on the export of agricultural products to finance the imports of intermediate and capital goods, the constant trade deficits as the result of the rise of those imports, the limits of the internal markets, and the failure of regional integration attempts. Both countries experienced a severe economic crisis at the beginning of the 1980s and as a result embarked on a new model of development, based on the exports of nontraditional agricultural products, assembly manufacturing, and tourism. By the end of the 1990s, both countries have outward-oriented economies.

The course of the adjustment policies shows the peripheral character of both countries and the pervasive dependence on U.S. policies. During the 1980s, geopolitical concerns led the United States to promote the CBI, which helped the Dominican export assembly industry, and to pump aid into Costa Rica, which allowed the country to avoid the worst social costs of structural adjustment. In the 1990s, with the geopolitical concerns gone, the aid to Costa Rica dried up, and the North American Free Trade Agreement's (NAFTA) textile exports elbowed Caribbean textiles from the American market, causing severe problems for the export-oriented model of development.

Yet, the two countries went through these common processes in ways that were importantly different. During the import-substitution period, the Costa Rican state constructed more efficient institutions to intervene in the development process, leading to faster and more balanced economic growth with a higher standard of living for the whole population. Following the debt crisis, both states diminished their intervention in the development process, but the Costa Rican state managed to conduct a more successful adjustment process with fewer social costs than did the Dominican Republic. The Costa Rican welfare state suffered from structural adjustment, but it was not dismantled. These differences show that even peripheral states have margins of action and that it is necessary to pay close attention to their regulatory regimes.

How did neoliberal policies affect the regulatory regimes of the two countries? Neoliberalism may have different effects on different regulatory regimes. I characterized the regulatory system in Costa Rica as developmental protective and the regulatory system in the Dominican Republic as predatory repressive. This differentiation was neater under ISI, and it can be argued that both countries moved closer to the x axis of Figure 1.1. The adoption of the neoliberal model of accumulation led the Costa Rican state to move toward the middle of the developmental-predatory continuum. Structural adjustment reduced the spaces opened to the Costa Rican state to engage in developmentalist or social policies. In the Dominican Republic under Balaguer, neoliberalism met neopatrimonialism; the result combined the worst of both worlds. Under the Fernández administration, neoliberal policies certainly helped to rein in some of the worst aspects of the predatory state. Under a predatory regulatory regime, reducing the scope of state intervention may diminish the sources of rents available to the state and may impose some constraints on its behavior. If that happens, the reduction of the scope of state intervention may actually help efforts to reform the state apparatus, bringing the Dominican state closer to the developmental side of the continuum. On the other hand, without an improvement in the working conditions of the public sector, the remainder of the state apparatus will continue its predatory behavior; without state policies aimed at integrating the excluded sectors, poverty will continue to be rampant; and without strong regulatory institutions, the private sector will behave in a predatory way.

There is no necessary relation between the size of the state and its efficiency in promoting economic growth and social welfare. Large state apparatuses are not necessarily effective; on the contrary, big predatory states are a major burden on society. On the other hand, small states can be effective in controlling key economic parameters and in that way promoting economic growth. Indeed, neoliberalism in Latin America has, in some cases, led to successful economic growth. In all cases, however, it has exerted a profound social cost in terms of increasing poverty and inequality. One can characterize the successful cases of neoliberal reform as developmental-repressive regulatory regimes. It seems that although neoliberal reforms may help to reform a predatory apparatus, going far beyond the limits of neoliberalism is necessary to transform a state into a developmental-protective regulatory regime.

A last point should be made about the labor laws in both countries: These laws were the result of the initiative of elite groups. The Costa Rican state, hegemonized by a reformist group in the local bourgeoisie, followed a policy of promoting social peace by granting a minimum level of welfare for the whole population. The Dominican state, dominated by Joaquín Balaguer leading an alliance of the traditional elites and the military, followed a policy of development based on cheap labor and repression of protest. The state policies toward the labor market that accompanied the implementation of structural adjustment policies should be noted. In both countries, a de facto deregulation of the labor market was accompanied by labor code reforms that extended labor protections. The Dominican congress legislated a new labor code that is similar to the previous one but that extends workers' rights to unionize. The new law guarantees legal protection for union members against arbitrary dismissal, a guarantee that did not exist in the former code. In Costa Rica, trade unions suffered a decline in their strength during the 1980s, as a result of severe defeats in the banana sector at the beginning of the 1980s and the successful challenge posed by *solidarista* organizations, a challenge fully supported by the state. Despite these defeats, the parliament introduced reforms to the existing labor code, reforms that were also designed to protect the right to unionize. This change was the result of American Federation of Labor-Congress of Industrial Organizations (AFL-CIO) pressures in the U.S. congress to deny preferential status in trade to countries that do not respect union rights (Pérez Sáinz 1998b). In both countries, the gap between labor laws and actual employment practices is growing.

In spite of the changes of the 1980s, the Costa Rican regulatory regime continues to be located in the developmental-protective space, whereas the Dominican regulatory regime continues to be predatory repressive. The differences and similarities between the two countries make them ideal cases for a comparison of the effects of state policies on the labor market and the informal economy. The comparison of these two countries allows one to answer questions such as: How and to what extent are the size and structure of the informal economy in each place affected by the commonalties in the development histories and the world-system position of the Dominican Republic and Costa Rica? How and to what extent are the size and structure of the informal economy in each country shaped by the differences in state development policies and labor regulation? These questions are the topics of the next chapters.

3

Industrialization, Regulatory Regimes, and Labor Absorption

The process of industrialization in Latin America led to an expansion of formal wage labor and at the same time to the emergence of large urban informal economies. The combined growth of formal and informal employment is a common characteristic of processes of peripheral modernization. The history of work under capitalism is that of the expansion of production organized around the use of wage labor, labor "bought and sold" in labor markets. Proletarianization is one of the central trends of the capitalist world system. The proletarianization of the peripheral labor force, however, is always partial. The total labor force of the periphery of the world system is not incorporated into modern wage relations, as this would put the full cost of labor reproduction on capital's shoulders. The result of the process of partial proletarianization is the rise of a variety of partially proletarian income-producing activities that are commonly referred to as the informal economy (Smith and Wallerstein 1992; Tilly and Tilly 1998).

This chapter addresses the macrodimension of the analysis. It looks at the broad process of urban labor absorption in Costa Rica and the Dominican Republic during the process of industrialization. First, I compare the evolution of the labor markets under import-substitution industrialization (ISI), roughly between 1950 and 1980.[1] Then I compare the labor market experiences of the

---

1. As argued in the previous chapter, the process of import-substitution industrialization began in both countries in the 1960s. I include the decade of the 1950s in my analysis for three main reasons: first, to get a perspective on the starting point of each country; second, the Costa Rican regime of regulation was established in the 1950s, and I want to capture its effects; and third, looking at the 1950s allows taking into account the industrialization efforts in the Dominican Republic under Trujillo.

two countries and the two cities of San José and Santo Domingo under neoliberalism and export-oriented development. The goal is to examine the process of labor absorption under different state regulatory regimes, as well as under the same regulatory regimes but under different models of development. My working hypothesis is that different development and labor market policies can alter the shape and size of the informal economy.

I chose to compare the cities of San José and Santo Domingo because they share similar structural positions in the two countries being compared. Both cities are the capitals of their respective countries and dominate their respective urban systems as their countries' centers of administrative and economic activities (Lozano and Duarte 1992; Lungo, Pérez, and Piedra 1992). During the 1950–90 period, the Dominican Republic and Costa Rica went through a process of accelerated urbanization. In 1950, the proportion of the urban population was 24 percent in the Dominican Republic and 34 percent in Costa Rica. In 1990, 63 percent of the Dominican population and 49 percent of the Costa Rican population were urban (United Nations 1989; World Bank 1995). In 1990, the estimated population of Costa Rica was 3.1 million people, while that of the Dominican Republic was 7.3 million people; the estimated populations of the metropolitan area of San José (AMSJ) and the city of Santo Domingo in 1990 were 861,300 and 1.5 million, respectively (Portes, Itzigsohn, and Dore 1994).

In Costa Rica and the Dominican Republic (and in the rest of Latin America and the Caribbean), the parallel processes of industrialization and urbanization created urban systems characterized by the concentration of population in one major urban center. In 1990, the population of San José represented 33 percent of the total population of the country and 71 percent of the urban population, whereas Santo Domingo encompassed 31 percent of the country's population and 51 percent of people living in cities. The population's rate of growth in these urban centers was faster than the rate of creation of formal employment, a fact leading to the emergence of a segment of the urban population that made its living from informal economic activities.

A surplus labor force is an important factor in the formation of the informal economy, affecting its size and rendering law enforcement more difficult, because there is more competition for jobs and workers are less willing to risk their jobs by demanding the observance of labor laws (Portes and Schauffler 1993). How much of the urban labor force becomes surplus labor, however, is not only determined by raw numbers; the size of the labor surplus is also strongly related to the development policies followed by the state, to the absorption of labor in the public sector, and to the willingness and capacity of state institutions to legislate labor laws and enforce that legislation. The size and shape of the informal economy are affected by the different state regulatory regimes. The comparison between Costa Rica and the Dominican Republic offers a frame of reference in which to assess the effects of different regulatory regimes on the broad processes of labor absorption.

To compare the labor market trends in the two cities, it is necessary to follow the changes in a number of employment dimensions. For that purpose, the narrative in this chapter shifts from theory and history to tracking statistical trends. I ask readers to bear with me through this admittedly dryer narrative as it is essential to pursue the macro level of the comparative analysis and to begin to address a number of theoretical issues about the informal economy and labor markets.

Several important issues in the public debate concern labor markets. One is the role of regulations in promoting informal employment. A closely related issue at the core of current debates is whether regulation leads to increasing unemployment. The mainstream position of economists and policymakers in developing countries argues in favor of deregulating labor laws to reduce unemployment and the number of people who have to engage in informal economic activities (Edwards and Lustig 1997; Portes 1994a; World Bank 1995). Eliminating regulation, it is argued, diminishes labor market distortions, which in turn allows for the clearing of the labor market. Some sociologists and economists have argued, however, that the relation between regulation and unemployment is not that clear and that it needs to be researched while taking institutional contexts into account (Itzigsohn 1996; Peck 1996; Standing 1991; Tardanico and Menjívar Larín 1997; Weeks 1991). The comparison between the labor market evolution in San José and Santo Domingo helps to clarify these debates.

Measuring the Informal Economy

The operationalization of the informal economy is a complex issue that often forces researchers to settle for available rather than ideal indicators. I have defined the *informal economy* as activities that avoid labor regulations. Given this definition, the indicators of informality should be related to the way in which firms comply with or avoid those regulations. However, most of the official statistics used to analyze the labor market macrotrends do not address this issue. Most studies of broad labor market trends use the ILO definition of the informal economy as an informal sector characterized by small firms with low capital and simple technologies. The ILO (and formerly PREALC) operationalizes the informal sector as including the self-employed (excluding those with university degrees), the owners of microenterprises—defined sometimes as those that employ up to five workers and sometimes as employing up to ten workers—and the microenterprise's workers. In some instances, but not always, domestic workers are also included in the informal sector. It is important to analyze how this operationalization relates to the adopted definition of the informal economy (Charmes 1990; Feige 1990).

Self-employment is an example of a type of activity not covered by labor regulations. In Costa Rica and the Dominican Republic, at the time of my research, it was not compulsory for self-employed workers to have medical insurance or to contribute to a pension fund. In Costa Rica, the social security administration (Caja Costarricense del Seguro Social—CCSS) offered optional insurance for self-employed workers. In the Dominican Republic, this option did not exist; self-employed people could buy only private medical insurance. Self-employment poses a problem for my definition of the informal economy. A strict application of the definition should leave self-employed people outside the boundaries of the informal economy. One can apply, however, a more inclusive definition and argue that self-employment should be considered an informal activity because it entails work carried out without any of the protections that the state regulations afford to similar forms of work that take place within wage employment relationships. Owners of microenterprises can also be considered part of the informal economy, because they are seldom covered by any form of social security while working long hours in their businesses, which generally do not present a sharp division of labor between microentrepreneurs and workers. This operationalization stretches the boundaries of the definition, but it is true to the analytical goal of looking at the forms and scope of unprotected work in urban labor markets in the periphery. Moreover, as many studies have shown, self-employed people and workers in microenterprises are often disguised employees of large formal firms (Benería and Roldán 1987; Birkbeck 1978; Bromley 1978). Indeed, the fact of linkages between formal firms on the one hand and informal firms and self-employed people on the other, and the inclusion of the latter in the production chains of the former, constitutes the core of Portes's approach to the study of the informal economy. In addition, to the extent that regulatory regimes affect the form and extent of labor absorption, they also affect the form and extent of self-employment and linkages between the formal and informal economies (these issues are explored in Chapters 5 and 6).

Workers at very small businesses, or *microenterprises* as they are usually called, are informal workers if their employers do not fulfill the existing labor regulations. Generally these employers do not, although it is arbitrary to set five workers as the upper limit in terms of size. In fact, many studies use ten workers as the limit, but this number is just as arbitrary. Empirical evidence shows that as businesses grow they tend toward more compliance with labor laws and introduce more productive technologies. Neither of these developments, however, happens necessarily when the business reaches five or ten workers. In spite of these problems, the size of the microenterprise is generally an acceptable proxy for the presence of unregulated labor in the firm.

Thus, self-employment and employment in microenterprises can be taken as indicators of labor market trends, indicative of the growth or shrinkage of a sector that is not likely to engage in formal work relationships. Focusing on those groups, however, tends to underestimate the size of the informal economy because a number of workers in medium and large firms do not enjoy the protection stipulated by the labor regulations. Many workers in medium and large firms are paid below minimum wages or are not covered by social security or other benefits to which they are entitled. Two indicators that capture part of this population—and at the same time correspond more closely with the definition of the informal economy adopted in this book—are the rate of invisible underemployment (i.e., the number of people that work full time but earn less than the legal minimum salary) and the number of workers who are not covered by social security. These two indicators show clear violations of labor regulations aimed at guaranteeing a minimum subsistence level for a worker's household.

A weakness of all the measures mentioned above is the fact that people often work both in the formal and in the informal economies. An ideal measure of the informal economy would need a twofold strategy. First, it would need a business survey to establish which labor regulations are most commonly violated at each enterprise by size and industrial sector. Such a survey would help define the relevant indicators of informality. Second, an ideal measure would need a household survey to establish the diverse strategies of labor market insertion of individuals and households. The semistructured interviews provide a small example of how such a study can be conducted; they look at the labor practices of the microenterprise and also inquire about the forms of insertion in the labor market of its owner and workers. The number of interviews, however, is small and the sample nonrepresentative. In the absence of such an ideal study, I use the available indicators mentioned in this section: the extent of self-employment and employment in microenterprises, the rate of invisible unemployment, and the proportion of the economically active population (EAP) not covered by social security. I see whether these indicators provide a consistent picture of the evolution of the labor markets in the two cities. First, I look at broad trends in labor absorption under import substitution; then, I look at the changes that took place under structural adjustment; finally, I look at the trends in indicators that refer to noncompliance with labor regulations.

This chapter traces the changes in the labor markets of the two cities until the beginning of the 1990s. The reason for this temporal choice is twofold. First, the empirical research on which this book is based was conducted at the beginning of the 1990s (during the 1991–93 period). Second, my task here is not to report the latest developments in these two countries (a task impossible for a book that always takes a long time to be produced), but to conceptualize regulatory regimes and their effects. This comprehensive look at macro-level trends allows us to begin to assess empirically the effects of regulatory regimes on labor absorption, the informal economy, and unemployment. This macro comparison is also a first step in the evaluation of the explanatory power of the different theoretical approaches reviewed in Chapter 1.

Economic Development and Labor Absorption

Labor Absorption Under Import-Substitution Industrialization

The import-substitution model of development was based on the assumption of the expansion of the internal market, and for that purpose it needed the absorption of labor into formal and stable wage relations. Large private firms and the public sector were the candidates to fulfill this task. The actual implementation of ISI did not fulfill the expectations of policymakers and planners about labor absorption. The countries of Latin America and the Caribbean did succeed in creating a relatively large stratum of formal manufacturing and service workers and public employees who had stable employment and relatively good incomes. At the same time, all these countries saw the rise and growth of a sector of people who did not have access to modern wage employment. As shown in the first chapter, different theoretical approaches attribute the rise of the informal economy to different causes. Although researchers linked to the ILO argued that it was the result of the particular form of industrialization that led to a structural surplus of labor, others attributed the surplus to the effects of different forms of state regulation of the economy (De

Table 3.1 Labor absorption in Costa Rica and the Dominican Republic during the import-substitution period (national trends in percentages).

	1950		1960		1970		1980	
	Costa Rica	Dom. Rep.	Costa Rica	Dom. Rep.	Costa Rica	Dom. Rep.	Costa Rica	Dom. Rep.
Wageworkers	66.5	34.0	--	43.0	75.3	51.7	75.4	53.7
Owners and self-employed	22.0	49.2	--	3.4	18.1	40.7	20.6	42.2
Family workers	11.5	16.8	--	13.6	6.6	8.1	4.1	4.3

SOURCES: IEPD (1991), Table 4.8; Soto (1982), Table 8 (chapter 1).

Soto 1989; Portes 1994a; Tokman 1989a). Comparing the experience of Costa Rica and the Dominican Republic can shed light on this problem.

Table 3.1 shows the general trends for the urban labor markets in the two countries. A first look at the data indicates that the overall trends in labor absorption are similar. For the 1950–80 period, the table shows an increase in wage employment in both countries, accompanied by a small decrease in the proportion of owners and self-employed people and a large decrease in family workers. In both countries, labor absorption into formal employment reached its peak in the 1970s. The proportion of wageworkers did not change during that decade, and there was a small increase in the proportion of self-employed people. During the whole period, the growth rate of wage employment was higher in the Dominican Republic, but this was due to the fact that Costa Rica had a much larger proportion of wage employment at the beginning of the period. At the end of the ISI period, there was a much larger proportion of wageworkers in Costa Rica than in the Dominican Republic, whereas the proportions of owners and self-employed were twice as large in the Dominican Republic

An important source of formal employment during the ISI period was public-sector employment. In Costa Rica, public-sector employment grew from 6.2 percent of the labor force in 1950 to 19.7 percent in 1980. In the Dominican Republic, on the other hand, 9.1 percent of the labor force was employed in the public sector in 1960 and only 10.2 percent in 1980 (Oficina Nacional de Estadística 1990; Soto 1982). These numbers underscore the fact that the Costa Rican state played a role in the reproduction of the labor force not only through the regulation of labor relations and the provision of social services, but also through being a source of stable and relatively well paid employment.

Table 3.2 takes a closer look at the urban labor market in the two countries during the import-substitution period. Throughout the whole period, urban formal employment in Costa Rica was larger than in the Dominican Republic.[2] In Costa Rica, urban formal employment grew steadily during the ISI years. The case of the Dominican Republic is different. Between 1950 and 1960, urban formal employment experienced a sharp reduction as a proportion of total urban employment, followed by a rapid growth between 1960 and 1980. These numbers suggest that under the Trujillo dictatorship the industrialization process developed at a very slow pace, and the people who migrated to the cities inserted themselves into informal activities. Trujillo, however, prohibited internal migrations, and only after the end of his regime in 1961 did both internal migration to the cities and industrialization accelerate. As a result, at the end of the ISI period, urban formal employment represented only 3 percent more of total urban employment in the Dominican Republic than it did in 1950, whereas in Costa Rica, it represented 10 percent more. The urban economically active population (EAP) in the Dominican Republic, however, grew during the period from 28 percent to 58 percent of the total EAP, a larger proportional growth than in Costa Rica, where the urban EAP went from 42 percent of the total EAP in 1950 to 69 percent in 1980.

Table 3.2 shows the presence and size of the structural labor force surplus in each country. Despite the growth of formal employment, a large number of industry and trade workers remained excluded from wage employment. Again, the proportion of the unwaged EAP in the Dominican Republic was much larger than in Costa Rica. For the latter, Table 3.2 shows that the proportion of unwaged labor was reduced during the 1960s and remained stable during the 1970s. In the Dominican Republic, there was a small reduction of nonwage labor in manufacturing during the 1960s, but nonwage labor in trade actually experienced a very small growth during the same period. Moreover, the growth of the formal sector in the Dominican Republic shown in the previous table may be misleading if one considers that invisible underemployment reached 43.4 percent of the total urban EAP and 38.7 percent of the urban wageworkers in 1980. In the same year in San José, invisible underemployment among the salaried workforce reached only 6.6 percent (Lozano 1987; Tardanico 1992).

---

2. The operational definition of informal employment used in this table is that of PREALC—that is: the self-employed, workers in firms of less than five workers, the owners of those firms, and family workers. Thus it overestimates the size of the formal sector because it includes in it people who work in firms with more than five workers, but who have no social security coverage.

Table 3.2 Trends in urban labor absorption in Costa Rica and the Dominican Republic during the ISI period (percentages).

	1950		1960		1970		1980	
	Costa Rica	Dom. Rep.	Costa Rica	Dom. Rep.	Costa Rica	Dom. Rep.	Costa Rica	Dom. Rep.
Urban EAP (% of total EAP)	42.0	28.2	--	33.2	--	45.6	69.5	58.6
Formal employment (% of urban EAP)	70.7	69.8	73.4	57.5	73.4	66.0	81.0	72.7
Percentage of unwaged EAP in manufacturing	27.6	--	26.5	34.8	16.5	30.2	17.8	--
Percentage of unwaged EAP in trade	47.5	--	39.8	62.0	33.4	63.2	34.6	--
Urban unemployment	--	12.2	--	--	3.5	24.0	6.0	19.0

SOURCES: IEPD (1991), Tables 4.8, 4.9, 4.10; Lozano (1987), Tables 1, 4; Ramos (1984), Table 4; García and Tokman (1984), Table 4; Katzman (1984), Table 3.

To sum up, during the import-substitution period, general trends in labor absorption in the two countries were rather similar. In both countries, formal employment grew, but a part of the labor force remained outside formal wage relations. These common trends are the result of the common pattern of peripheral industrialization, and they lend support to the ILO/PREALC argument about the origin of the informal economy in Latin America. Yet, the comparison between the two countries also indicates that the type of regulation regime indeed affects the process of labor absorption, although the effects of the regulatory regimes seem to be the opposite of those suggested by the literature that argues in favor of deregulating the labor market. Despite stricter enforcement of the labor laws, labor absorption into formal wage relationships was much higher in Costa Rica than in the Dominican Republic. Moreover, unemployment and underemployment were considerably lower in Costa Rica. The evidence shows that a developmental-protective regime was much more successful in promoting labor absorption and in reducing the informal sector, unemployment, and underemployment than a predatory-repressive regulatory regime.

What matters seems to be not the "amount" of state intervention but the type of intervention and the overall institutional context in which it takes place. In Costa Rica, in spite of a stricter regulation of the labor market, the informal economy was smaller. One could argue that this was the result of a higher level of development, but I have already showed that the higher level of development was achieved in the context of a stricter regulatory regime. Indeed, the regulation of the labor market and the protection of the conditions of work were some of the elements that allowed Costa Rica to achieve a higher level of development.

Exports, Structural Adjustment, and the Informal Economy

The new export-oriented model of development is based on the comparative advantage offered by cheap labor. As a result, Latin America as a region went through a process of de facto deregulation of labor regulations. The quality of the jobs created in the new growth sectors—mainly assembly manufacturing, new agroindustries, and tourism—measured in terms of salaries, fringe benefits, and job stability is much lower than those created in the growth sectors of the former period. At the same time, the region witnessed the rise of a number of precarious hiring practices such as part-time and temporary work, hiring of workers through employment agencies, and extensive subcontracting (ILO 1991). During the economic crisis, the public sector performed a countercyclical function, absorbing part of the workers expelled from the private formal sector. This increase in employment led to a large reduction in the salaries of the sector. As the decade went on and structural adjustment programs were applied, employment in the public sector also decreased. During the first half of the decade, open unemployment reached levels previously unknown in the region, being reduced during the mild recovery of the second half of the 1980s (Infante and Klein 1991; Jatoba 1989; Portes, Itzigsohn, and Dore 1994).

How did these trends affect the two cases? How did the differences in state regulatory regimes affect the evolution of the labor markets after the debt crisis forced a change in development models? Table 3.3 shows general trends in the urban labor markets in both countries for the 1980s. Between 1980 and 1991, the urban economies of both countries went through a process of informalization, expressed in a reduction of waged work and a rise in self-employment and unpaid work. These trends point again to the commonalties of peripheral insertion and strengthen Pérez Sáinz's (1998a) argument about the need to rethink the informal economy under the new model of development. Nevertheless, important differences remained in the particular form that these common trends took in each country. Despite the common trends, the previous differences in the structures of the urban labor markets persisted. The table

Table 3.3 Evolution of urban employment by occupational categories in the Dominican Republic and Costa Rica during the 1980s (percentages).

Occupational Categories	Dominican Republic[a]		Costa Rica[b]	
	1980	1991	1980	1991
Employers	2.1	3.8	6.0	5.0
Self-employed	25.1	27.9	12.2	19.0
Wageworkers	70.5	62.2	79.9	73.9
Unpaid workers	2.3	4.6	1.9	2.1
Unemployment[c]	18.2[c]	21.9[d]	5.0[d]	6.0[e]

SOURCES: Itzigsohn (1995, 1997); Tardanico and Lungo (1997).

[a] The data for urban Dominican Republic appear in Itzigsohn (1997).
[b] The data for urban Costa Rica appear in Tardanico and Lungo (1997).
[c] This percentage is taken from Ariza, Duarte, Gómez, and Lozano (1991).
[d] These percentages are only for the cities of Santo Domingo and San José, and they appear in Itzigsohn (1995).
[e] This percentage was calculated based on information gathered in the quarterly household survey conducted by the local Bureau of the Census (DGEyC 1991).

shows that under the new development model, the formal sector remains larger in Costa Rica than in the Dominican Republic; self-employment and unpaid work are considerably higher in the Dominican Republic during this period, whereas wage work is considerably higher in Costa Rica.

Table 3.4 takes a close look at the labor market trends in Santo Domingo and reveals a consistent trend in the rise of self-employment throughout the whole decade and a reduction in salaried employment and in the number of owners.[3] Unpaid family work increased during the peak of the economic crisis and decreased later, but its 1991 level was still higher than in 1981. Open unemployment remained constantly high during the decade. The data suggest that the main mechanism of the labor market's adjustment in Santo Domingo was a rise in self-employment and a small increase in unpaid family labor.[4] Open unemployment did not seem to play a role in the adjustment of the labor

---

3. Part of the large increase in self-employment for 1991 may be the result of the inclusion of casual workers under this category, but even if this is the case, there is a consistent trend toward the rise of self-employment.

4. The adjustment of the labor market in Santo Domingo was probably different from that in other cities of the country, such as Santiago, La Romana, and San Pedro de Macorís. This is so because the large growth in assembly-manufacturing employment—which was one of the main sectors of wage-employment growth—took place in those three cities. In 1992, out of a national total of 142,000 persons employed in EPZs, those three cities concentrated 81,000 jobs, whereas the EPZs of Santo Domingo and neighboring areas employed around only 11,000 people (figures calculated on the basis of information compiled by the author at the Consejo Nacional de Zonas Francas de Exportación—National Council of Free Export Zones).

Table 3.4 Evolution of the labor market in Santo Domingo in the 1980s.

	1980	1983	1991
Employers[1]	5.1	3.3	2.9
Self-employed[1]	14.5	17.7	25.2
Wageworkers[1]	73.5	71.1	70.0
Unpaid family workers[1]	1.2	2.2	1.9
Casual workers[1]	5.8	5.8	--
Unemployment[3]	21.4	21.7	21.9[2]

SOURCES: Duarte (1986), Table 4 (chapter 3); Lozano (1987), Table 1; IED (Instituto de Estudios Dominicanos) (1992); and Central Bank of the Dominican Republic (statistical information compiled by the author).

[1]The figures for the years 1980 and 1983 are from Duarte (1986), Table 4 (chapter 3). The figures for 1991 are from the IED, information compiled by the author.
[2]Figure for March 1990.
[3]The figures for 1980 and 1983 are from Lozano (1987). The 1991 figure was calculated by the author based on data obtained from the Central Bank of the Dominican Republic.

market, although the apparent stability of open unemployment may mask important changes. A national household survey carried out in 1991, Encuesta Demográfica de Salud '91 (ENDESA '91), found that the rate of urban open unemployment for men was lower than in the 1981 census, 13.6 percent as opposed to 17.7 percent. Open unemployment for women rose from 19.9 percent in 1981 to 46.7 percent in 1991.[5] Moreover, the survey found very high rates of participation in the labor force for both urban men and women. For men between 25 and 40 years, the rates of participation were above 90 percent, and for women between those ages they were close to 80 percent (Ramírez 1993).[6]

These numbers suggest that what happened was a massive incorporation of people into the EAP. Men most likely inserted themselves into self-employed activities, whereas women found jobs in export manufacturing or joined the ranks of the unemployed (Itzigsohn 1997). But the notion of inactive people in a city with low salaries and without a welfare system is problematic. A large number of the "unemployed" are made up, in fact, of casual workers, who

---

5. The survey Encuesta Demográfica y de Salud 1991(ENDESA '91—Demographic and Health Survey 1991) found a rate of urban unemployment of 27.4 percent. The larger rate of unemployment, as well as the large rate of unemployment for women, is probably the result of a methodological change in the measure of unemployment. ENDESA '91 classified as unemployed not only those people who searched for a job during the week of the survey, but also those who did not look for a job but expressed their willingness to work for a salary (Ramírez 1993). Given this method of measurement, the decline in male unemployment looks remarkable.

6. Even for urban boys between ten and fourteen years, the rate of participation in the labor force was 42.1 percent (IEPD 1993).

switch from job to job as jobs arise. Among unemployed people, for example, many engage in unrecorded gainful activities such as selling illegal lottery tickets and organizing *sanes* (rotating saving schemes).[7]

These facts are consistent with Lozano's (1987) model of the Dominican labor market. Lozano finds that urban open unemployment remained stable during the years of rapid industrialization, at a rate of around 20 percent of the urban EAP. He explains this apparent contradiction by asserting that in the Dominican cities a sector of underemployed people serves as a labor reserve for the modern sector and behaves countercyclically during economic crises. In periods of growth, the formal sector absorbs labor from the ranks of the underemployed; in periods of recession, formal workers join the ranks of the self-employed or the underemployed. The high proportion of the unemployed is constantly nourished by internal migrations and by the growth of the urban EAP.

The picture is different in San José. In this city, at the peak of the economic crisis the informal sector grew mildly, whereas unemployment absorbed most of the people expelled from the formal sector. Table 3.5 shows that as the economy recovered there was a large decrease in unemployment, which in 1989 was below its precrisis level, as well as a slow decrease in the informal sector, which remained above its precrisis level. Formal wage employment experienced a sharp fall during the crisis and a mild subsequent recovery. The data presented in Table 3.5 seem to indicate that the labor market in San José was basically unchanged by the economic crisis. The numbers for 1989, however, may be misleading because 1989 was a year of high GDP growth (5 percent yearly), and perhaps more important, it was an electoral year, one of the results being that the government stimulates the economy. There were important changes, however, in the informal sector. The proportion of self-employed people grew from 47.2 percent in 1980 to 67.5 percent in 1989, whereas over the same period the proportion of owners was reduced from 11.2 percent to 8.6 percent and the proportion of wageworkers was reduced from 35.6 percent to 20.9 percent (Trejos 1991). Thus although the size of the informal sector remained stable, there was a change in its internal composition.[8]

7. Unemployment in Third World cities needs to be studied in the context of household strategies for survival. In fact, the household surveys of the Costa Rican Dirección General de Estadística y Censo (DGEyC) have incorporated questions to try to capture the kind of gainful activities that otherwise go unrecorded.

8. The data for Costa Rica after 1987 are not strictly comparable with previous years. This is so because of methodological changes introduced into the household surveys that year. It is impossible to know how much of that growth is real and how much is the result of methodological changes.

Table 3.5 Evolution of the labor market in San José in the 1980s.

	1980	1982	1989
Formal Sector	71.6	66.7	70.7
Domestic workers	4.6	5.4	4.3
Informal Sector	22.1	25.1	23.2
Open unemployment	5.0	11.3	2.7
Global unemployment[1]	10.7	22.2	9.7

SOURCE: Trejos (1991), Table 2.

[1]This index is defined as the sum of open unemployment and visible and invisible underemployment transformed into the equivalent unemployment rates. (Visible underemployment refers to the people who work less hours than the legal working week and would like to work more hours per week. Invisible underemployment refers to the people who work the number of hours stipulated in the legal working week and earn less than the legal minimum salary.)

Tardanico and Lungo (1995, 1997) find some evidence of informalization of the urban labor markets in Costa Rica. Employment in microenterprises—those employing less than five workers—rose from 29.5 percent of total employment in the city in 1980 to 36.1 percent in 1991 whereas nonwage employment grew from 19.1 percent to 26.9 percent during the same period. These authors show that there was an increase in nonwage, small firm,[9] part-time, and subminimun wage employment in the cities of Costa Rica. These trends point to the increasing downgrading of employment for labor in San José, but this increase seems to be a moderate one and tempered by the electoral cycle. Cordero and Mora (1998) find that the trends for the whole country in the 1983–92 period show a small rise of employment in the private formal sector, a minimal increase in the informal sector, and a decrease in employment in the public sector. These authors argue that the fastest-growing sector in the Costa Rican labor markets is that of people employed in the new tradable sectors (export-processing zones and *maquilas*). This segment is equivalent to the assembly-manufacturing sector in Santo Domingo, and it is composed mainly of young single women with primary education (Bodson, Cordero, and Pérez Sáinz 1995).[10]

---

9. A note of caution is necessary about the growth of small firm employment in Costa Rica. Apparently, an important part of this growth is the result of skilled and professional workers going into self-employment. This points to a deterioration of working conditions for these segments, but not of small firms behaving countercyclically by absorbing semiskilled and unskilled people expelled from the formal sector (Tardanico and Lungo 1997).

10. Assembly manufacturing suffered during the 1990s in both countries, although for different reasons. After the peace agreements in El Salvador and Guatemala, Costa Rica lost employment in assembly manufacturing to these locations that have lower labor costs. Costa Rica has

An important difference between the two cities of San José and Santo Domingo is the behavior of open unemployment. In San José, open unemployment played an important countercyclical role at the peak of the economic crisis and then experienced a large reduction. The very low rate of unemployment shown in Table 3.5 may be hiding the retirement of discouraged workers from the labor market. Indeed, in 1989, discouraged workers represented 54.1 percent of the total of the underutilized labor force, which consists of the open unemployed, the underemployed, and discouraged workers (Trejos 1991). Hence, instead of showing a recovery in employment, the data may be a sign that people have given up finding gainful formal employment. In 1991, a year of slow growth, unemployment rose to 5.6 percent, showing again its countercyclical nature in Costa Rica. In any case, open unemployment in San José remained at much lower levels than in Santo Domingo.

The data on the labor market trends under structural adjustment point to the same picture of convergence on common trends with differences arising from the actions of different regulatory regimes. Both cities experienced processes of downgrading of employment and informalization of employment similar to those documented for the rest of Latin America. Yet, these processes were much more pronounced in Santo Domingo. In San José, public policies managed, to a certain extent, to limit the deterioration of employment conditions.

These findings address the public debates described at the beginning of this chapter. The implementation of labor market regulations apparently does not lead to a larger informal economy or higher unemployment rates. How did state intervention lead to a larger formal sector and less unemployment? The answer to this question has to do with the increase of the general income level and with the role of the state as employer. The general income level is higher in Costa Rica than in the Dominican Republic, affecting the size of the population that enters the labor market; the lower the level of income, the more people must households send into the labor market to survive (Itzigsohn 1997; Tardanico and Lungo 1997). In 1991, the net rate of participation in the Dominican Republic was 55.0 percent, whereas in Costa Rica it was 52.0 percent. At the same time, the employment rate in the Dominican Republic

---

tried to attract other types of firms that demand a higher skilled labor force. In that sense, it was successful in convincing Intel to open an assembling and testing facility. The Dominican Republic suffered from the signing of NAFTA, which affected Caribbean textile exports to the United States. Textiles being the largest sector in assembly manufacturing, this agreement has created serious problems for Caribbean EPZs. The Dominican Republic (and other Caribbean countries) has been lobbying the U.S. Congress to obtain parity with NAFTA for Caribbean textiles.

was 49.3 percent, and in Costa Rica it was 44.3 percent (Banco Central de la República Dominicana 1996; DGEyC 1992).[11] In other words, more people enter the labor market in the Dominican Republic. On the other hand, fewer good jobs are available in that country.

The number of existing good jobs is related, in part, to the role of the state as employer. Public employment is one of the main sources of employment in Latin America. In 1991, public employment constituted 23.4 percent of urban employment in Costa Rica, but only 19.7 percent of urban employment in the Dominican Republic (Ramírez 1993; Tardanico and Lungo 1997). Equally important, public employment in Costa Rica was one of the better remunerated sectors, and although working conditions in the public sector have consistently deteriorated since the beginning of the 1980s, remunerations were still better than in much of the private sector (Gindling 1991; Tardanico and Menjívar Larín 1997). In the Dominican Republic, on the other hand, public employment expanded during the 1990s, but it was among the worst-remunerated sectors (Itzigsohn 1997). The size and quality of public employment had a lot to do with the differences in labor market trends.[12]

State intervention has a direct effect on employment creation and an indirect effect on the rate of participation in the labor market, and these two factors affect the rate of unemployment and the relative size of the labor market segments. The size and quality of public employment constitute one of the main differences between Costa Rica and the Dominican Republic. However, the trends of the 1980s point in the direction of a slow convergence between the two countries. Public employment in Costa Rica grew during the 1980s but at a smaller pace than private employment, so that its importance declined

---

11. The net rate of participation equals the economically active population (EAP) divided by the working-age population, which indicates the relative size of the population in the labor force. The employment rate equals the number of employed people divided by the working-age population. The differences in the net participation rate and in the employment rate are actually larger than these percentages indicate. The reason is that the two countries use a different baseline for the working-age population—the denominator in the calculation of these rates. In the Dominican Republic, the baseline includes the population of workers ten years of age and over, whereas in Costa Rica it refers to the population twelve years of age and over.

12. These days, it is common to criticize state employment as inefficient and unproductive. Reducing state employment is a major goal of labor market reformers in the periphery and the center. My research indicates that state employment can indeed be inefficient and unproductive (the Dominican Republic provides many examples of that), but it can also be efficient and productive: A large state need not be a cumbersome state. Whether the state needs to be reinvented or reduced should be a matter of empirical evaluation that takes into account the goals of state employment and all the consequences—positive and negative—of its reduction, rather than a declaration of principles.

proportionally (Tardanico and Lungo 1997). Moreover, public-sector salaries have been affected by years of adjustment. Although they are still better than much of the private sector, particularly the new tradable sector, there is a trend toward the deterioration of public-sector work (Cordero and Mora 1998).

The Rise of Underemployment and the Decline of Social Security

Some available labor market indicators are close to the definition of the informal economy used in this book, that is, economic activities that avoid existing labor regulations. These indicators refer to the presence of invisible underemployment (i.e., those people who work during the legal working week but receive less than minimum wage) and the scope of social security coverage. These indicators also shed light on labor market trends that are not revealed by the indicators of labor absorption.

In Santo Domingo, a large sector of underemployed workers has been a constant element of the labor market since the beginning of the industrialization process. A labor force survey conducted in 1980 by the Oficina Nacional de Planificación (ONAPLAN—National Planning Office)[13] found that in Santo Domingo, underemployment encompassed 38.7 percent of wageworkers and 56.1 percent of the self-employed (Lozano 1987). A survey of manufacturing and construction workers conducted in Santo Domingo in 1981 by the sociologist Isis Duarte (1986) found that 7 percent of workers in import-substitution industries, 30.2 percent of construction workers, and 12.0 percent of export zones workers were paid less than the minimum salary.

No exactly comparable numbers exist for the beginning of the 1990s, but a survey of the labor force in the export zones, tourism, and agroindustry conducted in October 1991 found that the number of people earning less than the minimum salary in those sectors was 18.9 percent, 25.5 percent, and 20.6 percent, respectively (BID-FUNDAPEC 1992; CIECA 1993a, 1993c). A longitudinal survey of small firms and microenterprises conducted in 1992 and 1993 found that 56.3 percent of those employed in those types of businesses earned

---

13. ONAPLAN is one of several official agencies in the Dominican Republic that conduct research on the labor force. The main agency in charge of the collection of statistical information is the Oficina Nacional de Estadística (ONE—National Statistics Office), the parallel to the Bureau of the Census in the United States. The Central Bank has also conducted two surveys of the labor force, in 1986 and one in 1991. These efforts, however, are unconnected, with apparently little coordination between the different agencies. In Costa Rica, the Dirección General de Estadística y Censo (DGEyC—General Bureau of Statistics and Census) conducts annual household surveys that serve as the main source of information for the labor market.

less than the minimum salary (Cabal 1993). The underemployed encompassed 42.5 percent of those working in manufacturing, 62.0 percent in retailing, and 63.8 percent in services. This research lends empirical support to the expectation that the larger the firm, the lower the proportion of underemployed people. In firms with four to ten workers, the number of people earning less than the minimum salary was 27.1 percent, whereas in firms employing from eleven to fifty workers, underemployment was only 7.0 percent.

These figures point to a number of trends in the Dominican labor market. First, informal work is substantial in the growing segments of the formal sector—that is, EPZs, tourism, and agroindustry. Second, informal work is widespread in small firms, those with less than ten workers. Third, informal work, while widespread, is less extensive in medium and large firms. The rate of invisible underemployment in those firms is equivalent to that found in 1980 in the import-substitution industry, whereas the rate of underemployment found in the export zones is higher than both and higher at the beginning of the 1990s than at the beginning of the 1980s.

As for social security coverage, researchers found that coverage of the IDSS grew during the 1980s, both in absolute numbers and as a percentage of the EAP. Duarte and Tejada (1991) estimate that the proportion of workers with stable jobs covered under social security insurance grew from 7.4 percent of the EAP in 1981 to 17.0 percent in 1989. A study by a Dominican business organization, the Consejo Nacional de Hombres de Empresa (CNHE—National Businessmen Council) (1992), calculates that the population covered increased from 8.5 percent of the EAP in 1985 to 13.9 percent in 1991. This extension in coverage suggests, against all expectations, an extension of the formal economy in Santo Domingo during the 1980s. These figures, however, mask a number of trends that point in the opposite direction. First, violations of the social security law are widespread in the growing sectors of the economy: export zones, tourism, and agroindustry. These sectors are supposed to constitute the formal economy of the new model of development. Nevertheless, social security coverage encompasses only 75 percent of workers in the export zones and 72 percent in tourism and agroindustry; in other words, one-quarter of the labor force in these sectors is informal (CIECA 1993c).

Second and more important is the deterioration of services provided by the IDSS. A study of the demand for health services in Santo Domingo found that among people who consulted a physician in 1987, only one-half of those insured under the IDSS actually turned to its medical facilities for care, and one-third turned to private health services (Gómez, Bitrán, and Zschock 1988). The actual trend is for large formal businesses to offer workers affiliation with private health organizations. Most people who enjoy health insurance are members of private health organizations, and about one-third of the people who contribute to the IDSS are also covered by private health insurance. In addition, 96.5 percent of those receiving retirement pensions from the IDSS in 1992 qualified for only a minimum pension of RD$500, the equivalent of $40 (CNHE 1992). These facts indicate that in spite of an increase in the population covered, social security is becoming increasingly unimportant for the reproduction of the labor force. The reproduction of the working population of Santo Domingo is carried out more and more by private means. Santo Domingo witnessed the blurring of the distinction between formal and informal work.

Until the 1980s, formal labor relations were predominant in San José. The available information for the 1980s and the beginning of the 1990s shows a clear rise in "precarious" forms of work in the city and in urban Costa Rica in general. In San José, invisible underemployment grew from 6.6 percent in 1980 to 9.3 percent in 1987 (Tardanico 1992). In the urban areas of the country, underemployment grew from 17.6 percent of total employment in 1980 to 25.6 percent in 1991, and part-time work grew from 8.8 percent to 14.2 percent (Tardanico and Lungo 1995).[14] An analysis of the 1991 household survey of the Dirección General de Estadística y Censo (General Bureau of Statistics and Census) shows that invisible underemployment in the urban areas of the central region[15] was concentrated mainly among workers and employees in the private sector. Among the latter, 9.5 percent were underemployed, as opposed to 7.3 percent of the self-employed, 3.6 percent of owners, and only 0.5 percent of public-sector workers.

The private-sector underemployed workers were not exclusively located in the "informal sector." Trejos (1991) shows that at the end of the 1980s underemployment was more extended in the microenterprise sector, but it was also widely diffused in medium and large firms. Among microenterprises, 37.2 percent of the salaried workers earned less than the minimum salary. Among small firms (between five and ten workers), 29.7 percent of the workers earned less than the minimum salary, and among medium and large firms (above ten

---

14. I do not have specific numbers for San José for the beginning of the 1990s. However, it is likely that the trends in the city were not different from the trends in the country. The proportions, however, were probably lower in San José, as indicated by the 1980s data. The city, being the site of a large segment of public offices and agencies, probably had a larger proportion of formal workers than the country in general.

15. The urban areas of the central region encompass, beyond the metropolitan area of San José (AMSJ), the cities of Heredia, Alajuela, and Cartago. Since 1989, the household survey reports (Encuestas de Hogares) provide information at the level of the whole central region and do not provide data for the AMSJ in particular because the four cities of the central valley are in fact being transformed into a unified metropolitan area.

workers), 13.6 percent of the workers experienced invisible underemployment. These numbers are very similar to those found by Cabal in Santo Domingo for underemployment in medium and large firms. In both cities, then, informal labor practices are not confined to the "informal sector," and the rate of informality owing to subminimum wage employment in the formal sector seems rather similar in both places. In San José in the early 1990s, similar to Santo Domingo, an increasing number of complaints about violations of minimum salary regulations in the *maquila* firms, especially those of the textile and clothing sectors, have occurred (CEPAS 1992). The rate of underemployment in the microenterprise sector, however, is much smaller in San José (the next chapter shows why this is the case).

The growth of underemployment and its concentration in the private sector coincide with a proportional reduction in public-sector employment prompted by structural adjustment policies. For the analysis of the trends toward informalization of the urban labor markets in Costa Rica during the years of structural adjustment, the slow growth and later attempt at reduction of public-sector work may have been more important than the growth of an "informal sector." A study of the segmentation of the urban labor markets in Costa Rica in 1982 (Gindling 1991) found that, controlling for skill variables, public-sector workers had higher expected incomes than workers in the private formal and informal sectors. The real segmentation in San José appeared to be not between formal and informal workers but between public- and private-sector workers.

The social security system in Costa Rica covered 67.9 percent of the labor force in 1980. This level of coverage remained more or less constant during the decade; it was reduced to 63.5 percent of the EAP in 1982, but in 1991 it stood again at 67.0 percent of the labor force.[16] In 1989, 99 percent of public-sector workers in San José were covered by social security—showing again the importance of the public sector for formal employment in this city—as well as 93 percent of workers of medium and large firms.[17] Also, 80 percent of small firms' workers, 63 percent of microenterprise workers, and 52 percent of the self-employed were covered by social security (Trejos 1991). These data indicate that, although not universal, at the end of a decade of structural adjustment, social security coverage was still quite extensive.[18]

16. These figures were provided to the author by the CCSS.
17. This coverage is much higher than that found in the Dominican Republic in the new growth sectors (assembly manufacturing, tourism, and agroindustry).
18. In Costa Rica, social security coverage is mandatory for salaried workers and optional for the self-employed. The latter have the option to contribute separately to a health insurance

On the other hand, the services provided by the CCSS also deteriorated during the 1980s. As is the case in the Dominican Republic, the state bears a heavy responsibility for this situation. According to Costa Rican law, the state must contribute 0.25 percent of workers' salaries to the health insurance fund and a similar amount to the pensions fund, in addition to the payments the state owes as an employer. In fact, at the end of 1991, the state owed CCSS the sum of 13 million colones to the health program and 3 billion colones to the pension fund (the equivalents of $106,000 and $24.5 million). As a result, both quantity and quality of the health services declined, and there was an increasing demand for private health services (ILO 1992). The CCSS has attempted to reorganize its services to confront this situation. On the one hand, it promoted the formation of firms managed by former employees to whom the CCSS wishes to contract out the maintenance of hospitals. At the same time, it experimented with the transfer of part of health care provision to private and cooperative clinics (Mesa-Lago 1994). To avoid the bankruptcy of the pension fund, the CCSS increased the retirement age from 57 to 62 years for men and from 55 to 60 for women.

The analysis of the data for underemployment and social security coverage shows the already familiar pattern of convergence in labor market trends in both places with differences in the ways these trends are experienced. There is a rise of precarious work practices in both cities. Underemployment and noncompliance with social security regulations are extensive in both places, along with an expansion of informal labor practices. This informalization, however, is much deeper in the Dominican Republic. In that country, underemployment is more extended than in Costa Rica, and the coverage of social security is much more limited. More important, perhaps, in the Dominican Republic both the minimum salary and social security payments do not guarantee the minimum necessary for the reproduction of the labor force. The minimum salary does not come close to covering the needs of workers and their families, and the social security infrastructure is unable to provide the health and old age needs necessary for the subsistence and reproduction of workers.

Informalization in San José meant a de facto deregulation of labor relations, increasing violation of the labor laws, and changes in labor practices toward unprotected forms of hiring and work. The state has been unable, or

---

and to a retirement pension insurance (ILO 1992; Mesa-Lago 1990). Microenterprise owners commonly register their workers as self-employed to reduce the amount they pay in social security taxes. Employers have to pay the CCSS a payroll tax of 25.66 percent for each worker, whereas as self-employed, they have to pay only between 5 and 12.25 percent of their income.

unwilling, to control these processes. Yet, the minimum salary and coverage by social security still made a difference in that city; they were still meaningful indicators of formality. In Santo Domingo, the deregulation of the labor market meant a blundering of the lines between formal and informal work. With the exception of a small group of workers in the private sector who managed to protect their working conditions through their unions, most work in Santo Domingo was unprotected work.

Regulatory Regimes and the Informal Economy

This chapter shows the limits of the process of proletarianization under peripheral capitalism. The labor market trends portrayed show that Costa Rica and Santo Domingo went through similar processes of labor absorption and informalization. Under ISI, both countries experienced growth in the formal economy, but by the 1970s, the import-substitution model had reached its limit for labor absorption in formal economic activities in both countries. The data presented also show that the process of proletarianization is not a linear one (Smith and Wallerstein 1992). Despite a de facto deregulation in employment practices, export-oriented development did not provide a solution to the labor absorption problems in the two cities. On the contrary, the change in development models and the implementation of structural adjustment policies brought about a greater informalization of the labor market. In fact, the two countries experienced a process of partial deproletarianization.

Both countries experienced a rise in the informal sector, a rise in precarious forms of work, and a decline in the role of welfare institutions for the reproduction of the labor force. Evidence also shows that informal employment was widespread in the new growth sectors. In fact, the informalization process encompassed the entire economy and was not limited to those categories normally considered part of the informal sector. In the words of Castells and Portes, the two countries "*informalize themselves,* . . . *vis-a-vis their own formal laws*" (1989, p. 29). These similarities are the result of the similar insertion of Costa Rica and the Dominican Republic in the world economy and the similar pressures that both countries withstand as a result of their position in the world system.[19]

---

19. De Oliveira and Roberts (1993) show similar trends for Latin America in general.

Nonetheless, the processes of labor absorption and informalization were very different in the two countries. During ISI, labor absorption into the formal economy was much larger in Costa Rica than in the Dominican Republic. The larger formal economy was the result of the role of the Costa Rican state in promoting development, in expanding public employment, and in enforcing labor and social security laws. During the 1980s, the process of informalization of labor relations was more limited in Costa Rica. This fact was, again, the consequence of the presence of state institutions that enforced minimum standards of living and working conditions for the lower segments of the labor market. A more developmental-protective regulatory regime led, then, to a higher rate of labor absorption into the formal economy during ISI and to a lesser degree of informalization during structural adjustment.

The data presented in this chapter, as always, should be read with caution. The numbers are not always strictly comparable, and important information may be missing. Yet, the trends that emerge from the different types of indicators analyzed all point in the same direction. Table 3.6 summarizes the broad trends described in this chapter. In Costa Rica, a developmentalist-protective regulatory regime led to a smaller informal economy, less unemployment, and a more protected workforce than in Santo Domingo. These findings contradict much of what has lately been written on the topic of labor regulations and the informal economy and show the usefulness of constructing typologies for comparative endeavor. It is not the "amount" of state intervention that matters, but the general institutional context in which regulation takes place.

The picture of a labor aristocracy that enjoys labor protection amid a sea of informality suggested by Portes (1994a) corresponds to what I found in Santo Domingo where labor regulations are indeed ineffective, but it is very different from the situation in San José where the informal economy is relatively small and where a relatively large proportion of the labor force is protected by labor regulations. Portes's argument may in fact hold but only for one of the types in my typology of regulatory regimes. The PREALC/ILO argument correctly captures the broad trends in labor absorption, but misses important differences between the different types of regulatory regimes. The neoliberal argument about the importance of deregulating labor markets may hold for some conjunctures in some sectors of the economy, but it is far from being a universal truth.

The differences between the labor markets in Costa Rica and the Dominican Republic could be attributed to the higher level of development of the former country, rather than to the differences in state regulatory regimes. I discard this alternative explanation for three reasons. First, if one attributes

Table 3.6 Summary of the labor market trends in Costa Rica and the Dominican Republic under two development models.

	Costa Rica (Developmental-protective regulatory regime)	Dominican Republic (Predatory-repressive regulatory regime)
Import-substitution period	• Growth of formal employment • Relatively small informal economy Low unemployment	• Growth of formal employment • Large informal economy
Neoliberal export-oriented period	• Proportional reduction in public employment • Rise of employment in tradable sectors • Downgrading of employment in working conditions across the urban economy, but the divide between regulated and unregulated work is still relevant	• Rise in the informal economy • Rise of employment in tradable sectors • Downgrading of employment in working conditions across the urban economy, blurring of the line between regulated work

labor market differences to the differences in development levels, one must still explain the differences in development level. As shown in the previous chapter, at the onset of the industrialization process, the differences in the development level between the two countries were small, certainly smaller than after forty years of industrialization. My explanation accounts for the creation of these differences in development levels; I attribute them to the different development policies followed by each country and to the differences in the regulatory regimes institutionalized by each state. Second, the differences in the development level, although considerable, are not that large. Costa Rica's real GNP per capita is about one-third higher than that of the Dominican Republic, but it is not that high in itself. Nobody would consider a country with GNP per capita of $2,150 part of the core of the capitalist world system. Finally, for countries in the same range of development, a higher level of economic growth does not necessarily translate into a larger formal sector or a reduction of social gaps. Brazil and Venezuela, two countries with a higher GDP per capita than Costa Rica, have larger informal sectors and higher levels of poverty than the latter (World Bank 1995). The type of regulatory regime is the best conceptual tool to explain the differences I found in the labor markets in Costa Rica and the Dominican Republic. We cannot always disentangle the effects of the different components of the regulatory regimes. It is clear, however, that under a developmental-protective regulatory regime, labor market regulation leads to an increase in formal employment, rather than an increase in informal employment or unemployment.

Needless to say, state action should not be idealized. In a predatory-repressive context, state intervention can do more harm than help. Moreover, the declining role of social legislation and public employment in the reproduction of the labor force in both places poses the question of whether state regulation is still a good indicator of the differentiation between formal and informal economies.[20] This issue is particularly poignant in Santo Domingo, where the reproduction of the labor force is becoming increasingly privatized for all segments of society, both for the more protected sectors among formal workers who obtain access to private health care and private pension funds through agreements at the firm level, and for the rest of the labor force, which is compelled to find the means for its reproduction through household, family, or other private strategies. Labor regulations still make a difference in Costa Rica, but the question arises as to whether this will be the case if the present trends continue.

It is not my intention to argue that the search for more flexible labor relations is bad in each and every case. As Lagos (1994) shows, the concept of flexibility has many meanings—labor cost flexibility, numerical flexibility (i.e., flexibility in hiring and firing), and functional flexibility. Some of these forms of flexibility may be useful or necessary in different situations. The conclusions that emerge from this chapter, however, are a serious warning to those who praise flexibility and deregulation as an overall solution to the problems of labor absorption, informality, and unemployment, as well as a recognition of the central role that the state needs to play if the expansion of gainful and stable employment is to be a goal of development policies.

---

20. The structure of the labor market is related not only to the action of the state but also to the action of class actors such as unions, to the action of social movements, and to the gender and ethnoracial division of labor.

4

Labor Market Regulation and Labor Market Segmentation

Picture in your mind the workshop of a clothing microentrepreneur. It is located in a big room in the owner's house in a working-class neighborhood in San José. Reams of cloth and a few sewing machines fill the room. Between two and four workers, all women, usually work there. Now only two women are working, and they assert that they earn the same amount of money working there as they could earn working in a big factory. Both of them have worked in *maquilas* before, and both chose to work in the informal workshop. This snapshot provides a window through which to look at two key questions in the analysis of the structure of urban labor markets in Latin America. First, are the incomes of the people involved in the informal economy significantly different from the incomes of the people working in the formal economy? Second, are the sociodemographic characteristics of formal and informal workers different? These two questions are key aspects of the discussion on labor market segmentation.

Labor market segmentation refers to the idea that in a certain labor market there is more than one logic of income determination and job allocation. A segmented labor market has two defining characteristics: (1) People with observed equal characteristics (such as gender, age, or education) working in different segments of the labor market earn different incomes. (2) There are barriers to mobility between the segments. At the core of the world system, the discussion on segmentation revolves around the presence and size of primary and secondary labor markets;[1] in the periphery, the analysis of labor

---

1. The primary labor market is characterized by high wages, internal mobility ladders, and protected jobs, whereas secondary labor market jobs are low-wage, unstable, and unprotected.

market segmentation focuses on the comparison between the formal and informal economies (Funkhauser 1997; Gindling 1991). This chapter analyzes the effects of the different regulatory regimes on the structure of the labor market. The chapter also asks whether, and to what extent, the labor markets in San José and Santo Domingo are segmented labor markets, and if so, what that means for the working conditions in the formal and informal economies. A key point that emerges from this analysis is the centrality of gender in the structuring of labor market segmentation and individual strategies of labor market incorporation.

On Segmentation

Segmented labor market theories challenge neoclassical concepts that argue that the labor market is composed of atomized "buyers and sellers of labor" and governed by competitive rules (like any other market in neoclassical accounts). Labor market segmentation also challenges the idea that human capital is the main determinant of income. Segmentation theories argue that the labor market is a social construct, embedded in social and institutional relationships that encompass different forms of organization and governance, of which competitive rules are only a particular case. Scholars do not agree, however, on the causes and mechanisms of labor market segmentation. Explanations of labor market segmentation usually focus on the needs of the productive system, the interests and actions of class, political, or institutional actors, or both.

Tilly and Tilly (1998) distinguish between two logics of segmentation: functional and historical. Functional logics explain segmentation through considerations of efficiency. The authors point to three areas in which considerations of efficiency may lead to segmentation: (1) internal labor markets as incentive systems to deter shirking and to retain skilled workers; (2) division of demand into stable and variable portions; and (3) development of systems of incentive and mobility based on patterns of available information about workers' performance. Tilly and Tilly argue that efficiency considerations are important but not sufficient to explain patterns of segmentation. Patterns of segmentation vary between industrial sectors, regions, and historical periods. Thus, it is necessary to complement functional analysis with the study of the historical change of labor market structures, in other words, to bring together functional and historical logics of segmentation. Historical logics focus on the power of inertia and the defense of vested interests and on the outcome of class struggle.

Peck (1996) traces the history of segmentation approaches and discerns three generations of segmentation theories. According to Peck, the first generation introduced the concepts of primary and secondary labor markets. Labor market segmentation was associated with a dual productive structure and with a dual composition of the labor force. On the one hand, the primary labor market was associated with large firms in the key sectors of the economy and primary labor market jobs with white, middle-aged men. On the other hand, the secondary labor market was associated with small firms in backward economic sectors, and secondary labor market jobs were associated with ethnic minorities, women, and young people. The emergence of labor market segmentation was attributed to the skill needs of core firms in oligopolistic markets, needs arising from technical innovation. The intellectual origins of this generation of theories are in institutionalist economics analysis, and the main authors were Doringer and Piore (1971).

The second generation of segmentation approaches was associated with the work of Marxist labor market analysts (Gordon, Edwards, and Reich 1973). These scholars saw the emergence of labor market segmentation as the result of strategies used by monopoly capital firms to control workers by creating divisions in the labor force. Confronted with the historical tendency of declining skill levels—and hence the homogenization of working conditions and the consequently likely emergence of working-class solidarity—monopoly capital firms attempted to divide the working class by creating extended hierarchies in the workplace. Monopoly capital also attempted to further divide workers by exploiting racial and gender differences through different recruitment strategies for the different labor market segments.

Third-generation segmentation analyses combine functional and historical analyses (Tilly and Tilly 1998). These analyses recognize the importance of functional demands, such as technological requirements or labor control strategies, but they shift the focus of the analysis to the processes of social reproduction, the struggles of labor unions, and the regulatory action of the state. The third-generation approaches posit multicausal explanations for labor market segmentation, emphasizing historical contingencies, regulation, and institutional variability (Peck 1996).

There is an obvious parallel between the three approaches that attempt to explain labor market segmentation at the core of the world economy (described by Peck) and the different approaches to the study of the informal economy in the periphery (discussed in this book). The first-generation approach corresponds nicely with the ILO/PREALC analysis of the informal sector. For both, labor market segmentation is rooted in a dual structure of production, a structure characterized by technical dualism between large, capital-intensive firms and small, labor-intensive firms. Remember that PREALC explained the origins of the informal sector by reference to a peripheral industrialization process characterized by investment in capital-intensive production techniques that make it very costly to expand formal-sector jobs, limiting labor absorption in the modern sector (Tokman 1989b). The difference between these approaches is that at the core, labor market segmentation was associated with the technological needs of oligopolistic firms, whereas in the periphery, it was associated with insufficient labor absorption.

The second-generation approaches parallel Portes's analysis of the informal economy. In both cases, labor market segmentation is the result of strategies of monopoly capital. These strategies have different goals: At the core, the goal is to control labor, and in the periphery, the goal is to reduce labor costs. The underlying logic of the segmentation process, however, is the same. The approach that I develop here corresponds to Peck's (1996) third-generation strategies. This study focuses on the results of state intervention in the social reproduction processes through the regulation of the labor market and on the differences produced by different regulatory regimes. At the same time, it recognizes the importance of the structure of production that emerges from peripheral industrialization in understanding the informal economy.

The Structure of Labor Markets in the Periphery

From the workers' point of view, labor market regulation addresses the circumstances of their social reproduction. The stated goal of labor market regulation is to improve the living and working conditions of all workers. It is often argued that the actual results of labor market regulation are the opposite of those intended, that labor market regulation results in labor market segmentation (Portes 1994a). If that is the case, labor regulation has the paradoxical effect of worsening the living and working conditions of the lower ends of the labor market. This chapter discusses and illustrates the effects of different regulatory regimes on the concrete working conditions of workers in the formal and informal economies in both cities.

Costa Rica and the Dominican Republic have rather similar labor codes; in both countries, employers can fire workers easily, although they must pay severance payments. In both countries, employers must pay social security taxes, although only Costa Rica enforces social security regulations. Both countries have minimum salary laws, although in the Dominican Republic those laws are not enforced, and more important, the minimum salary does not guarantee the livelihood of the workers and their families. My claim is that the differences in the regulation regime led to different labor market structures. My work shows that, as is consistent with the results of the previous chapter, a developmental-protective regulatory regime can lead to a less segmented labor market and to better working conditions for the marginalized sectors.

Studying Labor Market Segmentation

As mentioned above, segmented labor markets have two main characteristics: different rewards for people with similar characteristics and barriers to mobility between the sectors. This chapter first analyzes the presence of segmentation in income between the formal and the informal economies; then it looks at the sociodemographic characteristics of the people involved in formal and informal activities; and finally it analyzes patterns of labor market insertion and mobility in the two cities. My investigation is based on the survey and the semistructured interviews mentioned in Chapter 1.

The survey was conducted in the summer and fall of 1991, encompassing three low-income neighborhoods in San José and four in Santo Domingo. Local research teams directed by senior social scientists interviewed 400 heads of households in each city. Budgetary limitations prevented the organization of a citywide representative survey; instead, local teams designed a two-stage survey. In the first stage, the local research team selected a number of neighborhoods in each city in an attempt to capture the variety of middle-low-income and low-income groups. The areas varied from those inhabited mainly by public employees and formal manufacturing workers to shantytowns inhabited mainly by informal workers. In stage two, households were selected randomly in each neighborhood, and the heads of these households were interviewed.[2] The interviews included a long series of questions on employment, which allowed me to analyze several aspects of informal work.

---

2. Because one of the goals of the survey was to capture the changes in economic position and the perceptions of the respondents as a result of economic changes during the 1980s, the respondents had to be thirty years of age or older. Thus, the younger cohorts were lost. This limitation of the sample is important because all the empirical evidence shows that young people play an important role in the informal economy. Nevertheless, the results still capture the core of the labor market structure.

Table 4.1 provides general information about the characteristics of the sample. Fewer than two-thirds of the heads of household interviewed were men. The mean age of the sample is quite high, and the average years of education are quite low: below high school. The mean education level of the sample is higher in Santo Domingo than in San José. The mean number of children per household is quite high in both places. In terms of other differences between the cities, the percentage of people married or living in unions is considerably higher in San José. The survey is limited in the population that it covers: The sample included only low-income sectors and did not include the younger end of the labor market. Therefore, these statistics are not representative of the cities in general, and the inferences that we make cannot be safely generalized to the entire urban population of these cities. Nevertheless, our research covers an important segment of the middle-low and low-income population in both cities and can provide some important clues about the structure of the respective labor markets. Moreover, the limitations of the survey are partially compensated for by the information collected in the semistructured interviews.

The qualitative interviews were conducted during the summers of 1992 and 1993. I conducted forty-four interviews in Santo Domingo and forty-seven in San José with microentrepreneurs and self-employed people in the manufacturing sector.[3] Seven microentrepreneurs in each city were interviewed twice, once in 1992 and once in 1993.[4] In addition, I interviewed ten microenterprise workers, four in Santo Domingo and six in San José. Respondents were contacted through the use of the snowball technique with multiple points of entry. This technique was used to avoid interviewing people belonging to the same social networks and hence to diversify the sample selection. The semistructured interviews lasted from half an hour to three hours, with an average length of one and one-half hours, which allowed me to check the information from different angles and at different points in the conversation, giving strength to the validity of the data. During the interviews, respondents were asked about the history of the microenterprise and its present economic linkages, the employment histories of the owners, and the owners' reliance on social networks for carrying out their businesses. In addition, I visited some of

---

3. Trade and not manufacturing is the largest sector in the informal economy. My reasons for choosing to focus the interviews in this sector is that in manufacturing one can better trace the character of the articulations of the formal and informal sectors.

4. I revisited six of the Dominican microentrepreneurs in 1997. Three were still in place, one could not be found, one was working as a security guard in a school, and one was in the United States (although the microenterprise was still in place, attended by the brother of the owner).

Table 4.1 Basic demographic characteristics of the sample.

		Santo Domingo	San José	Pooled Sample
Gender (columns' percentages in parentheses)	Women	153 (37.9)	138 (34.5)	291 (36.2)
	Men	250 (64.3)	262 (65.5)	512 (63.8)
Family status: married or living in consensual unions (percentages of total sample in parentheses)		259 (62.1)	296 (74.0)	555 (69.1)
Age (mean in years)		47.8	42.8	45.3
Education (mean in years)		7.3	5.9	6.5
Number of children (mean)		3.6	3.4	3.5

SOURCE: Survey.

the microentrepreneurs several times during my field trips and spent entire days observing the labor process and learning how they conduct their businesses. I also interviewed several people working in different microenterprise-promotion agencies.

The analysis that follows is based on the analysis of these sources of data. For the purpose of the analysis, I relied on different techniques, among them, two different forms of multivariate analysis: ordinary least squares (OLS) regressions and multinomial logit regression. These techniques are easy to follow for people with statistical training, but they may be cumbersome for those who lack that training. Therefore, for the benefit of the narrative flow, I have placed the more technical parts of the analysis in an appendix. Readers trained in statistical methods may refer to the appendix where the statistical results are presented, while untrained readers can choose to avoid the more technical parts of the analysis.

Income Segmentation

As for the analysis of income segmentation, one recurrent characteristic of informal economies everywhere is that they are not homogeneous. Three main types of economic actors can be distinguished in the informal economy: informal employers, informal workers, and self-employed people. Cross-national comparative studies have found that informal employers often have relatively high earnings, usually comparable to or even higher than formal workers have. Informal employers are often people who have acquired skills and experience in a formal job and have switched to independent work of their own volition, either because they can make more money than they could in the formal economy or because they value the flexibility and independence that informal work allows. The earnings of most of the self-employed and informal workers, on the other hand, are often at the bottom of the income scale (Fields 1990; Portes 1985; Roberts 1995; Tokman 1989b).

To analyze the structure of the labor markets in Santo Domingo and San José, I classified the sample into the following occupational categories:

- Self-employed: people working for themselves without employing paid workers.
- Employers: people employing paid workers.[5]
- Informal workers: wage or salary workers who are not paid social security benefits.
- Formal workers: wage or salary workers who are paid social security benefits.
- Nonworking: people who were not employed at the time of the survey.

These categories are based on Portes's (1985) analysis of the class structure in Latin America and the Caribbean. Portes distinguishes between the formal proletariat, the informal proletariat, and the informal petty bourgeoisie. Following Fields (1990), however, I also differentiate between two segments in the informal petty bourgeoisie: an upper segment consisting of informal owners and a lower segment constituted by the self-employed. The lower segment, together with the informal workers, constitutes the core of the informal economy. Table 4.2 presents the breakdown of the sample by occupational categories.

The size of the informal economy is about 40 percent of the sample in each city, although the distribution is different. Santo Domingo had a larger proportion of informal workers and a smaller proportion of self-employed people than did San José. The segment of formal workers is considerably larger in San José, 27.5 percent of the sample, as opposed to only 22.3 percent of the Santo Domingo sample; the proportions of people in the nonworking category are the inverse of those in the formal workers category: 22.0 percent in San José and 27.3 percent in Santo Domingo. The last point strengthens the findings in Chapter 3, which showed that the lack of labor regulations or, expressed in different terms, the presence of paternalistic-repressive regulations leads to a

---

5. I initially distinguished between formal and informal employers. The former paid social security taxes, and the latter did not. In fact, a large majority of the employers were informal, and only a handful were formal; for that reason, I collapsed all the employers in one category and considered them informal employers.

Table 4.2 Distribution of employment by occupational categories and mean income of occupational categories.

	Santo Domingo	San José	Pooled Sample
Employment by occupational categories (columns' percentages in parentheses)			
Employers	41	47	88
	(10.2)	(11.7)	(10.9)
Formal workers	90	110	200
	(22.3)	(27.7)	(24.9)
Informal workers	55	38	93
	(13.6)	(9.5)	(11.6)
Self-employed	107	117	224
	(26.6)	(29.1)	(27.9)
Nonworking	110	88	198
	(27.3)	(22.0)	(24.6)
Total	403	400	803
	(100.0)	(100.0)	(100.0)
Mean monthly income of occupational groups (in US$, calculated according to exchange rate in 1991). The numbers in parentheses are the ratios of the income in each category vis-à-vis their respective mean incomes.			
Employers	327.2	257.2	291.4
	(203.2)	(142.1)	(170.7)
Formal workers	191.6	217.4	205.7
	(119.0)	(119.9)	(120.5)
Informal workers	165.7	151.8	159.7
	(102.9)	(83.7)	(93.5)
Self-employed	152.6	171.8	162.3
	(94.7)	(94.8)	(95.1)
Nonworking	79.7	116.2	94.8
	(49.5)	(64.1)	(55.5)
Sample mean	161.0	181.2	170.7

SOURCE: Survey.

higher rate of unemployment. The nonworking category in my sample, however, is broad. It includes people who are actually searching for a job and people who are outside the labor force (e.g., housewives, people living on a pension or other sources of income not related to current employment). Only a small proportion of the nonworking group is unemployed, that is, people searching for a job. Some people in this category have some source of income such as remittances or pensions, and most of them probably engage in some form of casual gainful activities, albeit not in a regular way.

Are the earnings of workers in the different segments of the labor market in each city significantly different? Table 4.2 shows similarities and differences in the income stratification of both cities. The table shows that in both places the income hierarchy is topped by employers, followed by formal employees, with the nonworking at the bottom. In Santo Domingo, informal workers have a higher mean income than the self-employed, whereas in San José the opposite is the case. Table 4.2 shows that the mean income of the total sample is higher in San José than in Santo Domingo, although this is not the case for all the categories; employers and informal workers have higher incomes in Santo Domingo than in San José. On the other hand, formal workers, the self-employed, and nonworking people have higher incomes in San José than in Santo Domingo. The table also shows, however, that although formal workers and self-employed people earn more in San José than in Santo Domingo, the ratios of their mean income vis-à-vis the mean income in their respective city are similar.

Table 4.2, then, shows differences between the mean income of the different occupational categories. The table, however, cannot tell whether the two labor markets are really segmented and whether the structure of the labor market in each city is different. The differences in mean income between the occupational categories may be the result of the sociodemographic characteristics of the people who work in each of those occupational groups rather than the outcome of being employed in different labor market segments. To sort out the effect of the occupational categories on income, net of the effect of personal characteristics such as gender, age, and education, it is necessary to perform some form of multivariate analysis that accounts for the effect of employment in the informal economy on income, controlling for individual and family characteristics. For that purpose, I conducted an OLS regression of the logarithm of monthly earnings on a number of individual, family, and occupational variables (see Part I of the Appendix).

The regression is set up to show the effects on the workers' income of working in each of the five occupational categories, independent of the effects of the characteristics of the respondent. In other words, given a set of individual and family-household characteristics, the regression shows how the income of the respondent is affected by employment in the different occupational categories delineated above. The individual characteristics that I control for are gender, age, and education. The gender variable indicates whether women are discriminated against in the labor market through earning lower incomes. The variables of age and education stand as proxies of human capital characteristics: work experience and skills.

Human capital is the most accepted mainstream explanation of wage determination. According to this argument, pay is related to productivity—the more productive the worker, the higher the pay. Productivity, in turn, is related to human capital (abilities and skills); hence, differences in income are explained by individual endowments and investment in human capital. Labor market segmentation theories do not deny the importance of human capital, but argue that income is determined not only by the individual endowments of the employee, but also by the institutional characteristics of the labor market. Therefore, people with similar endowments of human capital working in different segments of the labor market earn different incomes.

To measure the effects of the particular characteristic of each city, I included a variable in the regression, indicating whether the respondent was from Santo Domingo or from San José. This variable captures the overall differences in regulatory regimes between the two countries. To see whether the determination of income is different in the two cities, I interacted the city variable with each of the occupational categories and with the gender variable. The family-household variables were included to control for the effects of the family and household situations of the respondents on their income. These variables were the respondents' number of children, whether they were married or living in a consensual union or not, the number of people in the household who had a job, and the stage of the family in the family cycle (the whole set of variables is described in more detail in the Appendix).

Combining the analysis of segmentation with the study of the effects of regulatory regimes, three possible scenarios can emerge from the analysis:

- If the structure of the labor market in both cities is similar and segmented, then the occupational category variables will be the most important determinants of income. This indicates that the income of the different occupational groups is significantly different, controlling for the sociodemographic characteristics and the human capital of the workers.
- If the structure of the labor market in both cities is similar and nonsegmented and human capital is the mechanism of income determination, then education, a proxy for human capital, should be the most important determinant of income.
- If the differences in regulatory regimes lead to different structures of the labor market, then the city and interaction variables will be the most important determinants of income. The city variable indicates whether income in the

two cities is significantly different, controlling for the sociodemographic characteristics of the workers. The interaction variables point to different dimensions in which the structure of the labor market in the two cities may differ.

The results of the multivariate analysis are mixed and involve elements of the three scenarios described above. The analysis shows that, in both cities, employers earn significantly more than formal workers whereas nonworking people earn significantly less. The presence of nonworking people in cities without unemployment compensation or with very low old age pensions poses the question of what the sources of their means of subsistence are. The people included in the nonworking category most likely perform some sort of income-earning activity, and as such we can consider them a proxy for the most marginal sector in the informal economy. There are no significant differences, however, between the incomes of formal workers, informal workers, and self-employed people. The analysis, then, yields some evidence of segmentation between the two occupational categories that represent the upper and lower ends of the labor market, but there is no evidence of segmentation at the core of employed people. On the other hand, the effect of education is significant and positive, stressing the importance of human capital.

How does the regulatory regime affect the structure of the labor market? The city variable indicates that incomes in San José are significantly higher than in Santo Domingo. Looking at how the city variable interacts with the occupational categories shows that the main difference between the two cities lies in the nonworking category. Although the incomes of formal, informal, and self-employed workers are not significantly different in the two cities, the income of the nonworking category is significantly higher in San José. This distinction could be the result of the presence of transfer payments in that city or the result of higher incomes in the more marginal sectors of the informal economy in San José. In either case, the analysis shows that the regulatory regime does not affect the overall structure of the labor market, which appears to be similar in both places—the result of a common process of peripheral industrialization. The effects of the differences in regulatory regimes are felt on the overall level of income, which is higher in San José, and on better incomes for the more marginal segments of the labor market.

The results of the analysis show that in both cities there is gender discrimination in wages. Women earn less regardless of their human capital or segment of employment. The analysis indicates that the gender gap in income is significantly higher in Santo Domingo. This result is consistent with the previous results that indicate that the effect of a developmental-protective regulatory regime is expressed in an improvement of the income of the less protected segments of the labor market.

How do these results compare with other studies of labor market segmentation in these countries? Gindling (1991) used the Costa Rican quarterly population surveys[6] to conduct a study of labor market segmentation in San José at the beginning of the 1980s. He found that the expected income in the public sector was higher than in the private-formal sector, which in turn had expected incomes higher than the informal sector. The quantitative data do not allow me to reproduce this analysis, as I cannot distinguish between people working in the public and the private sectors. Moreover, Gindling's private-formal sector was composed of skilled professionals and of people working in occupations associated with government sponsorship; as such, they were more likely to receive the protection of the state. Again, I cannot distinguish between occupations in this way in my sample, and it is very likely that a large part of this segment is not included in the sample to begin with.

Cordero and Mora (1998) conducted regression analyses of income in Costa Rica for the years 1988, 1991, and 1992. Their analysis differs from mine in that it is also based on the quarterly population surveys and tracks the labor market trends for the whole country. Their categories are based on PREALC's, but they differentiate in the analysis between public-sector workers, private formal-sector workers, and workers in the new tradable sectors (tourism, nontraditional agricultural exports, and assembly manufacturing). For the three years, and similar to Gindling, they find that informal-sector income is significantly lower than formal-sector income and public-sector income is significantly higher. An interesting finding is that the new tradable sectors have incomes significantly lower than the formal sector. As with Gindling's analysis, I cannot reproduce this analysis with my quantitative data. However, the qualitative information analyzed later in this chapter bridges some differences among the various quantitative analyses. An important finding of Cordero and Mora, which coincides with mine, is that controlling for employment sector, women earn significantly less than men do. Gender differences in income seem to be a pervasive characteristic of all segments of the labor market in the region. For example, Espinal and Grasmuck (1997), in their comparative analysis of male and female microentrepreneurs in Santiago, the second largest city in population in the Dominican Republic, found that men's microenterprises generate higher incomes than women's firms.

---

6. The Costa Rican Dirección General de Estadística y Censo (DGEyC—General Bureau of Statistics and Census) conducts quarterly population surveys.

Segmentation in Job Allocation

The second dimension of my analysis looks at the background characteristics of the people involved in the different occupational groups. Because the multivariate analysis did not provide clear evidence of income segmentation among formal, informal, and self-employed workers, the differences in earnings among these occupational categories shown in Table 4.2 could be the result of differences in the background characteristics of the people working in the different labor market segments. If certain characteristics, such as gender or age, are a condition for access to formal jobs, this finding would point to a nonrandom allocation of jobs, limited labor market mobility, and hence the presence of labor market segmentation. Indeed, in a comparative study of Central American labor markets, Funkhauser (1996) found that in all the countries of the region the informal sector is composed of mainly the youngest, the oldest, the least educated, and women. Also Gindling (1991), in an analysis of the composition of the sectors in the urban labor market in San José, found that women and less educated people are significantly more likely to be in the informal than in the formal sector. Thus, evidence shows that job allocation in the region is based on the ascriptive characteristics of the workers.

To sort out whether job allocation is random or segmented along certain individual characteristics, we need to perform a form of multivariate analysis that shows the effects of sociodemographic characteristics on determining the occupational category in which people work. Multinomial logit analysis does just that. This type of analysis indicates the likelihood that people with certain characteristics end up in certain occupational categories and not in others, controlling for other sociodemographic characteristics (see Part II of the Appendix). The analysis shows that gender affects the distribution of people in the labor market. Men are more likely to be formal workers or employers than self-employed or informal workers, and women are much more likely to be in the nonworking category. Education also has an effect on job allocation. People with more years of education are more likely to be formal or informal workers than self-employed or employers. People with very few years of education are more likely to be in the nonworking category. Interestingly, education has no effect on people's being formal or informal workers. Age increases the likelihood of people's being in the nonworking category. Younger people are also more likely to be informal workers than self-employed. This fact may be related to the often-found fact that many self-employed people are former formal or informal workers who accumulated work experience and chose to start their independent business.

The picture that emerges from this analysis shows a clear segmentation among the occupational categories mainly along gender lines, but also along education and age lines. Employers and formal workers are more likely to be men. Formal-sector workers are more educated than the self-employed and employers, although there are no significant differences in education between formal and informal workers. Self-employed people and employers tend to be older than informal workers. The more clearly defined segment is the nonworking category. Women, old people, and less educated people are significantly more likely to be in this category. The multinomial regressions show gender to be the main stratificatory variable between the labor market segments[7] and thus the main explanatory variable for the earning differences between workers in different occupational categories. The analysis of earnings shows that Santo Domingo is more segmented along gender lines than San José. These results, taken together, support the general claim that protective state intervention in the labor market tends to reduce the level of inequality.

Segmentation and Labor Market Mobility

The quantitative results show a complex picture concerning the structure of the labor markets in the two cities. Labor market stratification in the two cities is, in fact, rather similar. So far, the image that emerges from the analysis is that state protective intervention in the labor market leads to a larger formal economy, a reduced rate of unemployment, and the improvement of the conditions of the lower segments in the labor market, but not to differences in the segmentation of the labor market. The labor market structure is similar in both countries because of their common position in the world economy and the similar industrialization policies their governments pursued. The distribution of people in the different occupational segments appears to be nonrandom. Gender appears to be the main variable in determining job allocation and the main source of difference in income between the different occupation categories.

The quantitative analysis offers a broad view of the overall structure of the labor market, but one cannot infer from its results the type of choice that people confront and their reasons for the choices they make. One must turn

---

7. These results coincide with Cordero and Mora's (1998) and Tardanico and Lungo's (1997) analyses of labor market trends in Costa Rica, which show that during the adjustment years there was an increase in the participation of women in the labor market and that women entered the labor market in its more marginal and unprotected sectors.

to the qualitative interviews to study the people behind the numbers; these interviews provide a close look at the structure of opportunities in each city through the eyes of informal actors. They show the alternatives and choices that people involved in the informal economy perceive and the strategies they adopt to make the most of their opportunities.

This section focuses on patterns of labor market insertion and mobility to illustrate the choices open to the urban dwellers in each city. I address the concrete labor market situations faced by the urban poor in both cities. The interviews were conducted with informal economic actors (informal entrepreneurs, self-employed people, and informal workers) and allow a glance at the work history and aspirations of the people involved in the informal economy in each city. In the interviews, I asked people about their work histories, their reasons for working in the places where they were working, how they conduct their businesses, and under what conditions they would change occupation. The respondents were people who have gone through several jobs, who have friends and siblings in every sector of the economy, and who have made informed choices within the constraints of their position in the social structure of the city.

The qualitative interviews provide a window on the logic of the informal actors. Taken alone, they are interesting case studies that allow a glimpse at the types of decisions and situations that urban poor people often confront. Analyzed in combination with the quantitative data, they clarify the picture of the structure of the labor markets in Costa Rica and the Dominican Republic. They also help bridge the gap between my quantitative results and those of Gindling (1991) and Cordero and Mora (1998) (researchers who were able to distinguish differences between public and private formal workers in San José, differences that my data set could not account for). The combination of quantitative and qualitative analysis proved to be an indispensable tool for understanding the structure of the labor market and the informal economy.

San José: Upward Equalization of Informal and Low-End Formal Work

The qualitative interviews show that in San José, working conditions in the informal sector are not very different from the lower end of the private formal sector. The lower end of the formal labor market encompasses the growing export sector, particularly in the garment and textile industries; it also includes employment in the export-processing zones, and as Cordero and Mora (1998) show, this is the fastest-growing sector of employment in the country. Workers in these jobs earn close to the minimum salary and are covered by the social security system. Informal workers earn similar wages and sometimes even a bit more, but they are not covered by the social security system. The reason for the similarity in incomes is related to the presence of state regulations.

In San José, the most common indicators of informality are salaries below the official minimum, noncompliance with the social security laws, or both. Noncompliance often takes the form of paying the optional social security tax for self-employed people instead of the compulsory and more expensive tax for employees. In Costa Rica, employers must register their businesses at the Social Security Institute (Caja Costarricense de Seguro Social) and pay social security taxes for each of their workers. The compulsory social security insurance covers health services, pensions for disability because of work injuries, and retirement pensions. Self-employed people have the option of enrolling under social security if they so desire. They can choose to pay for a limited insurance that covers only health service or for an extensive insurance that also covers disability and retirement pensions. When informal employers register their workers as self-employed, they usually pay for only their health insurance and not disability or retirement. Moreover, because workers are registered as self-employed, the employers can fire them without making full severance payments.

For the workers, the possibility always exists of complaining to the Ministry of Labor about the violation of labor regulations. Such complaints can be a very real threat against their employers, because they imply the danger of having to pay overdue social security taxes and fines that can put the informal entrepreneur out of business. The real possibility of legal enforcement affects labor relations in informal businesses. Informal employers often bargain with their workers for slightly higher salaries in exchange for nonpayment of social security taxes. Workers have a short-term gain from this because they would otherwise have to contribute 12 percent of their salaries to social security taxes—in the long term, they lose the possibility of having a pension. Of course, this arrangement also exempts employers from paying their share of social security taxes.

As Gindling and Terrell (1995) show, enforcement of labor regulations in Costa Rica is by no means universal in terms of both the minimum wage and social security regulations.[8] However, the possibility of enforcement strengthens the position of informal workers in whatever agreement—most often, a

---

8. Gindling and Terrell (1995) show that about one-third of the full-time labor force earns less than the minimum wage. However, these authors show that most of the violations in the minimum wage occur in rural rather than urban areas.

verbal agreement—they reach with their employers. A complicated question is How do workers know what the appropriate minimum wage is? In Costa Rica, there are close to two hundred different minimum salaries for different industries and occupations (Gindling and Terrell 1995). In their negotiations, informal workers and microentrepreneurs use the earnings of people working in similar jobs in the formal sector as a comparison to establish an acceptable wage (in the interviews, the most recurrent comparison was with wages in assembly manufacturing).

The following examples illustrate the structure of opportunities open for low-income sectors in Costa Rica. They show the mobility among the lower tier of formal employment, self-employment, and informal employment in San José. The first case is the one with which I began this chapter. It involves two women, Olga and Xenia, working in an informal workshop located in a poor neighborhood of San José, which assembled clothes for local retail chains. They asserted that they could earn the same amount of money working in that place as they could in a big factory and that they enjoyed more flexibility in their working hours. Neither of them received social security benefits, but both were insured through their husbands' insurance,[9] although this option entails the risk of losing the benefits in case of separation. Both have worked in textile *maquilas* before, and for both working in an informal workshop was a choice. Xenia argued that although in the big *maquilas* it is possible to earn more money through incentives, it is necessary to work extremely hard; hence she preferred the less strenuous pace of the informal workshop. Olga claimed, however, that if she did not have her husband's social security insurance, she would not be working there, indicating that access to social security is an important consideration in choosing jobs.

Two points emerge from the previous account. The first one is the importance of the state social policies in the choice-making process of the urban poor. In extending the social security coverage of one member of the family to the whole family, the state expands the scope of choices open to the members of poor urban households. The other one is the confirmation of the gender segmentation of the labor market. For poor women, the employment alternatives in the formal economy are not very attractive. This conclusion was also confirmed in an interview with a manager of an electronic assembly firm in an export zone close to San José. The firm employed sixty workers in cutting and assembling electronic components. Most of the sixty workers were women,

---

9. This option does not exist in the Dominican Republic.

with the exception of the manager and some supervisors. He reported that the previous year the company was paying sixty cents per hour plus all the fringe benefits stipulated by the law and had a turnover of 100 percent. Most women leaving the job cited family reasons, but management reached the conclusion that it was due to dissatisfaction with the wages. Because the firm needed to provide some training to the workers and needed them to perform precision work, they raised the hourly wage to $1.10, and since then they have had a turnover rate of 18 percent. The high turnover shows that there was no scarcity of jobs at this level. The accounts of the women above show that there was extended mobility between this type of formal job and jobs in informal microenterprises, but not into other sectors of employment.

In addition to women, most of the people involved in the movements among the lower tier of formal employment, self-employment, and informal employment are Central American male immigrants and older men. Some women and immigrants involved in this segment of the labor market do manage to become informal employers; most of them, however, remain at the subsistence level. For example, Jaime was a Nicaraguan who had been living in Costa Rica for about ten years. He was married to a Costa Rican woman and had two Costa Rican children. By the time of the interview, he was still an illegal resident. Jaime was a self-employed sandal maker who learned his trade working in a midsize shoe factory (about fifty workers) for a number of years. In that factory, he was barely paid the minimum salary, and his employer did not pay social security taxes. With some help from his parents, he managed to open his business and quit informal employment, and he was making a bit more than twice the minimum salary. He would have liked his business to grow and to be able to hire people, but he could not afford that. His business was still in a very precarious situation, and he did not rule out the possibility that he might need to go back to work as a wageworker. He hoped to get his legal residency in the country so that he could get paid a better salary with social security benefits.

These examples of mobility exclude the public sector. In Costa Rica, despite the deterioration of salaries and government attempts to reduce the number of workers in the public sector during the last decade and a half, at the time of my interviews this sector was part of the higher tier in the formal economy. A manager of the Costa Rican Social Security Institute working on the transfer of hospital services to cooperatives of workers recounted that many public-sector workers who were laid off or accepted early retirement went into self-employment. These workers were mostly men in their mature years who employed themselves most commonly as craftsmen or skilled workers performing some specialized work for informal microenterprises. The first type belongs to what can be considered a more traditional petty bourgeoisie; the latter are informal workers who, because of their skills, command higher than average salaries. Some public employees who went into self-employment were successful in their new endeavor, but many were not, mainly because the necessary skills to succeed in those crafts are acquired in jobs different from those in the public sector. Many of those who failed as self-employed, the manager of the CCSS admitted, were readmitted to public employment.

Because the study focused on the informal economy, I did not get a clear picture of work in the public sector. This is a limitation, because I cannot know the types of mechanisms used to limit the entrance of people into that sector. Nevertheless, it was clear from the interviews that public-sector employment did not figure in the choices of informal workers or low-wage workers. In that sense, there appear to be clear barriers to mobility between the informal and low-end private formal sector and the public sector, which in spite of the deterioration of the working conditions that took place during the 1980s was still considered part of the protected formal economy.[10] The cases presented above—as well as the qualitative interviews in general—suggest a blurring of the line between the lower end of the formal economy and the informal economy. The blurring of the line is, on the one hand, the result of the deterioration of formal employment, but on the other hand, it is the result of state regulations that give tools to informal workers to improve their position.

Santo Domingo: Downward Equalization of Formal and Informal Work

The qualitative interviews also show the blurring of the formal-informal divide in Santo Domingo. Two elements contribute to this blurring of boundaries. First, social security benefits and the minimum salary do not at all guarantee basic economic survival. Second, employers use loopholes in the labor laws, such as firing workers at the end of the year, giving them full severance pay-

---

10. Cordero and Mora (1998) show that the public sector had the fastest-growing income between 1983 and 1989. Between 1989 and 1992, income in the public sector declined. Still, in 1992, public-sector workers earned more than private formal-sector workers did. However, both Cordero and Mora (1998) and Tardanico and Lungo (1997) find that in the early 1990s there was a decline in employment in the public sector for people with primary education or less, the kind of people who are likely to be in my sample. So one barrier to entry could be a change in the composition of public-sector work toward the employment of skilled personnel.

ments for that year, and then rehiring them at the beginning of the next year (many firms also illegally use the severance payment as a replacement for the compulsory Christmas bonus).

This practice is widespread because it allows employers a margin of flexibility in the use of their workforce. Informal producers in all sectors stated that at the beginning of the year, after the holidays, demand drops sharply. Because employees had been fired and paid their severance payment, employers were able to reduce their payrolls during a low-demand period simply by not rehiring some of their former employees. This practice is accepted and even demanded by many workers because the bad working conditions in formal and informal jobs prompt a high level of mobility among firms. Under these conditions, workers who do not hold high-salary jobs prefer to collect severance money at the end of each year rather than accumulate it. Access to severance payments through *desahucio* is one way of obtaining a minimum amount of capital—this is why often workers demand it, even workers in the core formal firms. In many instances, even unions demand the *desahucio* of a predetermined number of workers each year while negotiating collective contracts (Hernández Rueda 1989).[11]

In Santo Domingo, the mobility between formal and informal employment involves not only the more vulnerable groups—women and immigrants—as in San José, but also skilled men in their mature years, men who supposedly form the core of the formal working class. The cases of Raúl, Fernando, and Carlos illustrate additional choices open to the urban poor in Santo Domingo as well as the mobility between formal and informal jobs in that city. An electrician who worked as a maintenance worker at a formal factory, where he earned slightly above the minimum salary plus benefits, Raúl decided to quit his job and began producing aluminum windows with some friends. They installed their workshop in part of Hector's (Raúl's cousin) furniture workshop; Hector allowed them to use the space in exchange for becoming a partner in the business. Although Raúl had no secure income, he estimated that he made more than twice what he earned before.

Fernando is a cabinetmaker who has worked for Hector in the furniture workshop for two years. He worked for many years in a midsize furniture

---

11. As mentioned in the first chapter, the legality of this practice of massive *desahucio* is unclear. Hernández Rueda (1989), a Dominican expert on labor law, argues that this practice is illegal because of Dominican jurisprudence stipulations for the reduction of personnel. Those stipulations subject large reductions of personnel to the approval of the Department of Labor. However, the labor administrative authorities have argued that they do not have a legal base to act against massive *desahucio*.

factory where he earned about twice the minimum wage—a relatively high income for a blue-collar factory worker. Although while working for Hector his income was not steady, Fernando thought that on average he made the same amount of money, and he was able to work at a more steady pace. Moreover, he was talking about becoming a partner in the business.[12]

Hector's family encompassed many of the labor market situations that characterize the low-income sectors of Santo Domingo. Hector had four sons. The youngest one, about fourteen years of age, worked with him in the furniture workshop. Hector's other two sons were working in a medium-sized furniture factory, making about $160 per month, a bit less than one-and-a-half times the minimum salary in the private sector at the time of the interview. Hector wanted them to come to work with him, but he said that they preferred the security of their steady incomes. Carlos, the oldest son, had studied computing. In the past, he had worked as a supervisor in an export zone north of the city. His salary was very low, and after discounting what he paid for transportation nothing in fact remained, so he quit the job in the export zone and worked with his father for a while. He tried to open a small business teaching computing, but it did not take off. At the time of my interview, Carlos was working for a big national liquor company as a supervisor and making a good salary; he apparently had made it into the more protected part of the formal sector, which provides access to higher salaries and private health insurance, but accounts for a very small percentage of private employment. This small sector achieves those benefits not through state protections, but through worker-employer negotiations.

The examples above show that, unlike in San José, in Santo Domingo skilled men in their mature years, a group that supposedly constitutes the core of the formal working class, often choose to work as informal workers. These findings coincide with those of Murphy's (1990) research among the Santo Domingo *lechugheros:* mobile retail vendors who sell vegetables and fruits from their tricycles, a kind of pushcart mounted on a bicycle frame. Murphy found that almost all the *lechugueros* preferred their occupation to a minimum-wage job in the formal economy, not because they earned good salaries, but because they definitely earned more than did the minimum-wage workers in the formal economy.[13]

The following are additional examples of the preference often showed by

---

12. He had then a very close relationship with Hector. However, when I visited Hector in 1997, Fernando was not there anymore, and Hector did not want to talk about him.

13. Murray (1996) also finds an inclination among Dominicans toward self-employment. He attributes it partly to economic reasons and partly to cultural preferences.

skilled workers in Santo Domingo for temporary jobs in the informal economy. A common arrangement among informal enterprises is to hire skilled workers for very short periods. Skilled workers like this type of arrangement because they earn more money doing several short specialized jobs than they do as formal workers with stable employment. Possibly for this reason, human capital—education and skills—did not help distinguish between formal and informal workers in my previous analysis. Francisco is a case in point.[14] He had a small workshop producing jewelry in the backyard of his house. At the time of my interview, he employed three workers, but none of them was permanent. One explained that whenever Francisco needed workers he would call him; otherwise, he worked for other workshops or was unemployed. He claimed that he preferred this working arrangement over any other because it allowed him to take the job that gave him more income at any given moment, and in this way he made more money than he could as a permanent worker. The same type of arrangement appeared in many other interviews. Susana, for example, inherited a small furniture workshop from her late husband and transformed it into a small firm with about eight permanent workers, for most of whom she paid social security taxes. Nevertheless, for some parts of the production process, she would still call an independent worker and pay him by piece rate. Asked why she would not hire such workers permanently, she explained that they were very skilled and worked so fast that they preferred to work piece rate, and no micro or small enterprise could afford to hire them on a permanent basis.

These examples show the preference of skilled men in their mature years for informal over formal work. Skilled, mature men are supposed to constitute the core of the formal economy, but given the lack of good employment options, they chose casual informal work. As suggested in the previous chapter, in Santo Domingo, under the export-oriented model of economic growth, men switched to informal occupations whereas women occupied the low-end jobs in the formal economy and the most precarious informal jobs.

In Santo Domingo, different sources of quantitative data showed a high rate of unemployment or nonworking people, particularly among women. In that city, however, no welfare net of any kind protects the unemployed. An important number of households survive thanks to remittances sent from abroad, transforming emigration into a household survival strategy (Itzigsohn 1995).[15]

---

14. This is the case with which I open the first chapter.
15. Costa Rica is not a migrant-sending country. On the contrary, it receives immigrants from the rest of Central America.

In many other cases, the unemployed engage in all sorts of informal activities that go unrecorded in household surveys, such as selling lotteries (legal and otherwise), cooking for the neighbors, or organizing *sanes*. In the popular neighborhoods of Santo Domingo, many people, mostly women, make a living out of organizing *sanes* (a *san* is a rotating savings or purchasing arrangement; the organizer of a *san* takes a percentage of the quotas paid by the people involved in it). A *san* cannot be organized by just anyone, because the organizer must enjoy the trust of the people who want to participate. Nor can anyone who wants to participate do so, because the participants must enjoy the trust of the organizer. Organizing *sanes* is a demanding activity. Alicia is a case in point. At the time of the interview, she had a small *ventorrillo*[16] in a marginal neighborhood. She told me that before she opened her business she used to sell door to door and organize *sanes* to complement her income. She quit because it was too stressful and brought her too much trouble. The people who make a living from organizing *sanes* or other unrecorded activities such as selling tickets for clandestine lotteries or soaking the beans for neighbors who go to work are most often considered unemployed or out of the labor force in official statistics or surveys.[17] Nevertheless, they do engage in informal work.

In Santo Domingo, labor mobility among formal employment, informal employment, and self-employment includes the public sector where, at the time of my research, salaries for the lower echelons did not reach $100 per month. Ines, for example, had been a public employee for the last fifteen years, but the deterioration of the public-sector salaries did not allow her to live on her salary alone. Thus, after completing her working day in her public-sector job, she sewed clothes at home. A year and a half before the interview, she decided to join her sister in an attempt to expand the clothing business. Ines still kept her job because it guaranteed her a small but secure income; nevertheless, she claimed that as soon as their microenterprise is large enough, she would quit her job in the public sector.[18]

The qualitative interviews show that, in each city, the income and working conditions in the low-end formal economy and the informal economy are very similar. This fact helps explain the lack of effect of the informal worker occu-

---

16. A *ventorrillo* is a very small grocery store. Usually, only the basic items of the popular diet are sold there, and people buy in small quantities, such as a cup of oil or a handful of beans.

17. These people are probably included in my nonworking category.

18. The situation of public-sector workers having double employment and often not showing up for their work hours was very common in Santo Domingo, because of the very low level of public-sector salaries.

pational category in the income regressions. The qualitative interviews show an important difference between the cities. In San José, the presence of regulations raises the conditions of informal workers to those of the lower end of the formal sector. In San José, informal workers are aware of existing labor laws and aware that the relevant state agencies are likely to respond to their complaints. In Santo Domingo, the absence of regulations depresses the conditions of most formal employment to those of informal employment. These findings correspond to my quantitative results, which indicated that there were no differences in segmentation between the cities, but that in San José state intervention improved the conditions of the lower ends of the labor market. Moreover, by showing the differences in working conditions between the public sector and the low-end informal sector in San José—a distinction that I could not make in the survey data—the qualitative information helps bridge the differences between my quantitative results and those of Gindling (1991) and Cordero and Mora (1998). The low-end formal sector coincides with Cordero and Mora's (1998) tradable sector with incomes that are lower than the public sector and the rest of the private formal sector.

Two important findings, common to both cities, emerge out of this analysis. The first is that gender appears to be the main stratificatory variable in both income and job allocation. Several scholars have shown the gender biases of the neoliberal model of economic growth. Export-oriented policies lead to the incorporation of women in the labor market in low-income and unprotected jobs, reinforcing gender differences in the labor market. This new gendered division of labor is the direct result of state policies promoting assembly manufacturing and other low-wage sectors that employ mostly women (Benería and Feldman 1992; Pérez Sáinz and Menjívar Larín 1993; Safa 1995; Safa and Antrobus 1992; Standing 1989). In this case, there is no difference between the two regulatory regimes; both countries followed similar policies with similar results in terms of the incorporation of women into the labor force. Nevertheless, the quantitative analyses show gender segmentation in Santo Domingo to be deeper than in San José. The positive effects of the Costa Rican protective regulatory regime on women are not the result of laws designed to protect or empower women. The labor market in San José is indeed segmented along gender lines, and gender roles in Costa Rica suffer from the same male biases as in the Dominican Republic.

The improvement of the position of women in San José in comparison to Santo Domingo is the result of the presence of protective labor regulations. As the qualitative analysis showed, in San José informal workers have some access to state protection through the possibility of complaining to the Ministry of

Labor and through the extension of social security to the family of the formal worker. The qualitative interviews did not show any protection of women as women in the labor market in San José compared with Santo Domingo. On the contrary, many women I interviewed in both places referred to the lack of protection by the state for compelling former husbands or partners to help in raising families.[19] If citizenship means the possibility of enjoying equal political, civil, and social rights as a member of a community and if those rights are enforced by the state, in San José, in comparison to Santo Domingo, women obtain access to a measure of social citizenship as workers—although that city also shows gender segmentation in income—but they are equally discriminated against in their rights as women.

The last point raises the question of the relation between labor market incorporation and gender roles. As several studies show, these labor market changes affect gender structures in more ways than by the presence of jobs that are predominantly filled by women. The massive incorporation of women into the labor market affects gender relations in the household (Benería and Feldman 1992; Espinal and Grasmuck 1997; Goldenberg 1993; Safa 1995). The entrance of women to the labor market as waged workers or microentrepreneurs sometimes—although not always—led to a challenge of the gender hierarchies in the household. The qualitative research provided numerous instances in which the work aspirations of women conflicted with the household power dynamics. One example is that of Celia in Santo Domingo, a microentrepreneur who after attending a training course in clay crafts organized by a microenterprise-development nongovernmental organization (NGO) began to produce and sell crafts with considerable success. Her business success created tensions with her husband, who resented the independence that her income allowed her. The result was that she left him and went on with her business. By the time of the interview, she had a successful microenterprise and was building a house for herself and her family. A somewhat different case is that of Sonia, whom I interviewed twice in San José. At the time of the first interview, Sonia was a married woman attempting to build a clothing microenterprise. By the time of the second interview, her attempts to have an independent economic life had created tensions with her husband and brought an end to her marriage. Her business, however, did not provide enough income to sustain her family, so she had to quit the business and began working as an employee. As Safa (1995) points out, the result of the challenge to the gender hierarchies is often that the burden of

---

19. My interviews did not focus on family relationships. I bring up this issue because it came up repeatedly in the interviews, particularly in San José.

sustaining the family falls solely on women's shoulders, and in that sense, there are no differences between the two countries.[20]

The second important finding that emerged in both cities is that the informal workshop is not a sweatshop. Many respondents argued that they prefer to work in the informal economy because they had more control of the pace of work. The case of Helena illustrates the problem of labor control faced by informal microentrepreneurs. Helena had a clothing microenterprise in Santo Domingo employing about eight workers. At the time of the interview, she was considering the possibility of paying social security for them. She thought that by doing so she could reduce the number of workers' absences. At that point, workers could simply call her and tell her that they were not feeling well and would not go to work that day. They would lose the payment for that day, but they were not afraid of losing their jobs. Helena figured that if she began paying social security, workers would need doctors' permission to absent themselves from work, and the payment of social security would create incentives for workers to stay on that job.[21] Most of the respondents indicated that informal workers have some degree of control over their labor and associated the working conditions in the assembly-manufacturing plants in the export zones with sweatshops. This fact does not mean that the conditions of work in informal microenterprise are not exploitative, only that the people I interviewed agreed that, in comparison, the export zones demanded a more strenuous pace of work and allowed less control over the working process than informal microenterprises.[22]

State Regulation and Labor Market Segmentation

The analysis of the different sources of data presented in this chapter shows a clear picture of the labor market choices faced by the urban poor. As with all

---

20. Several studies show that structural adjustment policies increase the work burden on women who now have to deal with a triple shift—working as wage earners, working in the household, and working in "participatory" community projects that employ local women as unpaid labor (Benería and Feldman 1992; Safa 1995).

21. Goldenberg (1993) in her study of microenterprises in San José also finds that microentrepreneurs use incentives to avoid shirking and turnover.

22. In San José, the access to social security provided by "low-end" formal employment was still a consideration in favor of working in *maquilas* in spite of the more strenuous pace. In Santo Domingo, as a result of the deterioration of social security, this consideration was not an incentive to work in the export-processing zones.

investigations of the informal economy, the data suffer from several problems, and the conclusions should be made with caution. Nevertheless, the consistency among the results of the different sources reassures us about the strength of the conclusions. Table 4.3 summarizes the results of the investigations pursued in this chapter. In both cities, I identify three main segments in the labor market. The segments are the same in both places, but the composition of the segments and the relations between them are different. In San José, the public sector is in the primary formal sector, whereas in Santo Domingo the public sector is in the secondary formal sector. In San José, the working conditions of the informal workers are leveled up to the conditions of secondary formal employment through the partial extension of labor protections. In Santo Domingo, the working conditions of secondary formal employment are leveled down to the conditions of informal employment through the absence of labor protections. In both countries, gender appears to be a key dimension of segmentation.[23]

The analyses in this chapter show, again, the recurrent pattern of differences in a common general structure. As a result of similar development processes and a similar insertion in the world economy, the labor market structure of the two countries is, in fact, similar. Gender is the key dimension of segmentation in both cities; age and nationality are also important.[24] Nevertheless, my analysis shows that different regulatory regimes led to the reduction of inequalities in one case and to their exacerbation in the other. The quantitative analysis shows that in Costa Rica, a developmental-protective regulatory regime led to the improvement of the working and living conditions of the lower segments of the labor market. The qualitative analysis allows a more detailed look at the concrete effects of labor regulation. The cases presented here show that informal workers use the threat of existing labor regulations to negotiate their working conditions with informal entrepreneurs. Under a developmentalist-protective regulatory regime, the effects of labor regulation are different from those hypothesized by the advocates of deregulation.

23. When I began this research, I was aware, as is every scholar working on the informal economy, that gender was an important dimension of the analysis. I did not, however, structure my research around gender questions, as I saw this as one important dimension of analysis among others. The course of the research and the analysis showed gender to be a central element—if not *the* central element—in understanding the informal economy. If I were to conduct this research again, a gender perspective would have a much more prominent place in the definition of the research project and in the research design.

24. The qualitative interviews showed this to be the case in San José. Nationality and race are important dimensions of labor market segmentation in Santo Domingo, where Haitians occupy their own niches in the informal economy and some of the most menial jobs in the formal economy.

Table 4.3 Structure of the labor market in San José and Santo Domingo.

	San José	Santo Domingo
Primary formal employment	Workers with access to relatively high wages and access to social security benefits. Includes public-sector workers. Working conditions of informal microentrepreneurs and some self-employed people are equivalent to those in this segment.	Workers with access to private health and old age pension and protected by collective agreements. Excludes public-sector workers. Working conditions of informal microentrepreneurs are equivalent to those in this segment.
Secondary formal employment	Workers in the private sector with minimum wages and access to social security benefits. Includes workers in the export-assembly sector. The export-assembly sector is composed mainly of women and has very strenuous working schedules.	Workers with very low salaries and access to very deteriorated social security benefits. Includes public-sector workers and export-assembly workers. Export-assembly workers are mostly women, and the work schedules in this sector are very strenuous.
Informal employment	Workers with minimum wages and no access to social security benefits (or access to limited self-employed benefits). Wages are similar to secondary formal employment, and the working conditions are less demanding. The working conditions of most self-employed people are equivalent to this segment.	Workers without access to social security benefits. The range of salaries is large, often higher than in secondary formal employment. The working conditions are more flexible and less demanding than in the secondary formal segment.

The picture of a protected working aristocracy surrounded by a sea of unprotected informality, often invoked to support the deregulation of labor relations, corresponds neatly to the case of Santo Domingo. There, the unwillingness of the state to implement existing regulations has not led to a more dynamic formal sector but to an informalized formal sector and generalized poverty. Moreover, to the extent that there is a labor aristocracy in Santo Domingo, it is not the result of a partial application of state regulations but of whatever limited power unions have. In Santo Domingo, workers' rights are not obtained through the action of the state but through the action of organized labor. Given that labor is rather weak, the extent of the implementation of workers' rights is not very extensive. This fact shows the importance of class and class organization in addition to the state regulatory regime.

In Costa Rica, labor is also weak, with the possible exception of the public sector, a fact that explains why the public sector was still part of the protected formal sector. Nevertheless, formal and informal workers have access to some measure of protection through the implementation, albeit partial, of state labor regulations. It is certainly not my intention to idealize the Costa Rican case or to posit a Costa Rican model. Indeed, debunking the Costa Rican myth has become a line of work among academics, and rightly so because myths have no place in guiding social science analysis. Nevertheless, in spite of all its well-known problems, the presence of a developmental-protective regulatory regime—although worn out by years of structural adjustment—led to the improvement of the working conditions of the lower ends of the formal economy and of informal workers, particularly women.

Appendix

Part I: Income Segmentation in San José and Santo Domingo

For the purpose of sorting out the income effects of employment in the informal economy, I conducted an OLS regression of the logarithm of monthly earnings on a number of individual, family, and occupational variables. The occupational categories were included in the regression as a set of mutually exclusive dichotomous variables, one for each of the occupational groups. The formal workers category was omitted from the regression as the contrast category. The coefficients of the occupational variables should therefore be interpreted as increasing or decreasing income relative to the income of formal workers. The other independent variables include a set of personal variables and a set of family variables. To measure the effects of the particular characteristic of each city, I included a city dummy variable in the regression. To see whether the structure of income determination is different in each city, I interacted the city variable with each of the occupational categories and with gender. The set of variables included in the income regressions and in the multinomial logit regressions is described in Table 4.4.

The personal variables included gender, age, and education. Education and age stand as proxies of human capital characteristics: skills and work experience. Income regressions commonly include an age square variable to capture a possible curvilinear effect of age. However, because the younger end of the

Labor Market Regulation

Table 4.4 Independent variables included in multivariate analyses.

Variable	Description
Income	Logarithm of monthly earning
Occupational categories	Set of dichotomous variables, one for each occupational group. Formal workers was the contrast category in the income regressions
Gender	Women coded 0, men coded 1
Age	Age in years
Education	Number of years of education
Migrant	Born in the city coded 0, immigrants to the city coded 1
Number of children	Number of sons and daughters of the interviewed
Family status	Dummy variable. Married people or people living in consensual unions coded 1, the rest (single, separated, widowed) coded 0
Number of workers	Number of people in the household who have a job
Family stage	For the purpose of this analysis, the family cycle is divided into four stages. Families and single people without children coded 1, families with children younger than 15 coded 2, families where the older offspring has reached 15 coded 3, families where more than the older offspring has reached 15 coded 4. Fifteen years of age was considered the cutoff age to be included in the labor force. Children younger than 15 were considered too young to join the labor force (although this does not mean that in reality they do not work).
City	Dummy variable. San José coded 0, Santo Domingo coded 1

labor market is not included in the sample, I do not include an age square variable. The family variables include the number of children of the respondent, the family status, the number of workers in the household, and the family stage (this variable refers to the position of the respondent's family in the family cycle). These variables were introduced to control for the family and household situation of respondents. The rationale for this is that the presence of other breadwinners in the household or a higher or lower dependence ratio may affect the occupational options of the head of the household and thus his or her income.

If the structure of the labor market in both cities is similar and segmented, I expect the occupational category variables to be statistically significant and the interaction variables to be nonsignificant. If the structure of the labor market in both cities is similar and nonsegmented, I expect education (and perhaps age) to be statistically significant whereas the occupational and interaction variables are not.[25] If the regulatory regimes affect the segmentation of the labor market, then I expect the interactions of the city variable with the occupational variables to be significant whereas the occupational categories are not.

Raw coefficients and standard errors for these regressions are presented in Table 4.5. I run three models: Model 1 includes the individual, occupational, and family variables plus the city dummy variable. Model 2 includes the same variables plus the interactions between city and occupational categories. Model 3 includes the variables in Model 1 plus the interactions of city with the nonworking category and gender. I included only these two interactions in the last model because they proved to be consistently significant from a statistical point of view.[26]

All three models show that the nonworking category has a statistically significant and negative effect on income, even when the interaction between city and the nonworking category is included. Being in the owners' category has a significant and positive effect in Models 1 and 3, but is not significant in Model 2, most likely because of collinearity. An important result is that there is no statistically significant difference in any of the models between the categories of informal workers and self-employed and the contrast category of formal workers, and the joint effect of the informal and self-employed categories is not statistically significant.

These results suggest that there is segmentation in both cities between the income of owners, who earn more than the other occupational categories, and nonworking people, who earn less than the other occupational categories. There is no segmentation in the incomes of informal workers, formal workers, and self-employed people. The dummy variable for city is significant and negative in Models 1 and 3. It is not statistically significant in Model 2, probably because of collinearity problems. This result shows that the general income level in San José is higher than in Santo Domingo. Labor market stratification

---

25. The fact that the effects of education are significant, by itself, is not necessarily a rejection of the presence of segmentation. Segmentation analyses usually run separate regressions for the different segments of the labor market and then test for differences in the effects of the independent variables in the different labor market segments. The reason for this design is that segmentation theories argue that the effects of human capital variables such as education are different in the different labor market segments. Here I do not look at the structure of determination of income in each sector separately, so one cannot know whether education or other variables have different effects in the different segments.

26. I also ran analyses using all the interaction variables. Because interaction variables create problems of multicollinearity, I use the procedure TEST in STATA to check for the joint effects of variables that were not statistically significant. These results are available on request.

Table 4.5 OLS regression of the logarithm of personal income on personal, family, and occupational variables (standard error in parentheses).

Variables	Model 1	Model 2	Model 3
Gender	.36**	.45**	.17
	(.10)	(.09)	(.13)
Age	-.01	-.01	-.01
	(.01)	(.01)	(.01)
Education	.06**	.05**	.05**
	(.01)	(.01)	(.01)
% of children	-.03	-.02	-.03
	(.02)	(.02)	(.01)
Married	.32**	.26**	.24**
	(.10)	(.09)	(.09)
Family stage	.10	.13*	.13*
	(.06)	(.06)	(.05)
Number of workers	.01	.01	.01
	(.03)	(.03)	(.03)
Owner	.29*	.17	.26*
	(.14)	(.19)	(.13)
Informal	-.10	-.19	-.13
	(.14)	(.20)	(.13)
Self-employed	-.10	-.12	-.12
	(.11)	(.14)	(.10)
Nonworking	-1.27**	-.56**	-.67**
	(.12)	(.17)	(.16)
City	-.48**	-.23	-.56**
	(.08)	(.15)	(.15)
City*owner		.22	
		(.27)	
City*informal		.11	
		(.27)	
City*self-employed		.01	
		(.21)	
City*nonworking		-1.25**	-1.10**
		.22	(.19)
City*gender			.52**
			(.17)
Constant	4.37**	4.22**	4.41**
	(.21)	(.22)	(.22)
Test$_1$: Informal = 0. Self-employed = 0.	$F(2, 762)=.52$. $P>F=.59$.		
Test$_2$: Informal = 0. Self-employed = 0. Owner = 0.		$F(3, 758)=1.11$. $P>F=.34$.	
Test$_3$: City*informal = 0. City*self-employed = 0. City*owner = 0.		$F(3, 758)=.27$. $P>F=.84$.	
N:	775	775	775
R^2:	.37	.41	.42

*$p<.05$
**$p<.01$

seems to be the same in both cities, regardless of state intervention in the labor market. However, the statistically significant interaction between city and the nonworking category suggests that nonworking people in Santo Domingo have a considerably lower income than nonworking people in San José. This difference may result from the presence of some forms of transfer payments and higher pensions in San José. The regulatory regime, then, does have an effect, but this effect is felt on the general standard of living and the income of the lower end of the labor market, not on the overall structure of the labor market.

Gender has a significant and positive effect in Models 1 and 2, indicating that men have larger incomes than women do. In Model 3, however, when I introduce the interaction variable, gender is no longer significant. The interaction variable has a positive effect on income, indicating that gender has a stronger impact on income in Santo Domingo than in San José. In other words, the income gender gap is significantly larger in Santo Domingo than in San José. This finding also supports the conclusion that the main effect of the regulatory regime is to improve the income of the least protected groups in the labor market.

Part II: Sociodemographic Composition of Labor Market Segments

To analyze the sociodemographic composition of the different occupational categories, I use a multinomial logit model. This type of analysis shows the effects of each variable on the probability of belonging to a certain occupational category vis-à-vis a reference group, controlling for the effects of the other variables. Multinomial logit performs maximum likelihood estimation of models with discrete dependent variables. This method is ideal for cases such as this in which the dependent variable takes on more than two outcomes and the outcomes have no natural ordering. The probability that Individual i ends up working in Occupational Category j (vis-à-vis a reference occupational sector) is given as

$$P_{ij} = \frac{e^{x_i \beta_j}}{\sum_{k=1}^{5} e^{x_i \beta_k}}$$

where
x_i is a vector of characteristics of Person i, for which the first element is a constant,
β_j is a vector of corresponding coefficients associated with Choice j,

$j, k = 1, \ldots 5$ denote
(1) formal worker
(2) self-employed
(3) informal worker
(4) employer
(5) nonworking

The coefficients represent the effect of a unit change in the independent variable on the natural logarithm of the odds of ending in the respective category of the dependent variable. The dependent variable in this analysis is the group of five different occupational categories. The independent variables are the same as those included in Model 1 in Table 4.3, with the addition of the migrant variable. This variable needs some clarification. The sample included people with at least ten years of residence in the capital city. Thus, one can assume that the migrants in the sample have lived there long enough to integrate themselves into city life. If there is a difference between the labor market situation of migrants and that of the city born, this result will be very robust. If instead there is no difference, that finding would still not rule out the possibility that more recent immigrants have special modes of insertion into the labor market, but it does suggest that, over time, paths of mobility are not closed to them.[27]

I ran models including interaction variables between city and the other independent variables, and none of these models had better explanatory power than the basic model. None of the interaction variables was statistically significant. I ran tests of their joint effect using the TEST and LRTEST procedures in STATA. The first procedure checks for joint linear effects of groups of variables, whereas the second performs a maximum likelihood test of nested models. None of these tests was statistically significant. These results are available on request.

The results of the multinomial logit analysis are presented in Table 4.6. The table is presented in three panels. In Panel A, the log odds of being in the categories self-employed, informal workers, employers, and nonworking are contrasted with the category of formal worker. In Panel B, the three latter categories are contrasted with the self-employed category. In Panel C, the results for employers and nonworking people are contrasted with the informal workers category. I did not perform a comparison of employers and the

---

27. I excluded this variable from the income regressions because it proved to have no effect on income.

Table 4.6 Multinomial logit regressions of occupational categories.

Var./category	Base Category: Formal Workers			
	Self-employed	Informal workers	Employers	Nonworking
Gender	-.97**	-.95**	.09	-2.44**
Age	.01	-.03	-.01	.07**
Education	-.12**	-.04	-.07*	-.11**
Migrant	.13	.25	.09	-.46
# of children	.01	.16*	.03	.06
Married	.02	-.17	.60	.31
Family stage	.06	-.05	.16	.10
# of workers	-.25**	-.38**	-.02	-.15
City	.22	.76**	.22	.39
Constant	.74	1.01	-1.15	-1.55*

Var./category	Base Category: Self-Employed		
	Informal workers	Employers	Nonworking
Gender	.02	1.06**	-1.47**
Age	-.05**	-.02	.05**
Education	.08*	.05	.01
Migrant	.12	-.03	-.60**
# of children	.15*	.02	.05
Married	-.20	.58	.29
Family stage	-.11	.10	.04
# of workers	-.13	.23*	.09
City	.54*	.01	.17
Constant	.26	-1.90**	-2.30**

Var./category	Base Category: Informal Workers	
	Employers	Nonworking
Gender	1.04*	-1.49**
Age	.02	.10**
Education	-.03	-.07*
Migrant	-.16	-.72*
# of children	-.13	-.10
Married	.78	.49
Family stage	.21	.15
# of workers	.36*	.23
City	-.53	-.36
Constant	-2.17*	-2.57**

N: 800.
Chi-square (36): 316.88.
p>chi-square: 0.00.
Pseudo R^2: 0.13.
*$p<.05$
**$p<.01$

nonworking category because the latter emerges from the results as the most differentiated category. More important, the focus of the present analysis is on the differences between the categories of employed people.

The table presents a full picture of the differences in the background characteristics of the people involved in each segment of the labor market. In fact, all three panels present equivalent information, and the duplication is for ease of presentation only. Repeating the analysis changing the base category is unnecessary. One could obtain the values of all the coefficients presented in Column 3 of Panel B by subtracting Column 2 from Column 3 in Panel A. For example, to learn the size of the coefficient for the effect of gender on the odds of being in the category of informal workers vis-à-vis the self-employed category, one need only subtract the coefficient for gender under *self-employed* from the coefficient for gender under *informal workers*. A quick look at the first panel of Table 4 shows that the coefficient equals −.95 − (−.97)= .02. A look at the gender coefficient under the column *informal workers* in the second panel confirms that it is indeed equal to .02. The advantage of this form of display is a clearer presentation of the results, and more important, by performing the analysis and changing the base category, one also obtains the corresponding levels of statistical significance of the results. The analysis of the results is located in the body of the chapter.

5

The Organization of Informal Production

The production and marketing of goods or services can be organized in a number of different ways involving different commodity chains that guarantee access to capital, raw material, supplies, labor, and markets.[1] These commodity chains may encompass a number of formal and informal activities. Formal and informal economic activities are connected by a multiplicity of linkages, forming a unified urban economy rather than two separate sectors. To understand the structure of the urban economy, it is important to study how informal and formal activities are linked. What forms of productive organization encompass formal and informal activities? What types of activities are conducted formally, and what activities are carried out informally? What options exist for informal economic actors to improve their position in those linkages? In this chapter, I focus on the linkages of formal and informal firms in different commodity chains. The goal is to analyze the opportunities and constraints confronted by informal microentrepreneurs under the export-oriented model of economic growth, the strategies they adopt to subsist or grow, and the ways that the opportunities and constraints are affected by the differences in regulatory regimes.

During the last two decades, networks of producers and subcontracting chains have challenged the vertically integrated factory as the dominant form of productive organization. Flexibility is the keyword used to describe current processes of change in production processes—flexibility in the organization of production and flexibility in the use of labor (Harrison 1994). The analytic

---

1. Earlier versions of this chapter have appeared in Korzeniewicz and Smith (1996) (see Itzigsohn 1996) and in *Perfiles Latinoamericanos* (see Itzigsohn 1998).

link, however, between the informal economy and flexible forms of organizing production and using labor is not new. Several scholars have focused on the insertion of informal firms in commodity chains organized by formal firms as a way of reducing labor costs. For example, Birckbeck (1978) has shown that garbage pickers at a garbage dump could be considered hidden workers of the formal firms that use the products they collect. Benería and Roldán (1987) showed that home workers in poor neighborhoods of Mexico City are incorporated into the commodity chains of large electronic companies. Portes has made the insertion of informal firms in chains of subcontracting the cornerstone of his analysis of the informal economy, arguing that this is a universal phenomenon that arises from the need to reduce labor costs.

Some scholars have seen in the emergence of flexible forms of production an opportunity for informal microenterprises to play a central role in productive and social processes. Some analysts have detected in the informal economy the presence of relations of solidarity and cooperation that constitute an alternative popular economy or at least that have the potential to become such (Burbach, Núñez, and Kagarlitsky 1997; Palma 1988; Pérez Sáinz 1989). Others have described cases in which informal microenterprises are linked through relations of cooperation in some form of industrial districts with the capacity to create regional economies of growth (Capecchi 1989; Pérez Sáinz 1997). Recent scholarship has also looked at the opportunities for linkages for informal firms created by the rise of transnational communities as a result of the widespread migration movements in the region (Portes and Itzigsohn 1997).

Pérez Sáinz (1997, 1998a) has done some of the most recent and innovative research on the position of the informal economy under the new forms of organizing production. His research provides a good framework for the analysis pursued in this chapter. He distinguished three main scenarios of informal economies under the current model of accumulation: The first scenario is that of economies of poverty, based on a context of exclusion and a logic of subsistence based on very limited resources. The second scenario is that of insertion in the process of globalization through the provision of inputs or subcontracting for the growing tradable sector. The third scenario is that of the agglomeration of small businesses that find a niche in the global economy and create dynamic local economies.

The first scenario is linked to the deregulation of hiring and firing workers and the expansion of precarious activities. The second scenario is linked to the flexible use of labor by large companies through the subcontracting of activities and the establishment of transnational commodity chains that profit from different national regimes of regulating labor. The third scenario is linked to the rise of flexible forms of organizing production in conglomerations of small firms. Pérez Sáinz has expanded the geographical scope of the study of informal activities by looking at small urban and rural communities in addition to the main urban centers where most of the studies of informality are conducted. His first scenario, that of economies of poverty, is located in large urban centers. The other two he found in small urban locations or rural communities. My study focuses on the linkages of informal activities in big cities, because most informal activities are still carried out in that setting. It is thus important to continue analyzing the linkages of informal production in this traditional site of study.

The Organization of Production: Integrated, Vertical, and Horizontal Linkages

A central question for this study is how different regulatory regimes affect the articulations of formal and informal activities. If stricter regulations lead to subcontracting, then there should be more subcontracting links in San José. A related question is what kind of linkages do microentrepreneurs enter in their quest for subsistence or growth? To address these questions, I propose to differentiate between three types of linkages in the organization of commodity chains: integrated, horizontal, and vertical linkages. Integrated linkages are characterized by stable relations between firms and a division of labor in the productive process. *Integrated* linkages can be divided into two types: cooperative and centralized linkages. Cooperative linkages are those with some form of coordination in the productive activities and exchange of information and knowledge between autonomous small firms. In this organizational model, a large number of small firms, agglomerated in geographically close spaces, engage in "cooperative competition," and production is usually characterized by flexible specialization. This type of linkage is commonly associated with industrial districts (Capecchi 1989). In Latin America, there are few cases of this type of productive organization, with the possible exception of the famous village of Otavalo in Ecuador and perhaps the case of the Sarchi artisans described by Pérez Sáinz (1997). The centralized type is based on stable relations between one big firm and a dense network of subcontractors and suppliers, usually located in geographic proximity. Production in this organizational type is organized around the integration of small firms into the production process of the core firm. The schedules for the supply of goods are tightly arranged in the "just-in-time" system. In this form of organization, the small firms bear the brunt of economic downturns, but they are also afforded certain opportunities for growth by virtue of being an integral part of a dynamic productive organization. The typical case is that of the Japanese multilayered subcontracting system where there are institutionalized long-term relations between different layers of subcontracting firms (Arrighi, Ikeda, and Irwan 1993). The informal economy in Latin America has very few recorded examples of this type of subcontracting. Perhaps the case of some dynamic entrepreneurs in San Pedro Sacatepequez, Guatemala, who have been linked for many years to one American company that provides them with machinery and loans, comes close to this organizational model (Pérez Sáinz 1997, 1998a).

The *horizontal* type of linkage refers to arm's-length market relations. This form of linkage has been the focus of ILO scholars (Tokman 1978, 1989b) and others such as De Soto (1989). One can divide horizontal linkages into two types: stable and precarious. The first refers to those forms of insertion in which the informal business finds a market niche that allows it stability and perhaps some growth. This view of the informal economy corresponds to the image of the informal economy as the "true market economy" (De Soto 1989) and inspires the policies for microenterprise development (Rakowski 1994). The precarious form of linkage refers to those situations in which the informal business barely subsists in highly competitive markets. The second type corresponds to the image of the informal economy as a marginal subsistence sector—equivalent to the scenario of the economies of poverty proposed by Pérez Sáinz.

Finally, *vertical* linkages correspond to relations between formal and informal firms, which involve no integration of the informal firms into a stable productive system. Here too are two different types of linkage: supplier and subcontractor. A supplier type of linkage corresponds to those cases where informal businesses produce customized products on request for certain formal firms or retailers or where informal producers constitute the beginning of loosely organized commodity chains such as those described by Birckbeck for the garbage pickers in Cali. A subcontractor relation would be characterized by a more hierarchical relation between firms, where the formal firm provides the raw material, design, and very strict schedules of production. This relation differs from the one I have characterized as integrated linkages by the fact that the relations between the different firms are looser, the stability of the subcontracting relationship weaker, and the conditions of subcontracting worse (e.g., the home workers described by Benería and Roldán 1987). Table 5.1 presents the typology of the different forms of linkages.

Table 5.1 Typology of forms of commodity chains of informal firms.

Type	Subtype
Integrated: stable relations between firms and division of labor in the productive process	Cooperative: Coordination in the productive process and exchange of knowledge and information Centralized: Stable relations between firms and integration of the productive process
Horizontal: arm's-length market relations	Stable: Microenterprises with a secure market niche Precarious: Microenterprises in highly competitive markets
Vertical: subordinated firms without a stable integration of productive processes	Supplier: Provision of customized goods or inputs to firms in a single commodity chain Subcontracting: Production of specified goods under direct supervision of other firm but without a stable integration of the productive process

The analysis of the linkages of formal and informal activities is based on the information gathered through the semistructured qualitative interviews with informal microentrepreneurs in the cities of San José and Santo Domingo. During the interviews, respondents were asked about the history of their microenterprises, their economic linkages and organization, and the owners' reliance on social networks for carrying out their businesses. Table 5.2 shows the distribution of the interviews by city and by trade. The qualitative interviews provide an in-depth knowledge of a large number of informal businesses, but given the design of the study, it is difficult to generalize from them. The sample is not representative, and the number of interviews is small. Moreover, given the fact that I made many of my initial contacts through microenterprise-development agencies, it is likely that I encountered a relatively well-off sector in the informal economy.[2] My analytical strategy to deal with these sample problems is to present and discuss cases from three different sectors that illustrate the forms of linkages that appeared repeatedly in my interviews. Through discussion of these cases, I hope to show the structure of opportunities open to microentrepreneurs and the choices they make. I attempt to establish the most common forms of linkages between formal and informal firms and to

---

2. This is so because to get a loan from a microenterprise-development agency, a microenterprise must be established for a certain time and must show economic viability.

Table 5.2 Semistructured interviews by trade and city.

	Santo Domingo	San José
Garments and tailors	8¹ (3, 1)	19⁵ (6, 3)
Carpenters and cabinetmakers	8² (2, 2)	7⁶ (0, 1)
Shoemakers	4	5⁷ (1, 2)
Crafts	8³ (1, 1)	4
Metals and construction	7⁴ (1, 0)	2
Trade and services	5	3

SOURCE: Semistructured interviews.

[1] Three microentrepreneurs were interviewed twice; one worker was also interviewed.
[2] Two microentrepreneurs were interviewed twice; two workers were also interviewed.
[3] One microentrepreneur was interviewed twice; one worker was also interviewed.
[4] One microentrepreneur was interviewed twice.
[5] Six microentrepreneurs were interviewed twice; three workers were also interviewed.
[6] One worker was interviewed.
[7] One microentrepreneur was interviewed twice; two workers were also interviewed.

analyze the strategies for subsistence or growth of informal microenterprises in the different sectors in the two cities. By doing so, I can show elements that are particular to certain sectors or to a certain country and at the same time identify elements that are common to all informal businesses. The variety of settings covered by the interviews guarantees that the discussion provides a broad picture of the constraints and opportunities confronted by microentrepreneurs.

The analysis is based on cases from three sectors: clothing, shoemaking, and crafts. The three are important areas of informal economic activities and have been affected by the recent changes in the model of accumulation. The clothing sector has been "globalized" during the last two decades. Large assembly factories have moved from the center to the periphery of the world economy, where they are concentrated in export-processing zones. In core countries, this sector has moved underground to informal sweatshops (Portes and Sassen 1987). Linkages have been found between formal factories or contractors in core countries and small informal workshops in the periphery (Pérez Sáinz 1997). Thus, in this sector we can expect to find a large range of informal economic actors, from the person who repairs clothes for his or her neighbors to international subcontracting linkages. The case of shoemaking is similar to clothing. In this sector there are also reports of international commodity chains that link main core firms and periphery informal workshops and home workers (Portes and Schauffler 1993). On the other hand, studies show the permanence of craftsmanship and the disappearance of the sector as it fails to compete with the rise of imports that accompany trade liberalization (Lungo 1996). The crafts sector is linked to tourism, one of the most important sectors of the current development model. As such, we could expect to find craftspeople inserted into commodity chains that allow them a possibility of economic growth. Yet, existing reports point to the precariousness of the informal microenterprise in this sector (Lozano 1996). A look at these three sectors allows us to see differences and commonalties in the incorporation into commodity chains and to sort out differences that arise from the particular form of organization of production or market in these sectors. The comparison between San José and Santo Domingo shows the differences that emerge as a result of different regulatory regimes.

The Linkages of Informal Firms

Garments: Producing for Low-Income Markets

In this sector, the main types of linkages I found were of the horizontal and vertical types. I found three main forms of articulation of informal garment producers in the two countries: small informal producers selling to the public, to informal peddlers, or to middlemen (horizontal-precarious); informal entrepreneurs who manage to consolidate their position by obtaining some secure contracts with formal shops (vertical); and informal firms that are able to diversify their clientele and manage to have a number of vendors going around the city or the country selling their own production (horizontal-stable). The following cases illustrate the linkages of microentrepreneurs in this sector in the two cities. I chose these cases because they demonstrate the combination of linkages pursued by microentrepreneurs in their attempts to subsist and perhaps grow.

Helena[3] had a small workshop in her in-law's house, in a lower-middle-class area in Santo Domingo where she employed eight workers, mostly women, producing shirts. Helena opened her business in the late 1970s, but until 1991 she engaged mainly in quality dressmaking for women. In that year, a relative of her husband offered her a subcontracting job for a big local garment company. The company was heavily engaged in production for export, and for that reason its management decided to subcontract its production for the local market. Helena and her husband decided, in their own words, "to confront the challenge

---

3. Helena is the microentrepreneur described in Chapter 4 in connection with the question of social security and the control of labor.

because we saw an opportunity for our business to grow." Unfortunately, they were not prepared for the large amount of work on tight schedules that the job implied, and they ended up losing money. Nevertheless, they decided to go ahead with the production of shirts and began to sell to informal street peddlers and informal middlemen who bought their products to sell to formal stores. I visited Helena twice, in 1992 and 1993; the first time she was just recovering from the failure of the subcontracting endeavor. The second time, the business was in better shape and had a stable clientele. Helena and her husband, though, were looking to grow and claimed that to do so they needed to get orders from big stores. They had not ruled out the possibility of taking another subcontracting job, but only if it paid very well.

Víctor made blue jeans in a workshop in the eastern part of the city, across the Ozama River, where he employed eleven workers. He had been in the business for seven years, but until the winter of 1993 he and his brother were engaged in the production of shirts. At that point, they decided to divide the business, and Víctor switched to making blue jeans. Víctor and his brother learned to make clothes as apprentices in an informal workshop during their teens. Later, they worked in several jobs until an acquaintance offered them jobs sewing clothes for a new shop in the center of the city. Slowly they established contacts with several shops on Duarte Avenue—one of the main commercial avenues of the city—for which they made clothes, sometimes on the basis of their own designs and sometimes as subcontractors. When Víctor and his brother split, Víctor used those contacts as the basis of his new business. Instead of selling shirts, he was now selling trousers. At the time of the interview, in June 1993, Víctor calculated that three-quarters of his production consisted of orders from shops, and one-quarter was his own. The latter part, he sold independently to a number of middlemen; he also had a vendor who went to different shops offering his products.

Manuel was the largest and most successful of the entrepreneurs of the clothing sector I interviewed. He had a small factory in the northern part of the city, where he employed twenty-two people in the production of blue jeans.[4] Manuel began making jeans along with his brother in their grandmother's house in the mid-1980s. He had learned the trade as an apprentice in an informal workshop as a teenager. Later, he and his brother began to produce and sell their own production to people in the neighborhood. Slowly they built the business and enlarged the number of customers. When I interviewed him,

---

4. I contacted Manuel and Víctor through a microenterprise-development agency that provided me with their names. Thus, these agencies serve a clientele that is wider than the microenterprise sector. I return to this point in the next chapter.

Manuel was selling his own brand of blue jeans to a variety of clients who included informal street peddlers and middlemen who bought the trousers to resell them. He also had four vendors who sold the production of his factory for a commission, mainly in the interior cities of the country, because the market in Santo Domingo, according to Manuel, was saturated. Indeed, Manuel complained bitterly about the growing competition and declining rate of profit. He said that people realized that making jeans was a good business; three of his former workers had opened their own workshop. Manuel, though, was trying to confront competition with a more efficient organization of production (producing the same quantity of trousers with a reduced payroll) and was thinking about a marketing campaign.[5]

These cases show the different market options available for garment producers in Santo Domingo and the different strategies that they follow. They suggest a certain progression along the different forms of linkages: Some informal entrepreneurs begin as sellers in final consumer markets (or sell to people who sell in final consumer markets), continue as suppliers or subcontractors, and then return as independent sellers in consumer markets but in a much stronger position than at the beginning. Of course, not all the informal garment producers go through these stages, nor do all of them manage to progress; in fact, most remain at the microenterprise level. The interviews show that, although independent production (horizontal-stable articulations) seems to be the goal, microentrepreneurs often enter into subordinated linkages to stabilize their businesses. Vertical linkages, either of the supplier or subcontractor type, provide more stability and security than horizontal-precarious linkages. These cases suggest that it is important not to equate independence with accumulation and subordination with subsistence. In many cases, the opposite is true.

The three cases discussed above have moved beyond being microenterprises. These three microentrepreneurs shared their intentions to make their businesses grow; they were guided by a logic of accumulation. The cases also show the tremendous difficulties that microenterprises face in this task. In the clothing sector in Santo Domingo, there seem to be clear market limits to the growth of even the most successful microenterprises. Perhaps the best strategy for these firms is to search not for growth but for a stable market niche.

How are the linkages of the microentrepreneurs affected by the different regulatory regimes? The following cases show the structure of opportunity confronted by garment producers in San José. They show that in San José, clothing microentrepreneurs confront even tighter limits than their equivalents

---

5. He learned these techniques in a seminar sponsored by a major American aid organization.

in Santo Domingo. Vicky lived in a small town on the west side of the San José metropolitan area. She used to sew clothes in her house until she got married, at which time she quit. The year before I interviewed her, she decided to go back into business. With the help of her husband's and brother-in-law's savings, she bought a number of machines to open a small workshop. She began producing with two employees, but very soon discovered that it was difficult to sell what she made. Her husband was able to sell part of her production to the workers at the company in which he worked, but the rest remained stockpiled. Soon Vicky learned that to keep her workshop, she had to produce for others. Thus, she began to take subcontracting jobs—to *maquilar* in the local parlance—for a store in her town and for a woman who sold to boutiques in San José.

Marta was a worker in a big formal garment factory in San José until she was fired for her involvement in a labor conflict. Marta then decided to open a workshop to produce clothes, and she used her contacts in her former job to convince them to give her subcontracting jobs. "I was the first to do *maquila* work for them," she claimed. At some point, she decided to take a loan from an official project to develop microenterprises in her neighborhood in the south of San José. With that money, she bought two new machines, hired six workers, and began to produce; but when the time came to sell her production, she had to rely on a middleman recommended by the owner of a neighboring workshop. The middleman ran off with the goods, leaving Marta and her neighbor bankrupt. Marta went back to subcontracting, but she claimed that she could barely employ one person that way and that there were no prospects for growth.

Grace was also trying to sell her production independently. She began sewing when her first child was born. When her husband was fired from his job in the public sector, the couple decided to try their luck producing clothes. They began producing underwear but did not succeed. To survive, they did subcontracting jobs for a woman who took the clothes to sell in Miami, but the woman disappeared at some point (although without owing them any money). When I first interviewed them, they were producing children's clothes; by the time of the second interview, they were also making coats. They were barely keeping their business above water, but they did not want to take subcontracting jobs. The reason was that the formal companies award the subcontracting jobs with the provision that the informal workshop must keep working for them during the good selling months, from September to the New Year. Grace and her husband wanted to be able to produce and sell their own clothes during those months. Grace, however, complained that people did not want to buy clothes from small enterprises. "If I put a label on this coat 'Made in Mexico'" she said, "people will fight to take it from me, but if they know that it is made here in San José they do not want to buy it." Nevertheless, she and her husband kept trying to become independent producers.

The main difference between these cases is that in San José the market for informal garment production seems to be narrower than in Santo Domingo, putting the microentrepreneurs of the sector in horizontal-precarious linkages. The reasons for this are twofold. First, the much larger presence in Santo Domingo of informal retailers offers an outlet for informal goods. This situation affects the way in which transactions are conducted. In Santo Domingo, middlemen have to pay for at least part of the merchandise before they take it. They also have no interest in disappearing without paying for the merchandise because they face tremendous competition and their contacts with informal producers are an important asset. In San José, on the other hand, middlemen are one of the most important outlets for informal production, and they face less competition. As a result, they hold a stronger bargaining position vis-à-vis informal producers than their counterparts in Santo Domingo. This allows them to take merchandise from producers without paying in advance and in many cases, to default on the payment.[6]

The second reason for the precarious position of clothing microentrepreneurs in San José is the higher purchasing power of large segments of the population in that city, which leads people away from informal production. In Santo Domingo, the informal microentrepreneurs provide the low-income consumer markets with cheap goods, and it appears from the interviews that the market for their production is large. In San José, a recurrent theme in the interviews was the microentrepreneurs' difficulty in finding markets. An important source of demand in San José was orders from public institutions. These institutions sometimes placed large orders for clothes for their workers (either uniforms or presents for the holidays). The recipients of these orders, however, are not the informal entrepreneurs, but middlemen who then outsource production to informal firms.

In both cities, formal businesses subcontract their production to informal businesses. Most of the subcontracting work does not come from factories, but from retail chains. To be sure, in both cities there are factories that subcontract to small workshops. In San José, Marta got a subcontracting job

---

6. In San José, I listened to many stories of middlemen who disappeared without paying for the merchandise they took. In Santo Domingo, I heard such stories only among craftsmen. In that city, craftsmen face a situation vis-à-vis middlemen similar to that of clothing microentrepreneurs in San José.

from her former company, but she was the first to do so, and it was due to her connections there. By the time I interviewed her, the factory was no longer giving jobs to informal workshops. In Santo Domingo, Helena also got a subcontracting job from a factory, a contract that almost overwhelmed her business. However, most of the subcontracting arrangements that I found were between retail chains or independent stores serving the low-income population and the informal firms.

According to this interpretation, state regulation affects the linkages of microentrepreneurs in the clothing sector more through its effects on the structure of the labor and consumer markets, than through its effect on labor costs. The larger labor surplus in Santo Domingo leads people to engage in informal economic activities. Street selling has low barriers to entry, and as a result more people compete to sell the products of informal enterprises, giving informal producers more outlets for their production. The low level of income in that city creates a large consumer base for informally manufactured products. Nevertheless, this is not the whole story. The following cases illustrate the effect of labor regulations on informal businesses in San José.

Silvia produced sweaters in her home's backyard with the help of one employee. In addition, she subcontracted her work to two other women who worked in their own homes. "I could enlarge my workshop and bring more employees," said Silvia, "but then I would have to pay them salaries. In this way, I get a subcontracting job, and I give it to them. I pay them much less than I am paid, and I earn the difference." This is a clear description of a widespread trend among informal workshops in all the economic sectors in San José. As the former chapter showed, informal workers have leverage in the informal working relationship by virtue of the real possibility of complaining to the Ministry of Labor. That possibility renders their work more expensive; higher salaries mean that the smaller workshops lose part of their comparative advantage, which they seek to regain by subcontracting work between informal workshops and home workers.

The case of Luis represents another example of the effects of labor regulation on the articulations of informal businesses. Luis had an informal workshop where he produced clothes for formal shops. Four years ago, he had a dispute with his workers, who complained to the Ministry of Labor about Luis not paying them social security. The ministry demanded the payments in arrears, and Luis went bankrupt. Bitter about his situation, Luis decided to try his luck in the United States. After a stay there, he decided he wanted to return to Costa Rica, and on his return he went back to his old trade, but in a different way than before. Luis began to design clothes and to offer them to formal shops. When he got an order, he went to one of a number of informal workshops and subcontracted the production of the clothes. Luis had only one employee, who helped him cut the pieces of cloth that they later took to the informal entrepreneur to be assembled. Luis was not the only one in this situation, and many informal producers I interviewed did subcontracting work for middlemen who specialized in the design and marketing of such designs but shied away from production.

The latter two cases present an interesting development of the articulations of informal firms in a regulated context. Because the informal labor force in San José is not entirely unprotected, informal entrepreneurs need to deal with labor costs that may be too high for them. For this reason, the informal commodity chains in San José have more stages than in Santo Domingo. In San José, I found two types of relations that I did not find in Santo Domingo: (1) subcontracting of production by informal firms to home workers; and (2) middlemen specializing in the design of products and subcontracting their production.

All the examples presented so far concern cases of subcontracting by local firms. In only one case were exports involved, but this was due to the initiative of a woman who took clothes to Miami herself, a case representing individual entrepreneurship rather than international commodity chains. Does this mean that there is no international subcontracting in these cities? Are the commodity chains that connect large multinational companies in the core with home workers in the periphery—the type of commodity chain described by Benería and Roldán (1987)—absent? International subcontracting takes place, but it does not reach the level of the small, informal firms.

In both cities, I asked the informal microentrepreneurs whether they had ever taken subcontracting jobs for international firms or knew about such cases. In all cases but one, the answer was that small firms did not get those kinds of jobs. In Santo Domingo, Helena took a subcontracting job from a firm that produced for export, but the production that it subcontracted was directed at the internal market. In San José, Silvia was explicit about the issue and claimed that international firms have schedules and quality demands that small workshops cannot fulfill. For that reason, international subcontracting work was carried out in export zones in Santo Domingo and in big *maquila* factories in San José. These large factories operated under special tax regimes, and as shown in the previous chapter, the cost of labor there was not higher than the cost of informal labor. The export zones and *maquilas* constitute an informalized formal sector, enjoying a formal firm's benefits of economies of scale and control of labor and the low labor costs of an informal workshop. As a result, there are no incentives to include informal workshops in the commodity chains.

The only exception that I found confirms the statement above. This exceptional case was a cooperative of women in a popular area west of San José, which had twenty-three workers, most of them members. At the time I conducted this research, there were several garment-producing cooperatives of women in San José, all of them dedicated to carrying out national subcontracting jobs. The members of the cooperatives were, in most cases, women who could not work far from their homes because they had to take care of their children. For that reason, the cooperatives were reluctant to impose strict working hours and discipline on their members. The problem with this form of work organization was that the cooperatives often failed to meet the schedules to finish the orders they received, and businesses were reluctant to give them jobs. As a result, the cooperatives that I visited were always in an unstable position, always on the verge of disappearing.[7]

What differentiates the exceptional case mentioned above is that the cooperative decided and managed to impose work discipline on its members, allowing it to take on contracts, deliver the work on time, and grow.[8] Hence, more than an informal workshop, it was a small informal factory with the capacity to meet the tight standards of international firms. The cooperative was informal by my definition, because most of the members were not covered by social security. When I first interviewed the manager of the cooperative, the cooperative was producing an order from a large U.S. retail chain, an order it got from a local middleman who had contacts with the U.S. firm. The second time I visited, the cooperative was working only for national firms. The manager of the cooperative complained that international subcontracting jobs paid less and were more demanding than national subcontracting jobs. Although the cooperative did not shy away from taking those kinds of jobs, it always took orders from national firms when it had the choice.

Meanwhile, Marta was trying to organize a number of small informal firms to jointly undertake a large international subcontract. She hoped that a number of small businesses working together could meet the tight schedules and quality demands of international firms. She also thought that international subcontracting jobs paid better than national ones. The experience of the cooperative refutes that belief. International subcontracting, then, exists and is

---

7. The case of these cooperatives shows another aspect of the relation between gender and labor market choices addressed in the previous chapter. The women involved in these cooperatives had no help taking care of their families and no access to public day care centers. As a result, they had limited labor market options. These examples also show how gender roles affect the organization of informal production.

8. They were able to impose labor discipline, in part, by creating a day care in the cooperative and in that way solving the problem of taking care of their workers' children.

widespread, but it stays at the level of the large and medium firms, seldom reaching the level of the microenterprises and small informal workshops.

To sum up, the interviews in both cities suggest that the main types of linkages are horizontal-precarious or vertical. This finding corresponds to Pérez Sáinz's economies of poverty scenario. Portes argues that the informal economy is functional for capital accumulation in two main ways: On the one hand, the informal economy supplies low-cost goods and services for working-class and middle-class consumers. In this way, the informal economy indirectly reduces labor costs. On the other hand, the informal economy allows formal firms a direct reduction of labor costs through subcontracting or hiring off the books. In the garment sector, the informal economy apparently fulfills mainly the first function, providing low-cost goods to low-income sectors. State policies that promote export-processing zones eliminate the incentive to include informal workshops in commodity chains. The export-processing zones and *maquilas* offer the advantage of tight control of the productive process, and, as shown in the previous chapter, there are no big differences in the cost of labor in the low-end formal and in the informal economies.

Shoemaking: Craftsmanship and Social Networks

Shoemaking and shoe repairs are important areas of concentration of informal firms. In this sector, as with garment production, I found that the main forms of linkages were horizontal-precarious or vertical. My interviews with microentrepreneurs in this sector highlighted the importance of craftsmanship and of social networks. Very often, the success, survival, or demise of informal microenterprises depends more than anything else on the contacts of the informal entrepreneurs. The following case exemplifies these points.

Pedro had a workshop in one of the popular neighborhoods of northern Santo Domingo, where he employed thirteen workers in two small, packed rooms. Pedro began as an independent worker eight years before I interviewed him, after working in a shoe factory for eight years. He began repairing shoes with two employees and in a period of three years managed to build a workshop with ten employees. A large number of the operations in Pedro's workshop were mechanized, although Pedro recently sold a very expensive assembling machine because the widespread energy shortages in the city made manual assembly more productive.[9] Pedro developed a large clientele by using

---

9. During the last two decades, the city of Santo Domingo experienced large energy shortages that would cut off electricity in different parts of the city for whole days (these shortages continue today). The shortages were more acute during 1990 and 1991, particularly during the summer. During my second visit, in 1993, the problem was under slightly better control. These

his networks from his days in the shoe factory. He knew the customers of that firm, and after quitting work there he approached these contacts directly, telling them that he now had his own business. I asked Pedro whether he had ever done subcontracting jobs, and he replied that he had once been approached by a large factory for that purpose, but rejected the offer. Because he had his own clientele he could afford to do so: "They want to exploit the little ones. This shoe, I sell it for 120 pesos; they wanted to buy it for 90 pesos."

This case illustrates the difficult choices faced by microentrepreneurs trying to find a niche between competitive markets that offer only precarious linkages and exploitative vertical forms of subcontracting. Pedro was able to find markets for his products only because of his knowledge of the field and his linkages with people in the field. There were, however, clear limits to his possibilities for growth, in part arising from the limitations of low-income markets and in no small part from the state's inability to provide basic services (electricity in this case). Thus the labor organization in this microenterprise was mostly of the craft type. Skilled workers made shoes manually and trained young apprentices (mostly teenagers). In that sense, Pedro's shop can be characterized as artisan production, where the workers have control over the production process, but only because of Pedro's inability to introduce machinery owing to the lack of electricity.

Craft forms of production are also important in San José but for different reasons. Hard hit by inflation during the 1980s and by the appearance of cheap imported shoes as a result of trade liberalization, the once-strong craft is languishing. Confronted with state policies of trade liberalization that resulted in a worsening of the market for informally produced shoes, Costa Ricans had left the trade of shoemaking to Salvadorans and Nicaraguans. Given the existing discrimination against other Central Americans in the Costa Rican labor market, Nicaraguan and Salvadoran shoemakers did not have much

---

energy shortages were more acute in the popular neighborhoods and have taken out of business a large number of microentrepreneurs who simply lost their clientele because the lack of energy meant that they were unable to finish jobs. The energy shortages hit microentrepreneurs particularly hard, because middle and large firms have their own independent energy sources and thus can continue to produce, thereby capturing the market. Pedro's workshop is a small firm rather than a microenterprise, but he does not have an independent energy source, and he is located in a popular neighborhood where energy shortages, although not as widespread as in preceding years, were still a problem in 1993. The magnitude of the problem is illustrated by the fact that the machine that Pedro was forced to sell was a machine that smaller entrepreneurs whom I interviewed would love to own. They told me that their productivity would be strongly enhanced if they could afford to buy one, but that it was just out of the realm of their financial possibilities.

choice but to try to subsist in the trade under the tougher market conditions. The following example illustrates the plight of shoemakers in San José.

Eloy, a Nicaraguan who had lived in Costa Rica since 1958, ran a workshop in a working-class neighborhood in the south of San José. Eloy had five workers, a Salvadoran and a Panamanian who had worked with him for a number of years, and three Nicaraguans who had been with him for only a few months. The work was carried out manually, as in all the small shoemaking workshops I visited in San José. Eloy sold his shoes mainly to one store in the center of the city and had done so for seventeen years. The store paid for his shoes on the spot (usually small workshops that sell to formal stores have to wait thirty days to get paid). He also sold some pairs of shoes to a middleman who bought from his shop every now and then; Eloy always tried to have some stock on hand in case she appeared. He said that until the crisis of the 1980s the demand for shoes was more stable (a recurrent theme in the stories of old shoemakers). Before the crisis, demand used to pick up in August, and Eloy would employ twice the number of workers from then until Christmas. At the moment of the interview, the good selling months were only October, November, and December. Eloy said that sometimes shoe stores came to him during those months and offered him jobs, but he did not take them because it was difficult to keep the workers during that period. All the workshops competed during those months to enlist more workers, who used the opportunity to jump between employers according to who paid better. Eloy said that in such conditions it was difficult to finish work on time. Other stores offered him higher prices for his shoes, but Eloy always made sure that he first provided the demand for the store to which he had been linked for so many years. Eloy's attitude was conservative, but that attitude allowed him to survive during rough times. His stable linkage with one store provided a more or less secure market during slack periods, and when demand picked up he used the workers he happened to have to produce as much as possible.

Daniel's workshop was a few blocks away from Eloy's. Daniel was also Nicaraguan, but he arrived in Costa Rica in 1976, almost twenty years after Eloy. The first time I interviewed him, Daniel had two employees: a Costa Rican who had been working with him for many years and whom he had trained and a Nicaraguan. The second time I visited him, he no longer employed anyone, and his workshop was on the verge of being closed. Daniel had opened his workshop in the beginning of the 1980s, and by 1985 he had ten workers and his business was growing. Daniel found a contact in Panama and was exporting his production to that country. He was proud to point out that even in those days of high demand, his shoes were completely handmade. As a good craftsman, he refused to introduce machines in his production process. Daniel claimed that in the mid-1980s the Panamanian market was closed to Costa Rican shoe production (he was not clear about the reason for this). In any case, since then, Daniel's workshop had gone through rough times. Daniel complained that the main problem was that the stores paid only thirty days after they got the shoes, and in this way the informal producer got decapitalized. He also complained that people preferred to buy cheaper imported shoes, instead of the "quality shoe" of the shoemaker. Daniel refused to use synthetic materials that would cheapen his shoes and insisted on using leather.

The cases of Daniel and Eloy represent the situation of the informal shoemakers in Costa Rica. Hard hit by inflation during the 1980s and by the appearance of cheap imported shoes as a result of trade liberalization, the once-strong craft was languishing and divided along national lines. Daniel and Eloy (as well as other people I interviewed) claimed that Costa Ricans had left the trade of shoemaking to the Salvadorans and Nicaraguans. A former Costa Rican shoemaker I interviewed, who became a wood craftsman, supported this opinion. Daniel and Eloy claimed that the Costa Ricans could not stand the tough conditions of the trade; they liked a secure income. The Costa Rican former shoemaker instead complained bitterly about the Nicaraguans who sold for less money and accepted worse working conditions. What this situation illustrates is a case of worsening market conditions as a result of state trade policies and the tensions it created among informal producers whose livelihood was threatened by trade liberalization. Under the new conditions, in the best of cases, the shoemakers managed to maintain a low level of business by using a conservative business strategy, as in the case of Eloy.

Lungo (1996) describes the refusal of the shoemakers in San José to mechanize their production, a refusal based on the "craftsman's pride" of the shoemaker, and argues that this craftsman's ethic has become a burden, prompting shoemakers to refuse to take the necessary measures to adapt to the new conditions, in other words, a case of negative social capital. This interpretation is plausible, because the Nicaraguan and Salvadoran shoemakers whom I interviewed did display pride in their trade and a strong preference for handmade shoes. However, Eloy's case may suggest another interpretation. The example shows that only a very conservative strategy of keeping relationships with buyers as well as with qualified workers can ensure the survival of informal microenterprises in conditions of extremely competitive markets. In this case, the attachment to craft production can be perhaps the only strategy of subsistence open to businesses that do not have the necessary capital to modernize and compete with imports.

The cases of Eloy in San José and Pedro in Santo Domingo show the importance of stable social networks in carrying out an independent business strategy. Eloy rejected offers from formal stores in the good months, and Pedro rejected an offer to carry out a subcontracting job. Both could do that because both had stable marketing networks. Eloy, however, did this as part of a conservative survival strategy, whereas Pedro did it as part of a strategy to keep his independence and growth. He could do that only because the market for shoes was then not as bad in Santo Domingo as it was in San José (although that may have changed as a result of the liberalization of imports enacted in 1993).

Shoemakers present a case of skilled workers navigating difficult market conditions by combining precarious market linkages with vertical linkages to stores that sell to low-income sectors. I did not find many cases of subcontracting in this sector. The only case of subcontracting that I found was that of a small shoe factory that I visited in Santo Domingo. The owner of this business, who employed between twenty-five and sixty workers according to seasonal demand, sometimes subcontracted small tasks such as sewing ornaments on top of shoes. He did that only in cases in which the workers in the factory were hard pressed to meet production schedules. Instability of demand is an important reason to informalize production. Formal businesses prefer not to incur large costs in fixed capital and a large payroll; instead they pass the cost of market instability onto informal firms or to their workers' families. This case also shows the gendering of tasks. Most of the employees in the factory were male workers; most of the people to whom the job was subcontracted were women. The owner of the factory subcontracted the work to the wives, daughters, or sisters of his employees. The owner of the factory claimed that the type of job that he subcontracted, jobs that needed attention to detail, were better done by women. In this case, contracting out to home workers (or small informal workshops) was more related to pressures of production than to reducing production costs.[10] This conclusion makes sense given the cheapness of labor in Santo Domingo and the flexibility with which firms manage their labor force through massive *desahucio*.[11]

The owner of the factory was also trying to get a loan to buy new machines to improve productivity. He thought that if he could buy new machines he could then take subcontracting jobs from companies in the export-free zones. He claimed that sometimes the export zone's firms received orders larger than

---

10. This use of home workers corresponds with that described by Chu (1992) for Hong Kong.

11. The factory I visited used to fire all its workers at the end of the year and rehire only those who were needed during the period of low demand after the holidays.

they could take, and so as not to reject them, they subcontracted them to factories like his. He emphasized, however, that to take that kind of job he needed better machinery than he had. This case shows that, as I found in the analysis of microenterprises in the garment sector, to participate in global commodity chains it is necessary to have a strong control of the labor process and a level of productivity that most microenterprises cannot afford.

Like Pedro, Juan, the owner of the factory, made and sustained his business through his social networks. Juan was an accountant, and although he worked in a bank for most of his life, his goal was always to have his own business. His first business was a shoe repair shop, run by a relative of his while Juan kept working at the bank. He got a loan to make the jump from repair workshop to small factory thanks to the ties he developed during his years at the bank. Juan had tried before to get a loan from a state industrial promotion agency to open a factory,[12] but he was rejected because he lacked the necessary guarantees. The second time, he had developed the right contacts to borrow the money to buy the factory.[13] Juan also obtained a big order from New York through the contacts provided by a Dominican friend who did business in New York.

The stories of Juan and Pedro illustrate the importance of social capital in building economic linkages and achieving business success, as well as the limits and opportunities created by state policies. Pedro managed to develop a clientele thanks to the ties from his former job. Nevertheless, the inability of the state to deliver basic services such as electricity imposed a very real limit in the capacity of his business to grow.[14] Juan got a big loan thanks to his ties at the bank. Also, thanks to the extended networks of Dominicans in New York, he managed to get a big production contract that helped him boost his production. He could not have done that by relying only on formal mechanisms, because even middle-class people like him had difficulties gaining access to state programs for industry promotion (or formal private financial institutions). These two cases also show the importance of class in creating social capital. Both Pedro and Juan made their businesses through social networks, but they both had access to different kinds of networks based on their class positions. Those class differences in their networks allowed Juan to buy a factory and Pedro only to create a small workshop.

12. He tried to get a loan from Fondo FIDE.
13. The factory was an old one. Juan changed the line of products the factory produced, but was unable to invest in new machinery because of lack of capital and difficulties in access to credit.
14. In the Dominican Republic, one company—a state-owned company—produces and delivers electricity. The Dominican state is trying to privatize the company or parts of its operations.

These examples show that state policies affect microenterprises in more ways than through labor regulations.[15] In Santo Domingo, the inability of the state to provide electricity to the population hampered Pedro's workshop's capacity for growth. The inaccessibility of loans, even to middle-class people such as Juan, hampered his factory's possibility for growth. In Costa Rica, the opening up of shoe imports eliminated the market for informal shoemakers and pushed the remaining shoemakers into precarious linkages with the urban economy.

Craftspeople: Market Straits

The following cases look at the crafts sector linked to the tourism industry in the two cities. Tourism is a growing sector under the new development model, and many informal entrepreneurs try to find a niche in this growing area. The following cases show the effect of market structure on the opportunities open to microentrepreneurs. In Santo Domingo, craftspeople find themselves pressed between an oligopsonic market (a market with very few buyers) for their products and oligopolistic (pertaining to a market with very few sellers) prices for their raw materials.[16] They can sell to only a small number of gift shops, often through intermediaries who have connections with those shops. The latter, thus, have the power to arbitrarily determine the prices of the products of the informal producers. Those informal entrepreneurs who have direct connections with the gift shops have more power in the market, because they are able to skip one link in the commodity chain and can sell more when demand is up. Even those craftsmen, however, are in a position of less power in relation to the gift shops.[17]

The following case illustrates this situation. Francisco worked in precious stones (amber, corals, and larimar), gold, and silver in his workshop in the eastern part of Santo Domingo. He produced a variety of jewelry and souvenirs. He claimed he needed to produce different kinds of products to sell, because the gift shops, his main market, wanted only a bit of each kind. Francisco knew many owners of gift shops and managed to sell large parts of his production;

---

15. See Liedholm (1994) for an analysis of the multiple ways in which state policies affect microenterprises.

16. Lozano (1996) vividly describes the situation of jewelry producers in Santo Domingo.

17. This situation repeats itself in other areas of crafts production such as ceramics. In Santo Domingo, an association of jewelry craftsmen had set as a goal to open independent retail channels for its members, among them export channels. By the time of this research, however, this association has not had great success.

nevertheless, during some periods he was unable to sell much. Moreover, even when he sold, he was at the mercy of the prices the shops wanted to give him. He said that competition among craftsmen was much tougher at the time of my interview than when he began twelve years earlier. He began producing jewelry in 1980, but stopped after three years because there was no market for his production. He then took part of his surplus to the United States, where he tried to develop contacts to sell it and establish himself as a craftsman, but after a year trying to sell in flea markets and working as a salaried worker he returned to the Dominican Republic. In the United States, though, he learned the trade to which he turned during the periods when he could not sell any jewelry: auto mechanics. Francisco had many contacts that allowed him easier and cheaper access to certain raw materials such as coral and turtle shells. Nevertheless, he was hard pressed by raw material prices, particularly those of amber and larimar, whose producers were organized and demanded high prices. Products made with these two stones were in the highest demand in the crafts market.

In San José, the situation was different. The market for souvenirs was larger in San José than in Santo Domingo. Competition among retailers of souvenirs was higher in San José, and crafts were sold in more areas of the city than in Santo Domingo. Moreover, crafts products were sold on the streets in San José—the one product that was not sold much in the streets of Santo Domingo. In Costa Rica, crafts products were sold mainly to tourists, but there was also a certain domestic market. The possibility of stable horizontal linkages allowed for the rise of more stable forms of employment and production organization. The following case exemplifies this. Magda had a small workshop in the north of San José where she produced ceramic figures of Costa Rican birds and other animals. Magda opened her workshop three years before I interviewed her, after quitting a job at an informal small factory where she learned the trade. At the time of the interview, she employed seven workers, who worked for fixed salaries slightly higher than the official minimum. She did not pay her workers' social security, but she was thinking about doing it. Magda was selling her products to a number of stores in town and had her own retail outlet in the northern part of the city.

Only among craftspeople did I find some cases of cooperation among microentrepreneurs. In most sectors, the pressure of the daily activities isolated microentrepreneurs from one another. In the crafts, the organization of production opened up some spaces for cooperation. Cooperation, however, took different forms in each city. In Santo Domingo, craftspeople sometimes lent their workshops and machines to fellow craftsmen. For example, in cases in which a craftsman got a request from a gift shop and did not have the necessary tools, he[18] could ask to use another craftsman's tools. So the instability of demand and the contacts that arose from belonging to the same trade gave space for some forms of cooperation in production, although I found that those instances of cooperation happened between people who came from the same town or who lived in the same neighborhood. At the time of my research, an association of craftsmen in Santo Domingo attempted to promote cooperation between craftsmen to expand the markets, but it has not been very effective. Moreover, it was plagued by rivalries between groups of craftsmen that were usually constituted on the basis of common regional origin.

In San José, I also found groups of craftsmen cooperating in attempts to open new markets for crafts either in the country or abroad. I even found cases of state support for these efforts. For example, I interviewed a group of craftspeople who were trying to open a store to sell their products in a town on one of the main tourist routes in the country. This group had been organized by a state agency for the promotion of crafts, an agency that was also advising the group on its project. This type of support is key to allow microenterprises to find better linkages in the global economy.

In summary, craftsmen in Santo Domingo were involved mostly in horizontal-precarious or vertical linkages. In San José, I found that it was apparently easier for craftsmen to move into horizontal-stable linkages, not because of the type of labor regulation in the two countries, but because of the structure of the particular markets in which they operated and the presence or absence of state support for craftspeople's activities.

Informal Microenterprises: On the Margins of the Global Economy

My research indicates that in both cities, as a result of a common form of insertion into the world economy, the forms of articulation of formal and informal firms are very similar. Almost all the informal micro- and small entrepreneurs whom I interviewed operated in the framework of horizontal-precarious or vertical linkages. In most cases, these linkages offered only subsistence opportunities. Some informal microenterprises managed to enter stable horizontal linkages that, combined with vertical ones, allowed for some opportunities for accumulation, but only on a small scale, and even then, their situation was precarious. In most cases, informal microenterprises supplied the low-income segments of the market.

18. I use the masculine pronoun only because the cases that I encountered involved men.

Most of the subcontracting opportunities for the informal microenterprises came from retailers that catered to the low-income sectors. Formal stores that catered to low-income sectors subcontracted production from informal enterprises to guarantee low prices, given the constraints of the markets in which they operated. As a result, they organized production in a sort of "putting out" system in which formal stores provided informal enterprises with raw materials that were assembled by the latter at low cost. Given the instability of the markets for informal goods, informal enterprises usually had little choice but to accept the deals proposed by this type of formal business, which in most cases was unfavorable for the informal producers (low prices and payment usually thirty days or more after delivery). Subcontracting by big factories is related more to pressure from production schedules than to pressure to reduce labor costs.

These conclusions are supported by the survey numbers. The mean number of workers of informal businesses was 2.9 in San José and 2.8 in Santo Domingo. In the microenterprise survey conducted by FONDOMICRO in Santo Domingo, the mean number of workers was 3.1. Moreover, that survey indicates that 92.1 percent of firms that employ one to four workers stay in that category and do not grow (Cabal 1993). My survey also indicates that in Santo Domingo 72.7 percent (twenty-four cases) of the informal microenterprises in manufacturing (including self-employed and employers) sell their products directly to the public; the percentage in San José is 61.5 percent (fifty-nine cases). In that city among those who do not sell directly to the public, 59.1 percent (twenty-one cases) sell their product to commercial establishments. In Santo Domingo, there are too few cases that do not sell to the public, only eight, but the FONDOMICRO survey indicates that 84.1 percent of microenterprises in manufacturing sell directly to the public; among the rest, the majority, 7.7 percent, sell to commercial establishments (the corresponding percentages among microenterprises in all sectors are 91.3 percent and 3.3 percent). The available quantitative data, then, strengthen the conclusions I reached from the qualitative analysis.

What are the effects of the regulatory regimes on the articulation of the formal and the informal economies? State export-promotion policies are important in understanding the absence of chains of international subcontracting in the informal economy. In both cities, international subcontracting does not reach the small informal workshops, but remains at the level of the medium and large firms. In both countries, the state provides international subcontractors with access to cheap formal labor in large factories—in the export zones in Santo Domingo and in the *maquilas* in San José—where they benefit from economies of scale and control of the labor process. Because of the similarity of policies, in neither city is there an incentive to extend the commodity chains to include informal microenterprises.

In the new export-based model of economic growth, informal microenterprises are mainly a subsistence sector. However, they are not thereby the most marginal sector of the economy. As the previous chapter showed, under the current export-free-zones-cum-tourism form of insertion in the world economy, labor flexibility encompasses the new formal sector. In this informalized formal economy, labor toils under strict control and with minimum or no protections. In this context, the informal microenterprise could even be a desirable alternative, both in terms of income and in terms of control of the labor process by workers.

Informal microenterprises are part of the urban economy mainly as producers of cheap consumer goods for low-income sectors rather than as providers of cheap labor. This conclusion corresponds to Pérez Sáinz's economies of poverty scenario, in which informal microenterprises are located on the margins of the global economy. Pérez Sáinz (1997, 1998a) describes some cases in which informal microenterprises are linked to global commodity chains. Two of these cases are relevant for this discussion. The first case is that of San Pedro Sacatepequez, a *kakchiquel* community near Ciudad de Guatemala, with stable linkages of subcontracting between small informal firms and an American retailer company. This case corresponds to the buyer-driven commodity chain described by Gereffi (1994). This example, however, does not contradict the general logic of my argument. San Pedro Sacatepequez is a small town whose geographic concentration allows for the control of the production process. Moreover, the ethnic networks in the village allow for social control over who gets access to contracts. The spatial agglomeration and ethnic ties, then, help to solve the problem of controlling the labor process. This control, however, is much more difficult to achieve in the context of a large city.

The second case, that of Puente Alto, a rural community in Northern Honduras, again emphasizes the importance of labor control in the form of organizing production. In this community, Pérez Sáinz found women home workers producing baseballs for export to the United States. The subcontracting firm had American and Honduran capital. The subcontracting firm first organized production in a big factory and turned to homework only after the workers in the factory unionized. The turn to homework was designed to break labor organization and to tighten the control over an atomized labor force.[19]

---

19. Pérez Sáinz shows the intersection of gender roles and the organization of production. He points out that the firm's turn to homework was accepted in the community because it fit local gender roles and expectations. Women approved of it because it allowed them to work at

As for the effects of regulatory regimes, my research shows that, as Liedholm (1994) suggests, there are other important areas beyond labor regulations in which regulatory regimes affect the linkages of microenterprises. Regulatory regimes affect the linkages of microenterprises through their effects on the overall structure of the labor market and the population's income level. In Santo Domingo, the proportionally larger number of people working in the informal economy creates opportunities for horizontal linkages between informal producers and sellers, and it also provides a market for informal production.

The state also affects the organization of informal production through its development policies. For example, I show that infrastructure policies, expressed in the provision (or lack of provision) of basic services, have a profound effect on the strategies of informal actors. Similarly, the regulation of different markets, from trade policies to the restriction of the use of certain parts of the urban space for informal activities, also affects the structure of opportunities opened to informal microentrepreneurs. For example, in San José, the opening of shoe imports almost eliminated the informal crafts producers. As shown in the comparison between shoemakers and craftspeople in Santo Domingo and San José, market structure is central in determining the different articulations of the informal firms in each trade. Whether the market is oligopolist, oligopsonist, or competitive, and whether informal goods have to compete with cheap imports, affects the way in which informal production is organized and the growth capacity of informal enterprises.

There is by now ample evidence that the new form of insertion in the world economy leads to social polarization. Gone are the integrationists' hopes—often more fictitious than real, but at least present—that characterized developmentalism during import-substitution industrialization. Is there in the informal economy a potential alternative popular economy? One element that emerges from the findings is the importance of social networks and social capital in the analysis of the strategies of informal actors. The informal economy is embedded in dense webs of social relations (Lomnitz 1982; Roberts 1990). One of the most important elements for the success of informal microenterprises is the presence of social networks that allow informal microentrepreneurs to reach an outlet for their products.

These social networks can be based on two different sources of social capital.[20] The first source I found is extraeconomic relationships, such as families

---

home and take care of their children. Men approved of it because they could maintain a tighter control over women when they were working at home rather than in the factory.

20. For a definition and discussion of social capital, see Portes and Sensenbrenner (1993).

or friendships, neighborhood relationships, or common migratory origin. These relationships form the foundation for the raising of bounded solidarities. The other source of social capital is relationships that emerge out of the economic activity itself, such as employment acquaintances. This type of social capital is based on reciprocity transactions. The presence or absence of these sources of social capital makes a big difference in the way informal microentrepreneurs conduct their businesses.

The relevance of social networks and social capital indicates the importance of going beyond the logic of state and capital in the analysis of the structure of the urban economy. One must take into account the logic of the informal actors. The latter are certainly constrained by the limits imposed by the logic of state and capital, but within those constraints there are margins for action, and the social capital that actors are able to mobilize makes a difference in the ways they conduct their economic activities. This chapter shows the importance of analyzing the social embeddedness of informal economic activities and the weak and strong links of the actors (Granovetter 1974, 1985). However, before we enthrone social capital as a solution to problems of development, let us remember that social networks and social capital are stratified by class and by other social categories of inclusion or exclusion such as gender, nationality, or race.[21]

Informality allows workers flexible conditions of labor in terms of control of their time. Nevertheless, before we begin celebrating the informal microenterprise as the realm in which labor controls the labor process or as the realm of a nascent popular economy, we must remember that this process occurs in conditions of extreme precariousness. Moreover, in most cases, cooperation between informal firms is hampered by the burden of daily survival on the microentrepreneur's shoulders. Left alone, informal microenterprises will continue to provide a mean for subsistence, sometimes better than in the low-end formal sector, but not much more. If there is a potential in them for more flexible forms of production—flexible in the sense of flexible specialization—it can emerge only, as Capecchi (1989) suggests, as a result of coordinated national and/or local state policies.

---

21. I showed that Salvadoran and Nicaraguan immigrants are often excluded from formal employment in San José, which leads them to engage in informal activities. Also, in Santo Domingo, social capital is stratified by race and national origin. In the Dominican Republic, there is a superposition of national and racial categories of classification. Dominicans see Haitians as black and themselves as non-black. Haitians are discriminated against and occupy their own marginal niches in the urban and rural economies.

6

The Informal Economy, Poverty, and Social Policy

Picture in your mind a small *ventorrillo* (a small grocery store) in a shantytown in the northern part of Santo Domingo. The store is, in fact, a table with a few fruits and vegetables. Usually, there are a few more things to sell, but Hilda, the owner, could not get to the market that day. The table is located at the front door to Hilda's house, a long and narrow shack made of tin, with holes in the roof. The street leading to the house is narrow, uneven, and unpaved; no cars can transit it. The shack has three rooms, and eleven people live in it (Hilda, her common-law husband, her six children, and three grandchildren). She started the store with a $40 loan when her husband lost a meat stand in a neighboring market because the freezer for the meat broke down and he had no money to replace or fix it. Hilda's husband was working again in the market, and between their two incomes they managed, although barely, to finish the month.

This snapshot provides a window into the subsistence efforts of the poor and the importance of informal entrepreneurship for those efforts. This snapshot is not peculiar to the current period, as the informal economy and marginal neighborhoods grew during the import-substitution period. What has changed is the mainstream attitude toward these phenomena. During the import-substitution period, analysts and policymakers associated the reduction of poverty and general upward mobility with the expansion of modern formal employment. Access to basic social services, pensions, and stable incomes was linked to formal employment. In other words, social citizenship—those social rights that allow every member of society to achieve an accepted basic standard of living—was achieved through work in the formal economy. Social citizenship was never universal, as formal work was indeed limited and the basic standards of living and social services were often low, but it was understood that the extension of social citizenship was related to the extension of the formal economy (Pérez Sáinz 1998b; Roberts 1998). As shown previously, Costa Rica was one of the countries that expanded social citizenship the most, whereas the Dominican Republic never expanded social citizenship very much.

The neoliberal model of economic growth leads to the downgrading of employment and labor market conditions. In the labor markets created by the Latin American export-oriented cum structural adjustment development model, both subsistence and success may be associated with a resourceful use of the opportunities opened by the informal economy rather than with formal employment.[1] Scholars, policymakers, and international agencies that previously looked at the informal economy as a burden to development now consider it a solution to problems of poverty and employment (De Soto 1989; Franks 1994; Rakowski 1994). Since the 1980s, the countries of the Latin American region witnessed the emergence of numerous programs of support and promotion for microenterprises. The assumption behind most of these programs is that support to informal microenterprises promotes employment and helps fight extensive poverty, alleviating the "side effects" of structural adjustment programs (Otero 1994; Otero and Rhyne 1994; Rakowski 1994). The "model citizen" under neoliberalism seems to be the individual, self-reliant entrepreneur.

This new situation poses the question of whether the informal economy can really help solve the employment problems under the new model of accumulation. It also poses the paradoxical question of whether social citizenship can be reconstituted based on informal entrepreneurship. Can the state expand access to basic living conditions through the expansion of unregulated activities? And if so, how? The purpose of this chapter is threefold. First, it describes the existing policies toward the informal economy in the two countries at the beginning of the 1990s and asks whether the differences in regulatory regimes affected these policies; second, it takes a closer look at microenterprise development programs and analyzes their effects on the different tiers of the informal economy. Finally, it discusses some policy measures through which the state can promote informal activities and asks whether the latter constitute a basis for the extension of social citizenship.

---

1. Two other avenues of upward mobility are migration, an option widely used in the Dominican Republic, and participation in illegal economies.

Informal Microenterprises' Development Policies

Otero (1994) identifies four types of state policy approaches to the informal sector. The four are (1) a detached role, in which the state does not show interest in the sector and lacks a defined policy; (2) passive collaboration, in which the state allows the operation of small programs but does not devise a specific policy for the sector; (3) active collaboration, in which the state designs and coordinates national-level policies toward informal microenterprises that are implemented through nongovernment organizations (NGOs); and (4) directive collaboration, in which the state plans and implements microenterprise development policies. Otero (1994) argues that the Dominican state pursued an active collaboration policy whereas the Costa Rican state pursued policies that were between active and directive collaboration.

At the time of my research, in Santo Domingo, the largest NGO involved in microenterprise development programs was—and still is—the Association for the Development of Microenterprises (Asociación para el Desarrollo de Microempresas—ADEMI). Several other important NGOs such as the Dominican Development Foundation (Fundación Dominicana de Desarrollo—FDD) provided trading in addition to credit; the Dominican Institute for Integral Development (Instituto Dominicano de Desarrollo Integral—IDDI) focused on development projects for the most marginal neighborhoods; and the Dominican Association for Women's Development (Asociación Dominicana para el Desarrollo de la Mujer—ADOPDEM) and Banco de la Mujer (Women's Bank) provided loans to women engaged in microenterprises. This list does not cover the whole field of NGOs working with microenterprises in Santo Domingo, but includes the largest ones. The Dominican state at the time of my research had a passive role. Its action was confined to donations, loans, or credit lines to the major NGOs. Although Otero classifies the Dominican state policy as active collaboration, I think that it is closer to her passive collaboration type.[2]

The lack of credit for starting, fixed, and working capital has been identified as one of the main bottlenecks confronted by informal microenterprises, and all programs for the promotion of microenterprises engage in providing loans. There are differences of opinion, however, about other areas, and the agencies listed above represent different approaches toward microenterprise

---

2. The Fernández administration (1996–2000) created a government agency for microenterprise development, but this took place after my research.

development. One of the key discussions in the field of microenterprise development is whether informal entrepreneurs need training in addition to capital. ADEMI represented the position that what microentrepreneurs need is capital; the FDD argued that microentrepreneurs also need training. The IDDI represented yet another approach; this NGO attempted to reach the poorest sectors in society and aimed to organize communities in addition to promoting microenterprises. This promotion was seen as part of larger community development projects. ADOPDEM and Banco de la Mujer had as their goal the empowerment of women through the development of entrepreneurship.

The importance of access to capital is emphasized by the findings of a FONDOMICRO[3] national survey of micro- and small enterprises in the Dominican Republic. The survey found that the increase in employment is significantly larger among those firms that received loans from banks, NGOs, or family and friends (Cabal 1992, 1993). The reach of all the microenterprise development programs, however, is very limited. FONDOMICRO's survey found that only 2.8 percent of microenterprises had ever received loans from an NGO. The main source of credit was family and friends, which encompassed 8.3 percent of the valid cases. The majority of cases, 76.1 percent, had never received any type of credit.[4]

Given the limited access to formal sources of capital, microenterprises often rely on informal mechanisms for raising capital, in the form of the neighborhood loan shark or of rotating saving or purchasing arrangements called *sanes*. The case of Mario and his wife Juana illustrates this type of arrangement. Mario was working for a big firm and wanted to open his own furniture workshop, but he did not have enough capital or access to loans. Juana, a public employee, organized a *san* among her fellow workers: Each week they contributed a fixed sum, in exchange for which her husband promised to build cabinets for them. When her husband finished a cabinet, it was allocated by lottery to one of the participants. In this way, the wife tapped a source of capital that allowed her husband to obtain the capital to become a microentrepreneur.

The situation in Costa Rica was similar in its basic contour, but, as could be expected, the state played a larger role. AVANCE, the Costa Rican parallel

---

3. FONDOMICRO is a Dominican institution whose purpose is to conduct research on microenterprises and to provide technical and financial assistance to institutions that support the development of microenterprises. It has conducted yearly surveys of microenterprises since 1992.

4. The 1996 follow-up survey found that 67.9 percent of microentrepreneurs have not received loans of any kind. According to that survey, the largest source of credit for microentrepreneurs is suppliers. Only 3.4 percent of the microentrepreneurs received loans from NGOs, whereas a similar percentage received loans from formal financial institutions (Ortiz 1997).

to ADEMI, was the largest NGO and was engaged in providing loans for microenterprises.[5] Other NGOs, such as Fundación Acción Ya, were interested in organizing microentrepreneurs into cooperatives or working groups in addition to providing loans. As with the case of IDDI in Santo Domingo, this approach saw microenterprise development as part of larger community-development programs.[6] In San José, there were also a number of state-sponsored programs for the promotion of microenterprises. The most prominent among those was, at the time of my research, the PRONAMYPE (Programa Nacional para la Micro y Pequeña Empresa—National Program for the Micro and Small Enterprise) implemented by the Ministry of Labor. This program set as its goal the creation of 30,000 new jobs (FAY 1992). The PRONAMYPE was the successor to the FRAME (Fondo Rotativo de Apoyo a la Microempresa— Rotating Fund for Microenterprise Support), implemented by the Arias administration. The two programs worked in a similar way: The Ministry of Labor set up a special fund and contracted private NGOs to identify candidates for loans and act as financial intermediaries. The NGOs' responsibility was to insure the repayment of the loans and to recuperate their operating costs through the loan interest rates.

The rationale behind this model of organization was to avoid red tape and bureaucratic delays in the implementation of programs. NGOs are considered to have a more flexible decision-making structure and to be able to reach people with the loans faster and more efficiently than can a public agency. This model of organization also reduces the organizational costs of the programs and avoids swelling public-employment ranks. However, because the NGOs need to finance themselves from the interest generated by the loans, interest rates are driven up, and the financial burden of the programs falls on the backs of loan recipients, who supposedly come from the most destitute sectors of society. In addition to these programs, during the time of my research, there was also a small loan program conducted by the IMAS (Instituto Mixto de Ayuda Social—Institute for Social Assistance), a welfare institution in charge of providing relief help to the poorest segments of

---

5. AVANCE and ADEMI both received aid from U.S. AID programs that sponsor this type of NGO. Both were then linked to ACCION International, a Boston-based NGO committed to the development of "popular capitalism" as a solution for the problems of poverty in underdeveloped countries (since then, ADEMI broke its relationship with ACCION).

6. Although the IDDI and FAY saw microenterprise development as a tool for community development, their approaches differed widely. IDDI focused on the development of community organizations and projects, whereas FAY focused on the organization of groups of microentrepreneurs that cooperate and help one another in common economic projects (FAY 1992).

society.[7] The IMAS program gave very small loans with easier conditions of repayment.

The differences in state policies between Costa Rica and the Dominican Republic correspond to what one might expect from their different regulatory regimes. Nevertheless, the different policies did not translate into different results. Although there is no evaluation of the scope of the Costa Rican government's different programs, it appears from the accounts of microentrepreneurs that their reach was not larger than the programs in Santo Domingo. Microentrepreneurs of all sectors complained about the difficulty of getting loans. Moreover, old microentrepreneurs who had been in business for a long time and had stable businesses recounted that in the past they had access to bank loans for small industries.[8] However, these microentrepreneurs complained that during the 1980s these types of loans were placed in the hands of NGOs and microfinance programs and that access to NGO loans was difficult because of the tough conditions that they imposed.

Microfinance and the Heterogeneity of the Informal Economy

To understand the effects of microenterprise development policies, it is necessary to take into account the heterogeneity of the informal economy. Marquez (1994) describes the informal economy by using the image of a pyramid. At the top of the pyramid are dynamic and stable enterprises; at the bottom are subsistence activities; and the middle is fluid, composed of some informal firms that are pushed up by good market conditions while others are pushed down by competition. The qualitative interviews show a similar picture, from which it is possible to distinguish three tiers of informal enterprises: first, those enterprises that have grown in terms of the number of employees and investments in machinery and have achieved a level of capital, employment, and output that lifts them to the rank of small firms; second, a large segment of informal microenterprises with a low level of installed capacity, which

---

7. The Figueres administration, 1994–98, consolidated all its social policies under its national antipoverty plan, which was under the administration of the second vice-presidency of the republic. The national antipoverty plan included a component in charge of providing loans to microenterprises. Its goal was to give 2,500 loans per year, not a very ambitious goal, pointing to the limits in the reach of these programs.

8. It is important to remember here that in Costa Rica the main banks were until recently state owned, that the state had the monopoly over medium- and long-term deposits, and that it had used its control over the financial assets of the country for development purposes.

struggle to maintain a niche in the market (through horizontal or vertical linkages) and experience a constant scarcity of working capital. Most of the interviews I conducted were among this second type of enterprise. Finally, there are those informal businesses operated by very poor, usually self-employed people, who function with very little capital, and whose permanence in business is based on self-exploitation.[9]

The upper tier is represented in the previous chapter by the case of Manuel in Santo Domingo.[10] The middle tier is represented by the cases of Helena, Pedro, and Francisco in Santo Domingo, as well as by those of Marta, Eloy, and Magda in San José (all these cases were discussed in Chapter 5). The cases of Hilda in Santo Domingo and Jaime, the Nicaraguan sandal-maker in San José, described in Chapter 4, represent the lower tier. My observations suggest that the middle of the pyramid may be less fluid and more stable than Marquez suggests. It is true that microenterprises at the middle of the pyramid can enjoy periods of growth caused by favorable market conditions that usually do not endure, as the case of Francisco in Santo Domingo or Eloy in San José attests. However, those microenterprises also show resilience and stability, and their incomes are clearly higher than mere subsistence activities.

The qualitative observations suggest that the significance of credit varies for each of these groups. Loans to firms on the upper tier may have a direct effect on capital accumulation and productivity by allowing the introduction of new technologies. They may also provide an injection of working capital that helps to expand the levels of production. This is the case with Manuel's firm in Santo Domingo, described in Chapter 4, which, after using a loan to buy raw materials and successfully maintaining the levels of production, was looking for new loans to introduce new production technologies. However, the amounts needed for this purpose are much higher than those usually provided by NGOs.

Loans aimed at the middle tier may help stabilize the situation of the firm or help it out of a financial strait. The firms most often use the credit for working capital.[11] The case of Francisco in Santo Domingo, also described in the previous chapter, who used the loans he got to purchase the expensive stones

---

9. The upper and middle tiers would be included in the entrepreneur category in the quantitative analysis in Chapter 4. The lower tier would be included in the self-employed category and probably also in the nonworking category.

10. I interviewed a furniture manufacturer in San José whose situation paralleled that of Manuel in Santo Domingo. However, given the stronger presence of state regulations, most of the cases that reach this level in San José become formal firms.

11. The FONDOMICRO survey in Santo Domingo found that most microentrepreneurs use their loans for working capital (Cabal 1993).

he needed for the jewelry he produced, exemplifies this case. Most of these businesses will not grow beyond a certain limit and will remain microenterprises. Loans to the lower tier have the effect of creating sources of livelihood, usually very modest, for people who are just striving to subsist. Hilda, the case with which this chapter begins, is a case in point. Jaime, the Nicaraguan sandlar in San José, is another example. He was asking the IMAS (Instituto Mixto de Ayuda Social) for a loan of 75,000 colones, the equivalent of $525. An official from one of the other loan programs described the IMAS loans as pocket money and said that only a microvendor could profit from them. Jaime's loan, however, would have allowed him to secure his business and escape the cycle of decapitalization caused by the fact that shoe stores usually take at least thirty days to pay for their purchases and would have allowed Jaime to settle in a trade in which he could earn a larger income than in a salaried job.

The heterogeneity of the informal economy is a fact well known by policymakers and NGOs. Lending to an established informal workshop employing ten workers is not the same as lending to a lone dressmaker with a sewing machine. For this reason, NGOs have developed a range of lending schemes: from loans for "solidary groups" of small, mostly self-employed informal entrepreneurs, where the whole group is responsible for the repayment of each individual loan, to loans to established medium-small businesses. Most NGOs and government lending schemes cater to the middle tier of informal enterprises. Loans to the lower and middle tiers sometimes have higher rates of default and do not cover the financial costs of the organizations. Some institutions, like ADEMI or the FDD in Santo Domingo, also target part of their loans toward the upper tier. This type of lending is relatively secure and more profitable than the smaller loans; thus it helps these institutions achieve a measure of institutional self-financing (ADEMI 1991, 1992; Castiglia 1993; Perfetti del Corral 1991). NGOs involved in informal microenterprise development are under pressure by many international donors to eventually become self-financing or at least to recuperate a substantial part of their operation costs, and the policy of high interest rates and tough credit conditions is designed to allow them to achieve this.[12] The belief is that microenterprises are in fact highly productive and that they can stand the tough credit conditions.

Most NGO programs work in the following way: Advisers from the NGO conduct feasibility studies of the microenterprises; if they approve the loan, then the NGO begins by providing a small loan, which might be fol-

---

12. By the time of my research, ADEMI was close to reaching the point of becoming an independent financial institution.

lowed by an additional amount if the original loan is repaid in a timely manner, and so on. The interest rate of the loans is generally a market rate or higher; the repayment periods are usually short; and there is no grace period. In fact, the NGO often deducts a commission from the loan at the time it grants it. These credit conditions are tough for very small businesses. In general, NGOs give loans to microenterprises that have been functioning for a certain period, usually one year.[13] The rationale for this policy is that the rate of mortality of microenterprises in their first year is about 40 percent.

The qualitative interviews portray a complex picture of microentrepreneurs' experiences with the tough conditions of NGO loans. Many informal microentrepreneurs indeed benefit from this type of credit. In several cases, however, the businesses were almost broke as a result of the lack of flexibility in the loans. Many microentrepreneurs confront situations in which they spend their loans in working capital but are unable to recuperate the costs immediately. Many stores, for example, pay microentrepreneurs only thirty to sixty days after delivery. The microentrepreneurs usually need to begin repaying their loans early, but they cannot because they have not been paid themselves. Thus, many people often prefer informal mechanisms of finance, such as loan sharks, that allow for more flexibility in payment—although at the price of putting the microentrepreneur in deep indebtedness—or *sanes* that allow the microentrepreneur access to the funds when needed.[14] Another problem with the high interest rates policy is that it often leads microenterprise development programs away from the poorest sectors.

As Márquez argues (1994), the need to repay loans and achieve sustainability leads most NGOs in the field away from giving loans to the poorest sectors in the informal economy. The more impoverished sectors are reached by NGOs such as the IDDI in Santo Domingo or state agencies such as the IMAS in San José, which specifically address these groups. The problem with programs focused on the poorest sectors is that it is almost impossible for such programs to become self-financing, and sometimes they have higher rates of default than programs addressed to the middle tier of entrepreneurs. As one NGO official working in a marginal neighborhood put it, "Once you see how people in this neighborhood live, it is difficult to go and ask them for their payments." This often makes such programs unpopular with international donors

---

13. One year was the cutoff period for ADEMI at the time of my research. That NGO later changed its policies, and currently, the minimum period that the informal firm must be in operation to qualify for a loan has been reduced to six months.

14. I found *sanes* only in Santo Domingo. I found no form of rotating credit associations in Costa Rica.

that finance the NGO's programs and that favor projects that have very low default rates and that can recuperate their costs.[15]

In sum, different policies of microenterprise promotion must be designed to address the needs of the different tiers of informal activities. Policies toward the upper tier should promote the creation and expansion of microenterprises capable of growing and accumulating capital; policies toward the middle tier should help stabilize the market position of microenterprises; and policies toward the lower tier should be designed to improve the standard of living of people in poverty. In other words, the policies toward the lower tier should guarantee informal producers their social reproduction.

Informal Entrepreneurship, Social Policy, and Social Citizenship

It is clear that the state's and the nonprofit agencies' policies previously discussed can help informal firms to stabilize their situation and in some cases also to grow. It is also clear that their reach is limited and that they are not unproblematic. Two questions then arise: What policies can achieve the goals put forward in the paragraph above? Can those policies constitute a base for the expansion of social citizenship? This section addresses these questions and advances some ideas about possible alternative policies toward the informal economy.

The evidence shows that common problems with microenterprise development programs are that they are isolated, do not reach large sectors of the population, and do not have continuity. These programs are implemented by NGOs that more often than not have good people and good ideas but not many resources. As a result, NGOs are constantly searching for funds and are dependent on the particular interests of the international donors that fund them (giving the latter an important say in local social policies) or must become self-financing with the most likely consequence of having to abandon certain areas of action. The state should take a leading role in integrating isolated institutions into a national strategy.[16] A greater state participation in the promotion

---

15. In my interviews, I encountered a number of instances in which programs addressed to the poorest sectors had to relocate to less marginal parts of town or change the type of microenterprise to which they gave loans because of demands from international donors that the programs cut their losses.

16. This position is also advocated by people involved in the promotion of microenterprise programs. See Otero (1994).

of these programs, in conjunction with the NGOs already working in the field, could bring much-needed stability and continuity to the programs and could assure a much greater access to the poor. NGO participation in the programs is important because it can provide a measure of community input in program design and help avoid clientelism in the implementation of these programs.[17] This model in fact guided the PRONAMYPE in Costa Rica, as well as its predecessor, the FRAME. These programs, however, were limited and focused exclusively on providing loans. The role of the state was limited to establishing the funds for the programs and contracting with NGOs that were interested in implementing them. The state should take a much more central role, going beyond the provision of credit. The state should link, coordinate, and finance existing scattered programs to develop an integrated national policy.

Another important point that emerges from my description of the three tiers of informal firms is that programs should have different goals and different means, depending on the targeted population. Programs aimed at promoting self-employment among the most vulnerable sectors of the population cannot work on the same assumptions as those aimed at established microenterprises with potential for accumulation. Programs based on the assumption of high productivity and capacity for repayment of high interest loans can reach only the better off among the microenterprises. Institutions that focus on this type of loan can fulfill a much-needed role in financing small producers. This role is indeed important in promoting those informal firms with the highest capacity for accumulation, promoting the formation of stable small- and middle-size enterprises, and filling gaps missed by financial institutions in the country. As we saw in the case of the shoe factory in Santo Domingo, even medium-size businesses often have problems to obtain loans from formal institutions.

Programs of self-employment for the most vulnerable sectors of society should not be based on the assumption of recovering full operating costs. These programs should indeed demand repayment, to stress the seriousness of their purposes and to engage the commitment of the recipients, but the conditions of repayment should be such that the targeted population can afford the loans. If well implemented, these programs could have a significant payoff for relatively small amounts of money. The case of Hilda, with which this chapter began, is a case in point. These programs focus social expenditures on the neediest segments of society, which is one of the cornerstones of

---

17. NGOs have the capacity to act as intermediaries between local communities and the state. However, one should not make the mistake of confusing NGOs and community organizations. The relations between these two sets of actors are always complex and sometimes conflicting.

the social policies promoted by international financial institutions—such as the World Bank and the Interamerican Development Bank—that are providing large chunks of funds for the development of social policies under neoliberalism.[18] These programs are important because they can improve the living conditions for the people involved in them; nevertheless, they cannot eradicate poverty in general or move most participants out of poverty. Again, as the case of Hilda shows, the *ventorrillo* improved her living conditions, but did not lift her family out of a marginal neighborhood, precarious employment, and even more precarious living conditions.[19] Moving people from extreme poverty to self-reliant poverty is indeed positive but does not solve the problem of poverty (Márquez 1994).

There are other important areas for state action beyond the financial aspects of microenterprise development. Chapter 5 illustrates the importance of social networks in the survival and growth of informal microenterprises. The findings of that chapter suggest that financial assistance is not informal microentrepreneurs' sole need. The state can play a role in developing the social capital of informal microenterprises. As Capecchi (1989) argues, the local state played a central role in the emergence of informal economies of growth in northern Italy by creating the conditions for the fulfillment of the potential of social solidarity. Of course, every situation is particular, and state action cannot reproduce the social and economic conditions of northern Italy. Nevertheless, there are a number of areas in which the state can act to promote and strengthen the social capital of informal actors.

One area of action is to promote the organization and cooperation of informal producers. The example of the emergence of an association of craftsmen in San José illustrates this point. The craftsmen were brought together by a state agency for the promotion of the crafts called ANDA (Asociación Nacional de Artesanos—National Association of Craftsmen) for the purpose

---

18. Emphasis should be made on the issue of the financing of microenterprise policies—and social policies in general. It is common these days for states to build their social policies on particular projects financed by international organizations. This approach gives international donors a wide input in the making of social policies and makes the continuity of those policies contingent on their continued interest and approval. States should take back into their hands the financing of the social sectors. This will be difficult given the financial constraints suffered by the states in the region. To do that, the Latin American states should do what they have seldom done, which is to tax the wealthy. The guiding principle of social policy should move from specific antipoverty programs to wealth redistribution. Only then will it be possible to design effective antipoverty policies.

19. Although this is a well-known point since Hart's (1973) work in Ghana, it has been blurred in recent years given the current emphasis on the self-sufficient informal entrepreneur.

of creating a market for crafts. That project failed for a variety of reasons, but the participants were already organized and went ahead on their own to create an association and open a craft store on one of the main tourist routes of the country. The creation of a national chamber of informal entrepreneurs in the tourism sector in Costa Rica provides another example. This organization, called TURCASA, was promoted by an NGO working to help microenterprises. Instead of providing loans to individual microentrepreneurs, the NGO organized the microentrepreneurs in this sector into a national organization that helped them address their common concerns and affect policies toward their activities.[20]

Organizing the cooperation of microentrepreneurs and developing social capital are by no means easy tasks. Two elements make these tasks very complicated: first, the difficulties in creating trust, particularly among a group of people whose daily activities take place in isolation from one another, and second, the burden of managing the firm and the workday. Microentrepreneurs usually do not have managers to take their place if they are not there, and their working day is often long. This leaves little time for meetings. As Capecchi (1989) argues, the emergence of informal economies of growth is based in the existence of previous bases of solidarity on which cooperation can be built. The interviews suggest that social capital can be built on two bases: first, if there are clearly defined common interests present (as in the case of the crafts association), and second, in those cases in which there is an existing base for trust and interaction, such as living in the same neighborhood or being of the same regional origin.[21] Although promoting cooperation is difficult, if it is successful it can begin to attract more people.

One element that appeared clearly in the interviews was that bottlenecks in the marketing of products could undermine all the benefits of financial assistance. Without a fast enough turnover of their production, informal microenterprises cannot pay their loans. As Márquez (1994) suggests, one possible

20. In 1998, TURCASA was still in place, although some of its more ambitious plans, such as creating a travel agency to serve its members, had failed. Moreover, some of the original members had left the organization, arguing that the group in control used its resources for its own benefit. Although I think that the development of this type of organization is a promising area of work, it is not easy, and success is by no means guaranteed.

21. The cases of Sarchi in Costa Rica and San Pedro Sacatepequez in Guatemala described by Pérez Sáinz (1997) are examples of the development of dynamic informal economies based on local solidarities. At the time this research took place, FAY has had some success in organizing some groups of microentrepreneurs in San José. These groups were based on locality and some of them on common trade. These efforts, however, were heavily constrained by the lack of resources of the organization. Unfortunately, I could not follow up on these groups.

policy direction is the creation of trading houses that allow a better integration of microentrepreneurs into the market. Such a policy can be implemented in different, complementary ways. One way is the promotion of marketing cooperatives among informal microenterprises.[22] These cooperatives can help them buy cheaper raw materials and find markets for their products. Although microentrepreneurs are often reluctant to cooperate in their production or marketing activities, such a policy could be very rewarding, because it might lead to increased cooperation among microentrepreneurs and hence to an emergent source of social capital. In the best of cases, this social capital may cement the growth of dynamic pockets of entrepreneurial activity.

Another possible policy directed at stabilizing the situation of informal producers is for state agencies to act as intermediaries in selling informal products, functioning as a marketing board. One of the main bottlenecks for informal producers is that they often have to wait thirty days or more before they are paid for their products. Because informal producers are vulnerable, stores often default on their payments. The state could promote the creation of neighborhood associations of microentrepreneurs, which, with the backing of the state and NGOs, could pay members their receipts and be in charge of securing payment from merchants. This action would free up the microentrepreneurs' working capital without forcing them to take out short-term, high interest loans and could lead to emerging forms of cooperation among these microentrepreneurs.

Two other ways in which the state can promote informal microenterprises are to privilege informal microenterprises in its procurement orders and/or to design incentives for formal firms that take orders or subcontract with informal firms. All these policies do not demand the commitment of large resources and have the benefit of being focused on specific sectors. The recommended policies could help the most vulnerable sectors of the informal economy to subsist in better conditions, stabilize the middle sectors of informal producers, and promote pockets of dynamism among the better organized. From the point of view of this study, however, one may ask whether the state should be engaged in promoting the informal economy, that is, in promoting activities that operate beyond its regulations—the equivalent of legitimizing a double-tier system of labor regulations (Márquez 1994). In other words, the state will be taking an active part in the informalization of the economy. The state may

---

22. I found two groups of microentrepreneurs, one in each city, trying to develop marketing cooperatives. Some microentrepreneurs also told me that the U.S. AID was emphasizing the need of cooperation in marketing between microentrepreneurs.

be promoting employment yet at the same time promoting the deterioration of social citizenship.

The answer to this paradox is twofold. First, there is a need for these policies in spite of their problems. The informal economy is not disappearing, and it is impossible to ignore it. Policies that focus on the informal economy can help create employment and alleviate poverty. Some of these policies, such as those that promote procurements or subcontracting with informal firms, could be linked to incentives to formalize. These policies would be directed to the upper tier of informal firms, which are the only ones that can comply with big orders, and they could be designed in such a way as to lead micro and small informal firms to become formal firms. Other policies can promote the rise of cooperation among the middle or lower tiers of informal microenterprises and in that way help dynamize local economies.

Second, again as Márquez (1994) suggests, the informal economy is not and cannot be the panacea for problems of poverty and employment. The informal economy does not constitute a base on which to build universal social citizenship. Microentrepreneurs and the self-reliant poor, the "model citizens" of the neoliberal realm, do not enjoy full social citizenship. The self-reliant poor are still poor and like microentrepreneurs—who are often only slightly above poverty—lack access to the basic services that guarantee social reproduction (health services, pensions, decent education). The belief held in several academic and policymaking circles that the informal sector can solve the problems of poverty and provide an engine for economic growth is not supported by my research. The promotion of informal activities is important, but it should be seen as complementary, not as an alternative to the rebuilding of gainful and stable formal employment. Moreover, because informal employment is often precarious, it is still imperative to explore new ways to expand social security, health care, and education to the whole population. The state has a central role to play both in the implementation of the policies proposed above and in any effort to promote formal employment and expand social security. It is imperative to develop regulatory regimes that are responsive to the social demands of the population and effective in expanding social citizenship.

7

Toward an Informal Future?

The State, the World System, and the Informal Economy

The previous chapters presented a complex picture of the informal economy in San José and Santo Domingo. The different individual elements that compose this picture are not new for those who study how people live and work in urban Latin America. The whole picture, however, with its multilayered view and comparative angle, provides new elements for the analysis of the informal economy in the region and for the assessment of different theories about the organization of work and production. This chapter first recaps the main findings of the book; then, it addresses the question of whether labor market deregulation is a solution to the problems of employment in the region; and it finishes with some reflections on the challenges of institutional change confronted by Latin American societies.

To begin, allow me to summarize the key theoretical argument. In this work, I have tried to bring together different theoretical approaches to bear on the study of the informal economy. In broad theoretical terms, I have set out to explore the explanatory possibilities of institutional analysis in a world-system framework. In other words, I am interested in studying the scope of the state institutional agency while accounting for the systemic limits on state action imposed by the world economy and the interstate system.

To capture the possibilities and limits of state action, I compared two countries with a similar insertion in the world economy but with different regulatory regimes. Regulatory regimes describe the institutional character of the state and are defined by positioning the state apparatus vis-à-vis two axes:

the developmental-predatory axis that refers to state development policies and the protective-paternalistic-repressive axis that refers to labor regulations. I believe that this approach has paid off. This comparative study shows the possibilities and limits of state-centered action in the world system. The previous chapters show that on the one hand, state institutional structures matter and can affect the lives of their citizens in different and important ways. On the other hand, state action has its limits; the policies pursued by the two states analyzed in this book affected the quality of life of their people but did not change the country's structural position in the world system. Moreover, in moments of crisis or changes in worldwide political-economic paradigms, states in similar structural positions are subject to similar world-system pressures and undergo similar socioeconomic processes. This fact is particularly true for peripheral states with little influence on the structuring of the world economy and the world interstate system.[1] Nevertheless, the character of the state institutional system has an effect on how those worldwide trends affect particular countries and individuals in those countries.

The comparison between the labor markets in San José and Santo Domingo shows a number of important similarities, the result of a common peripheral insertion in the world economy and similar policies of industrialization. First, the trends in labor absorption are parallel in the two cities: a growth of the informal economy until the 1970s, stagnation during that decade, and the downgrading of employment and informalization of the labor markets during the 1980s and 1990s. The structure of the labor markets, the income differences between different occupational categories, and the mechanisms of job allocation are basically similar in both places. The linkages between formal and informal firms also proved to be the same in both cities. Most informal activities are linked to the urban economy through horizontal-precarious or vertical linkages. In both cities, informal economic activities constitute mainly a subsistence economy whose function in the overall process of capital accumulation is to provide cheap consumer goods to the low-income sectors and subsistence for the people excluded by the new growth model. At the same time, both states have "informalized" formal work in the new tradable sectors, those that constitute the growth engine under the new development model. In that way, they eliminated incentives for the formation of transnational commodity chains that include informal workshops or home workers.

1. The world system shapes its constituent units and at the same time is shaped by them. However, in the process of shaping the structure of the world economy and the interstate system, core states have a much stronger influence while peripheral states often have no say in the international political and economic order.

Yet, in spite of these commonalties, the two cities also have important differences. Although the two cities experienced parallel trends in labor absorption, the informal economy is much bigger in Santo Domingo. Although during the 1980s and 1990s both cities experienced the downgrading of employment and the informalization of their labor markets, this trend was much more pronounced in Santo Domingo. In the two cities, the labor markets are segmented, but segmentation is more pronounced in Santo Domingo. In both cities, gender is a key variable explaining income differentials and job allocation between different labor market sectors. In Santo Domingo, however, gender differences in income are more pronounced. In San José, the presence of state regulation allows the weakest sectors in the labor market to enjoy a measure of protection and to improve their working conditions. Women in that city benefit from the possibility of gaining access to protective state institutions. The regulatory action of the state does make a difference in creating a more formalized and less segmented labor market. In San José, there are also a few examples of policies toward the informal economy that attempt to develop the potential of cooperation between informal firms.

I attribute these differences not to particular policies or legislation—although these are important—but to the overall institutional character of the state, to the type of regulatory regime. As the discussion in the first chapter indicates, the labor legislation in the two countries is similar in terms of minimum salaries and flexible use of the labor force. In both countries, access to social security is mainly tied to formal employment. The main difference between the two countries is that in Costa Rica labor laws are enforced in a stronger way than in the Dominican Republic; the minimum salaries in Costa Rica are low but still relevant for the social reproduction of workers; in the Dominican Republic, they do not begin to address the needs of workers and their families. In Costa Rica, social security has a much larger coverage and also includes workers' families. The differences then are not so much in the actual laws, but in how the laws are implemented, in the regulatory regimes.

The different regulatory regimes are the result of different processes of institution building in a common development model. The elites that fought for control of the Costa Rican state in 1948 shared a common vision of social reform. After the war, Figueres instituted a number of reforms that created an effective state apparatus. On the one hand, the dissolution of the army eliminated the one institution that could oppose the new regime. On the other hand, the nationalization of the banking and insurance systems gave the state apparatus the tools to carry out its policies of national development cum social reform. The basic agreement between the main elites on the principles of the sociopolitical regime guaranteed that the democratic alternation in government did not translate into an endless struggle over the basic functioning of the state apparatus. In Santo Domingo, the Balaguer government, which emerged after the 1965 U.S. invasion, was the result of the previous failure of the conservative business elites on the one hand, and the reformist popular sectors on the other, to impose their social and political projects in the post-Trujillo transition period. The Balaguer regime was a Bonapartist one, receiving support from traditional and new economic elites, the army, and segments of the popular sectors. The state apparatus developed as a neopatrimonial regime based on patron-client relations and access to the state apparatus and its benefits as a premium for political loyalty, a predatory state apparatus that only now, more than thirty years later, is slowly beginning to change.

It could be argued that the differences between the labor markets in the two cities are merely the result of the different level of development in each country. My argument is that one cannot simply attribute these differences to different levels of development. One must still explain how the differences in the levels of development were produced to begin with. As shown in Chapter 2, significant differences between the two countries in level of development—as measured by GNP per capita—only began to appear in the 1950s. The higher level of development of Costa Rica, compared with the Dominican Republic, was the result of the policies adopted by the government, policies that emerged from the 1948 crisis. Those policies included the legislation of protective labor regulations, the expansion of social security, and the construction of state institutions capable of implementing policies. The differences in regulatory regimes are what led Costa Rica both to higher levels of development and to a more protected labor market.[2]

The analysis presented in this book, then, shows the rewards of combining world-system analysis with an institutionalist perspective in the framework of comparative analysis. In terms of the concrete analysis of the informal economy in Latin America, I have combined Portes's analysis of the structure and linkages of the informal economy with De Soto's institutional insights, locating the analysis in the PREALC/ILO analytical framework of labor

---

2. Moreover, Costa Rica has a larger formal economy than countries that have a higher level of development—at least, as measured by GDP per capita—such as Venezuela or Brazil. The differences in regulatory regimes are the best explanation for the differences in the informal economy and the labor market in the two countries. As Tendler (1997) convincingly shows, institutional action makes a difference even in the context of low development levels.

markets under peripheral industrialization.³ The combination of different theoretical paradigms shows the strengths and limitations of the different approaches to the study of the informal economy. De Soto emphasized the importance of the institutional character of the state, and my research proves him correct. However, my research indicates that his characterization of the Peruvian state corresponds to one type of my regulatory regimes' typology and cannot be considered representative of the state in general. This book shows the importance of comparisons between different types of state regulatory regimes. Moreover, this study debunks De Soto's myth of the informal economy as a free-market realm. This book shows—as others have done before—the insertion of informal activities in economic structures that shape and constrain them and the ways that state policies can have a positive role in the creation of dynamic informal firms. It also shows the embeddedness of informal activities in social relationships and the importance of social networks for the subsistence and success of informal firms.

Portes argued that labor market regulation matters in structuring the informal economy, and this claim is supported by my research. However, he contended that state regulation in the Latin American region led to the formation of a worker aristocracy surrounded by a sea of informality. That situation proved to be the case in only one of the two typological cases studied in this book, that of a predatory-repressive case. The effect of state regulations in the case of a developmental-protective regulatory regime proved to be different; in the developmental-protective case, the effect of state regulation was to expand the informal economy and reduce segmentation.

Finally, my analysis shows the importance of taking into account the world-system position of the countries and the social structures derived from it. The many common elements in the labor markets of the two cities are the result of the parallel paths of peripheral industrialization described by PREALC researchers. The two countries went through similar processes of expanding—yet limited—proletarianization followed by a period of partial deproletarianization. Nevertheless, focusing exclusively on the commonalties of industrialization policies, labor absorption trends, and peripheral world-system position misses the differences in the labor markets caused by different

---

3. The PREALC/ILO analysis is not framed in world-system analysis; it is rooted in ECLAC structuralism. However, ECLAC structuralism and world-system analysis shared a vision of the world economy as constituted by a division of labor between the center and the periphery and by different economic dynamics in the different regions of the world economy.

regulatory regimes, differences that proved to have an important effect on the living and working conditions of the people in these two countries.

Should the State Deregulate the Labor Market?

Is labor market deregulation the solution to the employment and poverty problems of the region? Defenders of deregulation propose two main arguments: Deregulation leads to rapid employment creation and reduction of unemployment, and deregulation reduces the size of the informal economy. Portes (1994a) presents one of the more elaborated and less dogmatic arguments in favor of flexible labor market regulations. He differentiates between four different types of labor rights: basic rights (rights against the use of child labor, physical coercion, and involuntary servitude), civic rights (rights to free association and collective representation), survival rights (rights to a living wage, accident compensation, and a limited work week), and security rights (right against arbitrary dismissal, right to retirement compensation, right to survivors' compensation). He suggests that the first two types of rights should constitute international standards whereas the latter two should be applied flexibly according to local conditions. Márquez (1994) agrees that if the Latin American states cannot apply the labor laws that they legislated they should deregulate their labor markets rather than accept a dual system of protected and unprotected labor. Should the labor market be deregulated?

My research indicates that deregulation does not constitute a solution to labor market problems. Costa Rica's labor regulation regime is stronger than the Dominican one in all four sets of rights, yet in Costa Rica there is a larger formal economy and less unemployment than in the Dominican Republic. Moreover, the de facto deregulation of the labor market that took place in both countries during the last two decades did not eliminate the informal economy; if anything, it enlarged it. Moreover, in San José, the presence of stricter labor regulations has led to a less segmented labor market. It is true that in that city the presence of regulations led to longer subcontracting chains, particularly subcontracting chains in the informal economy. It is also true that labor regulations are not universally implemented, but the effect of relatively adequate regulations is the improvement in the position of those at the bottom of the labor market. The research indicates that the presence of stricter labor regulations and the existing threat of their implementation help improve the conditions of informal workers. State regulations equalized upward the working conditions in the informal economy and in the lower end of the formal economy. In Santo Domingo, a place where there is less regulation and less threat of enforcement, the floor is lowered for those who are supposed to be protected.

Should the state not deregulate the labor market? Should it, on the contrary, legislate tougher labor market protections? One should be cautious with this answer. The research reported in this book indicates that what matters is not legislation per se but the overall institutional context. As Portes (1994a) suggests, merely legislating labor protections in institutional contexts in which those laws cannot be applied does not result in an improvement of the general labor conditions. As Tokman (1989b) argues, the universal application of labor regulation would probably wipe out most informal microenterprises. Moreover, as Lagos (1994) shows, the concept of flexibility has many meanings—labor cost flexibility, numerical flexibility (i.e., flexibility in hiring and firing), and functional flexibility. Some of these forms of flexibility may be useful or necessary in different situations for reasons of either efficiency or competitiveness. In the context of the current growth model, without the development of export-processing zones and *maquilas*—the informalized formal sector—the employment problems of Costa Rica and the Dominican Republic would have been even more daunting than they are. Moreover, as I argue in the previous chapter, in the present conditions the promotion of informal firms should be a component of employment and antipoverty policies even if this policy means promoting deregulated activities.[4]

The previous analysis leaves us in an apparent dead end; one cannot support the call for flexibilization of labor markets, yet more regulation is not necessarily a solution. Nevertheless, this book does point in one clear direction: As long as improvement of the general standard of living and expansion of social citizenship are goals of the development process, the state should aim to design policies of effective protective intervention in the labor market. It is indeed true that to be effective, the protective intervention should be attuned to the state institutional capacity, to the development level, and to the broad socioeconomic context. This book shows, however, that even in a context of generalized deregulation (the Latin American context in the 1980s and 1990s) the protective intervention of the state can make a difference in

---

4. The need for flexibility in policies is not particular to Latin America. Esping-Andersen (1996) shows that the constraints imposed on European welfare states by the new global economic conditions are forcing them to search for new forms of welfare provision, new forms that often entail more flexible labor market conditions, although, as Esping-Andersen remarks, the inevitable need to adjust does not mean the nonviability of the welfare state.

the working conditions of the people—the comparison between Costa Rica and the Dominican Republic leaves no doubt about that.

Toward an Informal Future?

Toward the end of the 1990s, the Latin American countries restructured and reoriented their economies. These are much more open and outward oriented than two decades ago. The restructuring process, however, deepened the peripheral character of the economic structures. The countries of the region gave up the aspirations for a more auto-centered growth based on the development of the internal and regional markets, technological capabilities, and human capital. It could be argued that given the limits of import substitution, the region had no choice but to look for a different form of insertion in the world economy and that given the assets of the region, low-skill manufacturing and services were the only choices available. Perhaps, as scholars argue, no other choice is open to the countries of the region but to negotiate the best they can their position in the global economic order. Perhaps the only thing worse than being exploited in the world economy is not to be exploited by it, to be left out of the world circuits of capital, trade, and production (Castells and Laserna 1994; Kincaid and Portes 1994). One can also argue that this is what Korea and Taiwan did at the beginning of their take-off. These arguments are indeed strong, but they pose several questions: Are the countries of the region attempting to develop higher value-added manufacturing and services to move up along the commodity chains? Do these countries invest in education and in specialization in key advanced technologies that provide a dynamic comparative advantage? Those actions were the keys to the movement of the East Asian new industrialized countries from the periphery to the semiperiphery, and the state played a central role in that movement (Evans 1995; Wade 1990).[5] In the two countries included in this study, only Costa Rica has taken a few small steps in this direction, by convincing some high-tech manufacturers such as Intel to open facilities in the country. It is unclear, however, how and whether this investment will translate into an increasing technological capacity for the country.

5. Korea and Taiwan also benefited from being frontier states in the context of the Cold War. Thanks to that historical contingency, their states carried out agrarian reforms; they enjoyed more leeway to develop independent industrialization policies than the Latin American states did; and they also enjoyed easier access to American markets (Arseniero 1994).

The new model of development also begs the question of the purpose of economic development. Who benefits from economic growth? Who bears the burden of adjustment, and how is the new wealth distributed? The burden of the crisis fell on those who were the weakest link and the least responsible for it: the poor, the workers, and part of the middle classes. As a result, the region has seen a de facto deregulation of the labor market accompanied by increasing social inequality and social exclusion. The neoliberal developmental strategy has been to pursue competitiveness through the provision of cheap labor. Although only this strategy might have been available at a certain time, and although it may lead to growth, it leads to growth with poverty and inequality.

The challenge for the Latin American states at the beginning of the new millennium is to achieve economic development while addressing growing social inequalities and expanding hard-fought democratic gains.[6] To achieve this goal, it is necessary to create developmental-protective regulatory regimes that can promote both economic growth and social citizenship. The states of the region need to take a leadership role to move beyond the competitiveness model based on cheap labor and static comparative advantages in raw materials and to build institutions capable of intervening effectively in the protection of workers and the delivery of social service. The particular policies and institutional forms of intervention would differ between countries according to particular institutional histories and the strengths of different social actors. Certainly, the challenges of institution building and the forms of protective intervention should be different under different regulatory regimes. For Costa Rica, the challenge is to reform existing institutions so that they can be effective in confronting the new socioeconomic situation; for the Dominican Republic, the task is to shed a tradition of neopatrimonialism and to build effective public protective institutions. This book can only assert a modest, yet important point: The state protective intervention in the labor market can improve the living and working conditions of the low-income sectors and the people involved in the informal economy.[7] In other words, the state should not abdicate its social responsibilities and its central role in expanding social citizenship.

---

6. O'Donnell (1996) refers to the new democratic regimes in the region as delegative democracies, that is, regimes that respect the democratic forms, but in which increasing social polarization pushes increasingly larger numbers of people away from political participation and toward delegating the solution of social and economic problems to strong leaders.

7. I presented some recommendations about policies toward the informal economy in the previous chapter, and I cannot go beyond these suggestions in the framework of this book. Tokman (1989b) presents an interesting set of policies to deal with problems of employment and the expansion of social security.

The neoliberal structural adjustment process has led to a realignment of the relations between state and society and in that sense constitutes a critical juncture for rebuilding institutional systems. This realignment confronts state agencies both with opportunities and problems. On the one hand, by weakening old clientelist relationships and corporate interests, neoliberalism opens a window for institutional reform and the development of more accountable and responsive state institutions (Weyland 1996). On the other hand, the political conditions in Latin America are not very favorable for social reformism. The strong unions and large labor parties that led to the various welfare state models developed in Europe are not present in the region (Filgueira 1998).[8] The strong social actors in the new socioeconomic model are some local business groups that begin to behave as multinational groups at the regional level, multinational corporations, transnational financial investors, and international financial institutions (the World Bank and the International Monetary Fund). None of these groups is interested in addressing the expanding inequality or the need for a downward redistribution of wealth. At the end of the 1990s, the international financial institutions have abandoned the antistatist neoliberal orthodoxy of the 1980s. The state they promote, however, is a residual state that addresses some of the worst forms of exclusion through focalized policies (World Bank 1997). Although such a state and its policies may help address some forms of poverty, they do not constitute a basis for the construction of social citizenship.

The reconstitution of formal work and the expansion of social rights ultimately depend on the ability of the workers, formal and informal, to organize and mobilize to demand social and political inclusion in the global economic order. The last two decades have seen the rise of innumerable social movements and local organizations. These movements are often frail and short-lived, but they have opened a number of spaces for democratic expression and participation. The spaces of action and expression of human rights concerns, indigenous cultural autonomy, and gender issues seem to be wider than ever—

8. In Latin America, one does not find the three different worlds of welfare states described by Esping-Andersen (1990). Social provision in Latin America used to be based on the differential access to social services by different occupational groups, because most states legislated social rights to incorporate key groups of workers into the political system and left large areas of welfare provision in the hands of families and communities. Roberts (1998) likened this mode of social service provision to Esping-Andersen's corporatist model. During the last two decades, the model of social provision has moved toward the liberal model, in which welfare is provided through market mechanisms and social assistance to particular sectors. However, as Huber (1996) noted, there have been deviations from this general trend. Costa Rica and Brazil have tried to keep models of social provision that guarantee universal access.

although not everywhere, and in any case, much work is still needed in those areas. With questions of social citizenship, however, there is a feeling that not much can be done. The top-down, paternalistic model of extending social rights through which the state attempted to co-opt selected social groups—the model of social citizenship characteristic of the previous developmentalist period—is exhausted; and in any case, it was responsible for the limits of social citizenship in Latin America. The neoliberal state has replaced the old paternalistic model with different combinations of labor market deregulation, focalized social policies—new forms of clientelism—and the privatization of social services. In this context, the expansion of social citizenship can be the result only of the independent organization of subordinated groups and their pressure on the state for the institutionalization of social rights.

The shape of Latin American societies in the near future will be the result of the balance of forces between the different local and global social and political actors. Social science research has very little say in the outcome of these social and political processes. In the best of cases, it can hope only to predict the possible outcomes and to inform the political actors about some likely consequences of their actions. In that vein, I hope that this book provides some ideas to search for ways out of the current exclusionary development model.

Bibliography

Abreu, Alfonso, Manuel Cocco, Carlos Despradel, Eduardo García Michel, and Arturo Peguero. 1989. *Las Zonas Francas Industriales*. Santo Domingo: Centro de Orientación Económica.
ADEMI (Asociación para el Desarrollo de Microempresas). 1991. *La Microempresa: Alternativa de Desarrollo*. Santo Domingo: CENAPEC.
———. 1992. *Resumen Ejecutivo*. Santo Domingo: ADEMI.
Alt, James E., and Kenneth A. Shepsle, eds. 1990. *Perspectives on Positive Political Economy*. Cambridge: Cambridge University Press.
Amadeo, Edward J., and José Márcio Camargo. 1997. "Brazil: Regulation and Flexibility in the Labor Market." Pp. 201–34 in S. Edwards and N. C. Lustig, eds., *Labor Markets in Latin America: Combining Social Protection with Market Flexibility*. Washington, D.C.: Brookings Institution Press.
Anglade, Christian, and Carlos Fortín, eds. 1985. *The State and Capital Accumulation in Latin America*, Vol. 1: *Brazil, Chile, Mexico*. Pittsburgh: University of Pittsburgh Press.
Ariza, Marina, Isis Duarte, Carmen Julia Gómez, and Wilfredo Lozano. 1991. *Población, Migraciones Internas, y Desarrollo en la República Dominicana, 1950–1981*. Santo Domingo: IEPD.
Arrighi, Giovanni, Satoshi Ikeda, and Alex Irwan. 1993. "The Rise of East Asia: One Miracle or Many?" Pp. 41–65 in R. A. Palat, ed., *Pacific Asia and the Future of the World-System*. Westport, Conn.: Greenwood Press.
Arseniero, George. 1994. "South Korean and Taiwanese Development: The Transnational Context." *Review* 17, 3: 275–336.
Banco Central de la República Dominicana. 1996. *Mercado de Trabajo, 1991–1996*. Santo Domingo: Banco Central.
Benería, Lourdes, and Shelley Feldman, eds. 1992. *Unequal Burden: Economic Crises, Persistent Poverty, and Women's Work*. Boulder, Colo.: Westview Press.
Benería, Lourdes, and Marta Roldán. 1987. *The Crossroads of Class and Gender: Industrial Homework, Subcontracting, and Household Dynamics in Mexico City*. Chicago: University of Chicago Press.
Betances, Emelio. 1995. *State and Society in the Dominican Republic*. Boulder, Colo.: Westview Press.

Bibliography

BID-FUNDAPEC (Banco Interamericano de Desarrollo—Fundación APEC). 1992. *Encuesta Nacional de Mano de Obra.* Santo Domingo: Fundación APEC.

Birkbeck, Chris. 1978. "Self-Employed Proletarians in an Informal Factory: The Case of Cali's Garbage Dump." *World Development* 6: 1173–85.

Bodson, P., Allen Cordero, and Juan Pablo Pérez Sáinz. 1995. *Las Nuevas Caras del Empleo.* San José: FLACSO.

Booth, John A. 1998. *Costa Rica: The Quest for Democracy.* Boulder, Colo.: Westview Press.

Borón, Atilio. 1995. *State, Capitalism, and Democracy in Latin America.* Boulder, Colo.: Lynne Rienner.

Bromley, Ray. 1978. "Organization, Regulation, and Exploitation in the So-Called 'Urban Informal Sector': The Street Traders of Cali, Colombia." *World Development* 6: 1161–71.

———. 1994. "Informality, de Soto Style: From Concept to Policy." Pp. 131–52 in Cathy A. Rakowski, ed., *Contrapunto: The Informal Sector Debate in Latin America.* Albany: State University of New York Press.

Buchanan, James M., Robert D. Tollison, and Gordon Tullock, eds. 1980. *Toward a Theory of the Rent-Seeking Society.* College Station: Texas A & M University Press.

Buchanan, Paul. 1995. *State, Labor, Capital: Democratizing Labor Relations in the Southern Cone.* Pittsburgh: University of Pittsburgh Press.

Bulmer-Thomas, Victor. 1987. *The Political Economy of Central America Since 1920.* Cambridge: Cambridge University Press.

———. 1994. *The Economic History of Latin America Since Independence.* Cambridge: Cambridge University Press.

Burbach, Roger, Orlando Núñez, and Boris Kagarlitsky. 1997. *Globalization and Its Discontents: The Rise of Postmodern Socialism.* London: Pluto Press.

Cabal, Miguel. 1992. *Microempresas y Pequeñas Empresas en la República Dominicana.* Santo Domingo: FONDOMICRO.

———. 1993. *Evolución de las Microempresas y Pequeñas Empresas en la República Dominicana: 1992–1993.* Santo Domingo: FONDOMICRO.

Capecchi, Vittorio. 1989. "The Informal Economy and the Development of Flexible Specialization in Emilia-Romagna." Pp. 189–215 in A. Portes, M. Castells, and L. A. Benton, eds., *The Informal Economy: Studies in Advanced and Less Developed Countries.* Baltimore: Johns Hopkins University Press.

Castells, Manuel, and Roberto Laserna. 1994. "The New Dependency: Technological Change and Socioeconomic Restructuring in Latin America." Pp. 57–83 in A. D. Kincaid and A. Portes, eds., *Comparative National Development: Society and Economy in the New Global Order.* Chapel Hill: University of North Carolina Press.

Castells, Manuel, and Alejandro Portes. 1989. "World Underneath: The Origins, Dynamics, and Effects of the Informal Economy." Pp. 11–37 in A. Portes, M. Castells, and L. A. Benton, eds., *The Informal Economy: Studies in Advanced and Less Developed Countries.* Baltimore: Johns Hopkins University Press.

Castiglia, Miguel Angel. 1993. "El Diseño de Programas Masivos de Apoyo a la Microempresa." Pp. 86–111 in Y. Barrera, M. A. Castiglia, D. Kruijt, R. Menjívar, and J. P. Pérez Sáinz, eds., *La Economía de los Pobres.* San José: FLACSO.

Ceara Hatton, Miguel. 1990. *Crecimiento Económico y Acumulación de Capital.* Santo Domingo: CIECA.

———. 1991. "La Economía Dominicana 1980–1990." Paper presented at the third Conference of Caribbean Economists. Santo Domingo, July 16–20.

———. 1993. "De Reactivación Desordenada hacia el Ajuste con Liberalización y Apertura (1987–1990 y 1991–?)." Manuscript. Santo Domingo: CIECA.
CEPAS (Centro de Estudios para la Acción Social). 1992. *Costa Rica en el Umbral de los Años Noventa: Deterioro y Auge de lo Social en el Marco del Ajuste.* San José: CEPAS.
Charmes, Jacques. 1990. "A Critical Review of Concepts, Definitions, and Studies in the Informal Sector." Pp. 10–48 in David Turnham, Bernard Salome, and Antoine Schwarz, eds., *The Informal Sector Revisited.* Paris: Development Centre of the Organization for Economic Co-Operation and Development (OECD).
Chu, Yin Wah. 1992. "Informal Work in Hong Kong." *International Journal of Urban and Regional Research*, 16: 420–41.
CIECA (Centro de Investigación Económica para el Caribe). 1992. *El Gasto Público Social de República Dominicana en la Década de los Ochenta.* Santo Domingo: CIECA/UNICEF.
———. 1993a. "El Comportamiento del Salario." *Notas de Coyuntura* 23 (May).
———. 1993b. "La Distribución del Ingreso en 1991." *Notas de Coyuntura* 22 (February).
———. 1993c. *Impacto del Ajuste y las Reformas Estructurales en la Pobreza y el Desarrollo Humano en la República Dominicana.* Santo Domingo: CIECA.
CNHE (Consejo Nacional de Hombres de Empresa). 1992. *Diagnóstico Financiero-Actuarial y Costo de Factibilidad de la Ampliación de Cobertura sin Modificar el Modelo de Prestación del IDSS.* Santo Domingo: CNHE.
Collier, Ruth Berins, and David Collier. 1991. *Shaping the Political Arena.* Princeton: Princeton University Press.
Cordero, Allen, and Minor Mora. 1998. "Costa Rica: El Mercado de Trabajo en el Contexto del Ajuste." Pp. 219–79 in E. Funkhauser and J. P. Pérez Sáinz, eds., *Mercado Laboral y Pobreza en Centroamérica.* San José: FLACSO/SSRC.
Davidson, Basil. 1992. *The Black Man's Burden: Africa and the Curse of the Nation State.* New York: Times Books.
De Oliveira, Orlandina, and Bryan Roberts. 1993. "La Informalidad Urbana en Años de Expansión, Crisis, y Restructuración Ecónomica." *Estudios Sociológicos* 11: 33–58.
De Soto, Hernando. 1989. *The Other Path.* New York: Harper and Row.
Deyo, Frederic C. 1989. *Beneath the Miracle: Labor Subordination in the New Asian Industrialization.* Berkeley and Los Angeles: University of California Press.
DGEyC (Dirección General de Estadística y Censos). 1992. *Encuesta de Hogares de Propósitos Múltiples: Módulo de Empleo, Julio 1992.* San José: Dirección Nacional de Estadística y Censo.
Díaz, Alvaro. 1997. "Chile: Socioeconomic Restructuring, Neoliberal Policy, and Urban Labor Market." Pp. 159–88 in R. Tardanico and R. Menjívar Larín, eds., *Global Restructuring, Employment, and Social Inequality in Urban Latin America.* Coral Gables, Fla.: North-South Center Press.
Doeringer, Peter B., and Michael J. Piore. 1971. *Internal Labor Markets and Manpower Analysis.* Lexington, Mass.: D. C. Heath.
Duarte, Isis. 1986. *Trabajadores Urbanos.* Santo Domingo: UASD.
Duarte, Isis, and Ramón Tejada. 1991. "El Gasto Social y las Clases Trabajadoras Urbanas." Unpublished manuscript. Santo Domingo.
Dunlop, John T. 1988. "Labor Markets and Wage Determination: Then and Now." Pp. 47–88 in B. E. Kaufman, ed., *How Labor Markets Work.* Lexington, Mass.: D. C. Heath.

Bibliography

ECLAC (Economic Commission for Latin America and the Caribbean). 1991. *Statistical Yearbook for Latin America and the Caribbean.* New York: United Nations.

Edelman, Marc, and Rodolfo Monge Oviedo. 1993. "Costa Rica: The Non-Market Roots of Market Success." *NACLA Report on the Americas* 26, 4: 22–30.

Edwards, Sebastian, and Nora Claudia Lustig, eds. 1997. *Labor Markets in Latin America: Combining Social Protection with Market Flexibility.* Washington, D.C.: Brookings Institution Press.

Espinal, Rosario, and Sherri Grasmuck. 1997. "Gender, Households, and Informal Entrepreneurship in the Dominican Republic." *Journal of Comparative Family Studies,* 28, 1: 103–28.

Esping-Andersen, Gosta. 1990. *The Three Worlds of Welfare Capitalism.* Princeton: Princeton University Press.

Esping-Andersen, Gosta, ed. 1996. "After the Golden Age: Welfare State Dilemmas in a Global Economy." Pp. 1–31 in Gosta Esping-Andersen, ed., *Welfare States in Transition.* London: Sage Publications.

Evans, Peter. 1979. *Dependent Development: The Alliance of Multinational, State, and Local Capital in Brazil.* Princeton: Princeton University Press.

———. 1995. *Embedded Autonomy: States & Industrial Transformation.* Princeton: Princeton University Press.

FAY (Fundación Acción Ya). 1992. *Del Dicho al Hecho. . . .* San José: Fundación Acción Ya.

Feige, Edgar L. 1990. "Defining and Estimating Underground and Informal Economies: The New Institutional Economics Approach." *World Development* 18 (July): 989–1002.

Fields, Gary. 1990. "Labour Market Modelling and the Urban Informal Sector: Theory and Evidence." Pp. 49–69 in David Turnham, Bernard Salome, and Antoine Schwarz, eds., *The Informal Sector Revisited.* Paris: Development Centre of the Organization for Economic Co-Operation and Development (OECD).

Filgueira, Fernando. 1998. "El Nuevo Modelo de Prestaciones Sociales en América Latina: Eficiencia, Residualismo, y Ciudadanía Estratificada." Pp. 71–117 in B. Roberts, ed., *Ciudadanía y Política Social.* San José: FLACSO/SSRC.

Folbre, Nancy. 1994. *Who Pays for the Kids? Gender and the Structures of Constraint.* London: Routledge.

Franco, Eliana, and Carlos Sojo. 1992. *Gobierno, Empresarios, y Políticas de Ajuste.* San José: FLACSO.

Franks, Jeffrey R. 1994. "Macroeconomic Policy and the Informal Sector." Pp. 91–112 in Cathy A. Rakowski, ed., *Contrapunto: The Informal Sector Debate in Latin America.* Albany: State University of New York Press.

Fundación Economía y Desarrollo. 1989. *Impacto del Sector Privado en la Economía Dominicana.* Santo Domingo: Acción Empresarial.

Funkhauser, Edward. 1996. "The Urban Informal Sector in Central America: Household Survey Evidence." *World Development* 19 (March): 1737–51.

———. 1997. "Mobility and Labor Market Segmentation: The Urban Labor Market in El Salvador." *Economic Development and Cultural Change* 46, 1: 123–53.

García, Norberto. 1991. "Ajuste estructural y mercados de trabajo." *Crítica & Comunicación* 1.

García, Norberto, and Victor Tokman. 1984. "Changes in Employment and the Crisis." *CEPAL Review* (December): 103–15.

Garnier, Leonardo. 1991. "Gasto Público y Desarrollo Social en Costa Rica." *Cuadernos de Política Económica,* no. 2. Heredia: Maestría en Política Económica—Universidad Nacional.

Geller, Lucio. 1991. "Labor Market Adaptation: Towards an Action Agenda." Pp. 185–209 in Guy Standing and Victor Tokman, eds., *Toward Social Adjustment: Labour Market Issues in Structural Adjustment.* Geneva: ILO.

Gereffi, Gary. 1990. "Paths of Industrialization: An Overview." Pp. 3–31 in Gary Gereffi and Donald L. Wyman, eds., *Manufacturing Miracles: Paths of Industrialization in Latin America and East Asia.* Princeton: Princeton University Press.

———. 1994. "The Organization of Buyer Driven Commodity Chains: How U.S. Retailers Shape Overseas Production Networks." Pp. 95–122 in Gary Gereffi and Miguel Korzeniewicz, eds., *Commodity Chains and Global Capitalism.* Westport, Conn.: Greenwood Press.

Gerschenkron, Alexander. 1962. *Backwardness in Historical Perspective.* Cambridge, Mass.: Belknap.

Gindling, Tim H. 1991. "Labor Market Segmentation and the Determination of Wages in the Public, Private-Formal, and Informal Sectors in San José, Costa Rica." *Economic Development and Cultural Change* 39: 584–605.

Gindling, Tim H., and Katherine Terrell. 1995. "The Nature of Minimum Wages and Their Effectiveness as a Wage Floor in Costa Rica, 1976–91." *World Development* 28: 1439–58.

Goldenberg, Olga. 1993. "Género e Informalidad en San José." Pp. 483–544 in Rafael Menjívar Larín and Juan Pablo Pérez Sáinz, eds., *Ni Héroes ni Villanas.* San José: FLACSO.

Gómez, Luis Carlos, Ricardo Bitrán, and Dieter Zschock. 1988. "La Demanda de Servicios de Salud en el Distrito Nacional." *Población y Desarrollo* 24 (October–December).

Gordon, David M., Richard Edwards, and Michael Reich. 1982. *Segmented Work Divided Workers: The Historical Transformations of Labor in the United States.* New York: Cambridge University Press.

Granovetter, Mark. 1974. *Getting a Job: A Study of Contacts and Careers.* Cambridge, Mass.: Harvard University Press.

———. 1985. "Economic Action and Social Structure: The Problem of Embeddedness." *American Journal of Sociology* 91 (November): 481–510.

Gudmunson, Lowell. 1986. *Costa Rica Before Coffee: Society and Economy in the Eve of the Export Boom.* Baton Rouge: Louisiana State University Press.

Harrison, Bennett. 1994. *Mean and Lean: Why Large Corporations Will Continue to Dominate the Global Economy.* New York: Guilford Press.

Hart, Keith. 1973. "Informal Income Opportunities and Urban Employment in Ghana." *Journal of Modern African Studies* 11: 61–89.

Hartlyn, Jonathan. 1998. *The Struggle for Democratic Politics in the Dominican Republic.* Chapel Hill: University of North Carolina Press.

Hernández Rueda, Lupo. 1989. *Manual de Derecho del Trabajo.* 2 vols. Santo Domingo: Editorial Tiempo.

Huber, Evelyne. 1996. "Options for Social Policy in Latin America: Neoliberal Versus Social Democratic Models." Pp. 141–91 in Gosta Esping-Andersen, ed., *Welfare States in Transition.* London: Sage Publications.

IEPD (Instituto de Estudios de Población y Desarrollo). 1991. *Población, Migraciones Internas, y Desarrollo, 1950–1981.* Santo Domingo: Profamilia.

ILO (International Labor Office). 1991. "Políticas de Empleo en la Restructuración Económica en América Latina y el Caribe." WEP 1-4-07 (Doc. 1). Geneva: ILO.

———. 1992. "Estabilización, Ajuste Estructural, y Políticas Sociales en Costa Rica: El Papel de los Programas Compensatorios." *Documentos Ocasionales* 1. Geneva: ILO.

Bibliography

Infante, Ricardo, and Emilio Klein. 1991. "The Latin American Labour Market, 1950–1980." *CEPAL Review* 45: 121–35.

Instituto de Estudios Dominicanos (IED). 1992. *Carta de Información Sobre Empleo, Sector Informal, y Micro-Empresas.* Santo Domingo: APROFED.

Itzigsohn José. 1995. "Migrant Remittances, Labor Markets, and Household Strategies: A Comparative Analysis of Low-Income Household Strategies in the Caribbean Basin." *Social Forces* 74, 2: 633–55.

———. 1996. "Globalization, the State, and the Informal Economy: The Limits to Proletarianization in the Latin American Periphery." Pp. 101–16 in Patricio Korzeniewicz and William C. Smith, eds., *Latin America in the World Economy.* Westport, Conn.: Greenwood Press.

———. 1997. "The Dominican Republic: Politico-Economic Transformation, Employment, and Poverty." Pp. 47–69 in R. Tardanico and R. Menjívar Larín, eds., *Global Restructuring, Employment, and Social Inequality in Urban Latin America.* Coral Gables, Fla.: North-South Center Press.

———. 1998. "La Globalización y las Articulaciones de las Actividades Informales." *Perfiles Latinoamericanos* 13 (December): 153–78.

Jacobstein, Helen. 1987. *The Process of Economic Development in Costa Rica, 1948–1970.* New York: Garland Publishing.

Jatoba, Jorge. 1989. "Latin America's Labour Market Research: A State of the Art." *Labour and Society* 14: 297–332.

Katzman, Reuben. 1984. "Sectoral Transformations in Employment in Latin America." *CEPAL Review* 24 (December): 83–101.

Kay, Cristóbal. 1989. *Latin American Theories of Development and Underdevelopment.* London: Routledge.

Kincaid, A. Douglas, and Alejandro Portes. 1989. "Sociology and Development in the 1990s: Critical Challenges and Empirical Trends." Pp. 1–25 in A. D. Kincaid and A. Portes, eds., *Comparative National Development: Society and Economy in the New Global Order.* Chapel Hill: University of North Carolina Press.

Lagos, Ricardo A. 1994. "Labour Market Flexibility: What Does It Really Mean?" *CEPAL Review* 54 (December): 81–95.

Lewis, Arthur W. 1954. "Economic Development with Unlimited Supplies of Labor." *Manchester School of Economics and Social Studies* 22: 139–91.

Liedholm, Carl. 1994. "The Impact of Government Policies on Microenterprise Development: Conclusions from Empirical Studies." Pp. 75–90 in C. A. Rakowski, ed., *Contrapunto: The Informal Sector Debate in Latin America.* Albany: State University of New York Press.

Lomnitz, Larisa. 1975. *Como Sobreviven los Marginados.* Mexico: Siglo XXI Editores.

———. 1982. "Horizontal and Vertical Relations and the Structure of Urban Mexico." *Latin American Research Review* 16, 2: 51–74.

Lozano, Wilfredo. 1985. *El Reformismo Dependiente.* Santo Domingo: Editora Taller.

———. 1987. "Desempleo Estructural, Dinámica Económica, y Fragmentación de los Mercados de Trabajo Urbanos: El Caso Dominicano." *Ciencia y Sociedad* 12, 3: 360–88.

———. 1996. "La Vida Mala: Economía informal, estado, y pobladores urbanos en Santo Domingo." In Alejandro Portes and Carlos Dore-Cabral, coordinators, *Ciudades del Caribe en el Umbral del Nuevo Siglo.* Caracas: Nueva Sociedad/FLACSO-República Dominicana/PCID-Universidad Johns Hopkins.

Lozano, Wilfredo, and Isis Duarte. 1992. "Proceso de Urbanización, Modelos de Desarrollo, y Clases Sociales en República Dominicana, 1960–1990." Pp. 213–349 in A. Portes and M. Lungo, eds., *Urbanización en el Caribe.* San José: FLACSO.

Lungo, Mario. 1996. "La ciudad y la nación, la organización barrial y el estado: Los dilemas de la urbanización en Costa Rica a principios de los noventa." In Alejandro Portes and Carlos Dore-Cabral, coordinators, *Ciudades del Caribe en el Umbral del Nuevo Siglo*. Caracas: Nueva Sociedad/FLACSO-República Dominicana/PCID-Universidad Johns Hopkins.

Lungo, Mario, Mariam Pérez, and Nancy Piedra. 1992. "La Urbanización en Costa Rica en los 80." Pp. 37–188 in A. Portes and M. Lungo, eds., *Urbanización en Centro América*. San José: FLACSO.

Lustig, Nora Claudia, and Darryl McLeod. 1997. "Minimum Wages and Poverty in Developing Countries: Some Empirical Evidence." Pp. 62–103 in Sebastian Edwards and Nora Claudia Lustig, eds., *Labor Markets in Latin America*. Washington, D.C.: Brookings Institution Press.

Mahoney, James. 1999. "Nominal, Ordinal, and Narrative Appraisal in Macrocausal Analysis." *American Journal of Sociology* 104, 4: 170–211.

Márquez, Gustavo. 1994. "Inside Informal Sector Policies in Latin America: An Economist View." Pp. 153–76 in C. A. Rakowski, ed., *Contrapunto: The Informal Sector Debate in Latin America*. Albany: State University of New York Press.

———. 1995. *Reforming the Labor Market in a Liberalized Economy*. Washington, D.C.: Inter-American Development Bank.

Marshall, Adriana. 1994. "Economic Consequences of Labour Protection Regimes in Latin America." *International Labour Review* 133, 1: 55–73.

Marx, Karl. 1976. *Capital: A Critique of Political Economy*, vol. 1. Harmondsworth: Penguin.

Menjívar Larín, Rafael, and Juan P. Pérez Sáinz, eds. 1993. *Ni Héroes Ni Villanas*. San José: FLACSO.

Mesa-Lago, Carmelo. 1990. *La Seguridad Social y el Sector Informal*. Santiago de Chile: PREALC.

———. 1994. *Changing Social Security in Latin America: Toward Alleviating the Social Costs of Economic Reform*. Boulder, Colo.: Lynne Rienner.

Mezzera, Jaime. 1987. "Abundancia como efecto de la escasez." *Nueva Sociedad* 90: 106–17.

———. 1992. "Subordinación y Complementaridad: El Sector Informal Urbano en América Latina." *Crítica & Comunicación*, no. 9. Lima: Organización Internacional del Trabajo.

Moser, Caroline. 1978. "Informal Sector or Petty Commodity Production: Dualism or Dependence in Urban Development?" *World Development* 6: 1041–64.

———. 1994. "The Informal Sector Debate, Part I: 1970–1983." Pp. 31–50 in C. A. Rakowski, ed., *Contrapunto: The Informal Sector Debate in Latin America*. Albany: State University of New York Press.

Moya Pons, Frank. 1992. *Empresarios en Conflicto*. Santo Domingo: Fondo Para el Avance de las Ciencias Sociales.

Murphy, Martin. 1990. "The Need for a Re-evaluation of the Concept of 'Informal Sector': The Dominican Case." Pp. 161–81 in M. E. Smith, ed., *Perspectives in Economic Anthropology*. Lanham, Md: University Press of America.

Murray, Gerald F. 1996. *El Colmado: Una investigación Antropológica*. Santo Domingo: FONDOMICRO.

O'Donnell, Guillermo. 1994. "The State, Democratization, and Some Conceptual Problems." Pp. 157–80 in William C. Smith, Carlos H. Acuña, and Eduardo A. Gamarra, eds., *Latin American Political Economy in the Age of Neoliberal Reform: Theoretical and Comparative Perspective for the 1990s*. New Brunswick and Miami: Transaction Publishers and North-South Center Press.

Bibliography

Oficina Nacional de Estadística. 1990. *República Dominicana en Cifras*. Santo Domingo: ONE.

Ortiz, Marina. 1997. *Microempresas, Migración, y Remesas en la República Dominicana, 1996–1997*. Santo Domingo: FONDOMICRO.

Otero, María. 1994. "The Role of Governments and Private Institutions in Addressing the Informal Sector in Latin America." In C. A. Rakowski, ed., *Contrapunto: The Informal Sector Debate in Latin America*. Albany: State University of New York Press.

Otero, María, and Elisabeth Rhyne. 1994. *The New World of Microenterprise Finance*. West Hartford, Conn.: Kumarian Press.

Palma, Diego. 1988. *La informalidad, lo popular, y el cambio social*. Lima: DESCO.

Peck, Jamie. 1996. *Work Place: The Social Regulation of Labor Markets*. New York: Guilford Press.

Pérez Sáinz, Juan Pablo. 1989. *Respuestas Silenciosas: Proletarización urbana y reproducción de la fuerza de trabajo en América Latina*. Caracas: Editorial Nueva Sociedad.

———. 1991. *Informalidad Urbana en América Latina: Enfoques, problemáticas, e interrogantes*. Caracas: Editorial Nueva Sociedad.

———. 1994. *El Dilema del Nahual: Globalización, exclusión, y trabajo en Centroamérica*. San José: FLACSO.

———. 1997. "Entre lo global y lo local: Economías comunitarias de Centroamérica." *Sociología del Trabajo*, nueva época, no. 30 (Spring): 3–19.

———. 1998a. "The New Faces of Informality in Central America." *Journal of Latin American Studies* 30, 1: 157–79.

———. 1998b. "Mercado Laboral y Ciudadanía Social en Centroamérica." Pp. 117–46 in B. Roberts, ed., *Ciudadanía y Política Social*. San José: FLACSO/SSRC.

Pérez Sáinz, Juan P., and Rafael Menjívar Larín. 1993. "Género e Informalidad en Centroamérica: Una Perspectiva Regional." Pp. 11–98 in Rafael Menjívar Larín and Juan Pablo Pérez Sáinz, eds., *Ni Héroes ni Villanas*. San José: FLACSO.

Perfetti del Coral, Mauricio. 1991. "El Crédito y Programas de Atención a la Microempresa." Pp. 38–43 in ADEMI (Asociación para el Desarrollo de Microempresas), ed., *La Microempresa: Alternativa de Desarrollo*. Santo Domingo: CENAPEC.

Perlman, Janice E. 1976. *The Myth of Marginality: Urban Poverty and Politics in Rio de Janeiro*. Berkeley and Los Angeles: University of California Press.

Polanyi, Karl. 1957. *The Great Transformation*. Boston: Beacon Press.

Portes, Alejandro. 1983. "The Informal Sector: Definition, Controversy, and Relation to National Development." *Review* 7 (Summer): 151–74.

———. 1985. "Latin American Class Structures: Their Composition and Change During the Last Decades." *Latin American Research Review* 20 (Fall): 7–39.

———. 1994a. "When More Can Be Less: Labor Standards, Development, and the Informal Economy." Pp. 113–30 in Cathy A. Rakowski, ed., *Contrapunto: The Informal Sector Debate in Latin America*. Albany: State University of New York Press.

———. 1994b. "The Informal Economy and Its Paradoxes." Pp. 426–52 in N. J. Smelser and R. Swedberg, eds., *The Handbook of Economic Sociology*. Princeton and New York: Princeton University Press/Russell Sage Foundation.

———. 1995. *En Torno a la Informalidad: Ensayos sobre teoría, y medición de la economía no regulada*. Mexico City: FLACSO y Porrúa.

Portes, Alejandro, Manuel Castells, and Lauren Benton, eds. 1989. *The Informal Economy: Studies in Advanced and Less Developed Countries*. Baltimore: Johns Hopkins University Press.

Portes, Alejandro, and José Itzigsohn. 1997. "Coping with Change: The Politics and Economics of Urban Poverty." Pp. 227–52 in A. Portes, C. Dore-Cabral, and P. Landolt, eds., *The Urban Caribbean: Transition to the New Global Economy.* Baltimore: Johns Hopkins University Press.
Portes, Alejandro, José Itzigsohn, and Carlos Dore. 1994. "Urbanization in the Caribbean Basin: Social Change During the Years of the Crisis." *Latin American Research Review* 29, 2: 3–37.
Portes, Alejandro, and Saskia Sassen-Koob. 1987. "Making It Underground: Comparative Material on the Informal Sector in Western Market Economies." *American Journal of Sociology* 93 (July): 30–61.
Portes, Alejandro, and Richard Schauffler. 1993. "Competing Perspectives on the Latin American Informal Sector." *Population and Development Review* 19 (March): 33–60.
Portes, Alejandro, and Julia Sensenbrenner. 1993. "Embeddedness and Immigration: Notes on the Social Determinants of Economic Action." *American Journal of Sociology* 98 (May): 1320–50.
Portes, Alejandro, and John Walton. 1981. *Labor, Class, and the International System.* New York: Academic Press.
PREALC (Programa Regional de Empleo para América Latina y el Caribe). 1991. "La Incidencia del Ajuste Estructural en el Mercado de Trabajo de Costa Rica." *Documento de Trabajo*, no. 359. Santiago de Chile: PREALC.
Przeworski, Adam, and Henry Teune. 1970. *The Logic of Comparative Social Inquiry.* New York: Wiley.
Pyke, Frank, Giacomo Becattini, and Werner Sengenberger. 1990. *Industrial Districts and Inter-Firm Co-operation in Italy.* Geneva: International Institute for Labour Studies.
Quijano, Anibal. 1974. "The Marginal Pole of the Economy and the Marginalised Labour Force." *Economy and Society* 3, 4.
Rakowski, Cathy A. 1994. "The Informal Sector Debate, Part 2: 1984–1993." Pp. 31–50 in C. A. Rakowski, ed., *Contrapunto: The Informal Sector Debate in Latin America.* Albany: State University of New York Press.
Ramírez, Francisco, Jaime Lobo, and Marvin Acuña. 1991. "El Estado y la Crisis de los Regimenes de Pensiones." *Cuadernos de Política Económica*, no. 4. Heredia: Maestria en Política Económica—Universidad Nacional.
Ramírez, Nelson. 1993. *La Fuerza de Trabajo en la República Dominicana.* Serie Monográfica, no. 3. Santo Domingo: IEPD.
Ramos, Joseph. 1984. "Urbanization and the Labor Market." *CEPAL Review* 24 (December): 63–81.
Ranis, Gustav. 1989. "Labor Surplus Economies." Pp. 191–98 in J. Eatwell, M. Millgate, and P. Newman, eds., *The New Palgrave: Economic Development.* London: Macmillan.
Roberts, Bryan. 1990. "The Informal Sector in Comparative Perspective." Pp. 23–48 in M. E. Smith, ed., *Perspectives in Economic Anthropology.* Lanham, Md.: University Press of America.
———. 1995. *The Making of Citizens.* London: Arnold.
———. 1998. "Ciudadanía y Política Social en Latinoamérica." Pp. 35–70 in B. Roberts, ed., *Ciudadanía y Política Social.* San José: FLACSO/SSRC.
Rojas Bolaños, Manuel. 1979. *Lucha Social y Guerra Civil en Costa Rica.* San José: Editorial Porvenir.
Rovira Más, Jorge. 1982. *Estado y Política Económica en Costa Rica, 1948–1970.* San José: Editorial Porvenir.

———. 1985. *Costa Rica en los años 80*. San José: Editorial Porvenir.
Rueschemeyer, Dietrich, Evelyne Huber Stephens, and John D. Stephens. 1992. *Capitalist Development and Democracy*. Chicago: University of Chicago Press.
Safa, Helen. 1995. *The Myth of the Male Breadwinner: Women and Industrialization in the Caribbean*. Boulder, Colo.: Westview Press.
Safa, Helen, and Peggy Antrobus. 1992. "Women and the Economic Crisis in the Caribbean." Pp. 49–82 in Lourdes Benería and Shelley Feldman, eds., *Unequal Burden: Economic Crises, Persistent Poverty, and Women's Work*. Boulder, Colo.: Westview Press.
Schoepfle, Gregory, and Jorge Pérez-López. 1989. "Export Assembly Operations in Mexico and the Caribbean." *Journal of Inter-American Studies and World Affairs* 31 (Winter): 131–61.
Skocpol, Theda. 1985. "Bringing the State Back In: Strategies of Analysis in Current Research." Pp. 3–37 in P. Evans, D. Rueschemeyer, and T. Skocpol, eds., *Bringing the State Back In*. Cambridge: Cambridge University Press.
Skocpol, Theda, and Margaret Somers. 1980. "The Uses of Comparative History in Macrosocial Inquiry." *Comparative Studies in History and Society* 22, 2: 174–97.
Smith, Joan, and Immanuel Wallerstein, eds. 1992. *Creating and Transforming Households: The Constraints of the World-Economy*. Cambridge: Cambridge University Press.
Sojo, Carlos. 1991. *La Utopía del Estado Mínimo*. San José: CEPAS/CRIES.
———. 1992. *La Mano Visible del Mercado*. San José: CEPAS/CRIES.
Soto, Sergio R. 1982. *Capitalismo y Crisis Económica en Costa Rica*. San José: Editorial Porvenir.
Standing, Guy. 1989. "Global Feminization Through Flexible Labor." *World Development* 17: 1077–95.
———. 1991. "Structural Adjustment and Labor Market Policies." Pp. 5–51 in Guy Standing and Victor Tokman, eds., *Towards Social Adjustment: Labour Market Issues in Structural Adjustment*. Geneva: ILO.
Summers, Roberts, and Alan Heston. 1984. "Improved International Comparisons of Real Product and Its Composition, 1950–1980." *Review of Income and Wealth* 2 (June): 207–62.
———. 1991. "The Penn World Table (Mark 5): An Expanded Set of International Comparisons, 1950–1988." *Quarterly Journal of Economics* 2 (May): 327–68.
Tardanico, Richard. 1992. "Economic Crisis and Structural Adjustment: The Changing Labor Market of San José, Costa Rica." *Comparative Urban and Community Research* 4: 70–104.
Tardanico, Richard, and Mario Lungo. 1995. "Local Dimensions of Global Restructuring: Changing Labour Market Contours in Urban Costa Rica." *International Journal of Urban and Regional Research* 19, 2: 223–49.
———. 1997. "Continuities and Discontinuities in Costa Rican Urban Employment." Pp. 95–142 in R. Tardanico and R. Menjívar Larín, eds., *Global Restructuring, Employment, and Social Inequality in Urban Latin America*. Coral Gables, Fla.: North-South Center Press.
Tardanico, Richard, and Rafael Menjívar Larín, eds. 1997. *Global Restructuring, Employment, and Social Inequality in Urban Latin America*. Coral Gables, Fla.: North-South Center Press.
Tendler, Judith. 1997. *Good Government in the Tropics*. Baltimore: Johns Hopkins University Press.
Tilly, Chris, and Charles Tilly. 1998. *Work Under Capitalism*. Boulder, Colo.: Westview Press.

Tokman, Victor E. 1978. "An Exploration into the Nature of Informal-Formal Sector Relationships." *World Development* 6: 1065–75.
———. 1982. "Unequal Development and the Absorption of Labor in Latin America, 1950–1980." *CEPAL Review* 17: 121–33.
———. 1985. "The Process of Accumulation and the Weakness of the Protagonists." *CEPAL Review* 26: 115–26.
———. 1989a. "Economic Development and Labor Market Segmentation in the Latin America Periphery." *Journal of Inter-American Studies and World Affairs* 31 (Spring–Summer): 23–47.
———. 1989b. "Policies of Heterogeneous Informal Sector in Latin America." *World Development* 17: 1067–76.
———. 1991. "The Informal Economy in Latin America: From Underground to Legality." Pp. 141–60 in Guy Standing and Victor Tokman, eds., *Toward Social Adjustment: Labour Market Issues in Structural Adjustment*. Geneva: ILO.
Tokman, Victor E., ed. 1992. *Beyond Regulation: The Informal Economy in Latin America*. Boulder, Colo.: Lynne Rienner.
Torres Rivas, Edelberto. 1992. "Longeva Pero Lozana: Reflexiones sobre la Democracia en Costa Rica." *Documentos de Trabajo*, no. 13/92. San José: FLACSO.
Touraine, Alain. 1987. *Actores Sociales y Sistemas Políticos en América Latina*. Santiago: PREALC.
Trejos, Juan Diego. 1991. "Informalidad y Acumulación en el Area Metropolitana de San José, Costa Rica." Pp. 259–309 in R. Menjívar and J. P. Pérez Sáinz, eds., *Informalidad urbana en Centro América: Entre la acumulación y la subsistencia*. Caracas: Editorial Nueva Sociedad.
Ulate Quiros, Anabelle. 1992. "Exportaciones: Obsesión del Ajuste Estructural." In J. M. Villasuso, ed., *El Nuevo Rostro de Costa Rica*. Heredia: Cedal.
United Nations. 1989. *Prospects of World Urbanization*. New York: United Nations.
Valverde, José Manuel, María Eugenia Trejos, and Minor Mora. 1993. *La Movilidad Laboral al Descubierto*. San José: Universidad de Costa Rica.
Vincenzi, Atilio. 1991. *Código de Trabajo*. San José: Lehmann Editores.
Wade, Robert. 1990. *Governing the Market*. Princeton: Princeton University Press.
Weeks, John. 1991. "The Myth of Labor Market Clearing." Pp. 53–77 in Guy Standing and Victor E. Tokman, eds., *Towards Social Adjustment*. Geneva: ILO.
Weyland, Kurt. 1996. *Democracy Without Equity: Failures of Reform in Brazil*. Pittsburgh: University of Pittsburgh Press.
Wiarda, Howard J., and Michael J. Kryzanek. 1982. *The Dominican Republic: A Caribbean Crucible*. Boulder, Colo.: Westview Press.
Wilkie, James W., ed., Carlos Alberto Contreras and Catherine Komisarik, co-eds. 1995. *Statistical Abstract of Latin America*, vol. 31. Los Angeles: UCLA Latin American Center Publications.
Wilson, Bruce M. 1998. *Costa Rica: Politics, Economics, and Democracy*. Boulder, Colo.: Lynne Rienner.
World Bank. 1995. *World Development Report: Workers in an Integrating World*. Oxford: Oxford University Press.
———. 1997. *World Development Report, 1997: The State in a Changing World*. Oxford: Oxford University Press.
Yashar, Deborah J. 1997. *Demanding Democracy: Reform and Reaction in Costa Rica and Guatemala in 1870s–1950s*. Stanford: Stanford University Press.

Index

ACCION International, 157 n. 5
ADEMI. *See* Association for the Development of Microenterprises (ADEMI)
ADOPEM. *See* Dominican Association for Women's Development (ADOPEM)
American Federation of Labor-Congress of Industrial Organizations (AFL-CIO), 58–59
ANDA. *See* National Association of Craftsmen (ANDA)
Arias Sánchez, Oscar, 53
assembly manufacturing, 47, 74 n. 10
Association for the Development of Microenterprises (ADEMI), 155, 157, 157 n. 5
AVANCE, 156–57, 157 n. 5

Balaguer, Joaquín, 41–43, 45, 49–50, 58, 172
Bosch, Juan, 40–42, 42 n. 6

Cáceres, Ramón, 37
Calderón Fournier, Rafael Angel, 53 n. 13
Calderón Guardia, Rafael Angel, 38–39, 53 n. 13
capital accumulation, 9
capitalism, 1–2, 61
Carazo, Rodrigo, 52
Caribbean Basin Initiative (CBI), 48, 57
CBI. *See* Caribbean Basin Initiative (CBI)
CCSS. *See* Costa Rican Institute for Social Security (CCSS)
Central American Common Market, 44
centralized linkages, 127–28
clothing industry. *See* garment industry
commodity chains, 125–26
Communist Party (Costa Rica). *See* Popular Vanguard Party (PVP)
comparative research, 29–30
constitucionalistas (Dominican Republic), 41
cooperatives, 138
  linkage of, 127
  marketing, 166
Costa Rica. *See also* San José, Costa Rica
  as developmental-protective regulatory regime, 21–22
  development of state in, 35, 38–43
  effect of neoliberalism in, 57–58
  export-oriented policies of, 52–53
  gradualism in, 53–54
  import-substitution industrialization (ISI) in, 44, 46, 57
  labor absorption during ISI period in, 67–70
  labor laws in, 19–20, 58, 90–91, 171
  1980s economic crisis in, 52
  poverty data for, 54–55
  self-employed workers in, 64
  social security system in, 80–81
  social welfare expenditures in, 55–56
  socioeconomic characteristics of, 30–33
  state formation in, 37–38
  unions in, 21
  urban employment in 1980s in, 70–71
  U.S. foreign aid to, 54

Index

Costa Rican Institute for Social Security (CCSS), 55
crafts industry, 145–47

deregulation, 19
desahucio, 107, 107 n. 11
De Soto, Hernando, 7–8, 8 nn. 4–5, 173
  historical analysis of institutions by, 14
  role of state in informal economy, 10–11
development. *See* economic development
developmental states, 14–15
Development models. *See* export-oriented development (EOD) model; import-substitution industrialization (ISI)
Dominican Association for Women's Development (ADOPEM), 155, 156
Dominican Development Foundation (FDD), 155, 156
Dominican Institute for Integral Development (IDDI), 155, 156, 157 n. 6
Dominican Institute for Social Security. *See* Instituto Dominicano de Seguro Social (IDSS)
Dominican Republic. *See also* Santo Domingo, Dominican Republic
  development policies of, 45
  development of state in, 40–43
  early state formation in, 35–37
  economic policies in 1980s in, 48–49
  effect of neoliberalism in, 57–58
  export-oriented policies of, 47–50
  import-substitution industrialization (ISI) in, 44, 46
  import-substitution period of, 57
  labor absorption during ISI period in, 67–70
  labor laws in, 19–29, 58, 90–91
  labor legislation, 45
  migrant remittances to, 47–48, 48 n. 11
  modern state formation in, 38
  as predatory-repressive regulatory regime, 21–22
  reform efforts by Fernández administration in, 51
  self-employed workers in, 64
  social polarization of, 50–51
  social security system of, 50
  socioeconomic characteristics, 30–33
  underemployment in, 81
  unions in, 21
  urban employment in 1980s in, 70–71

Dominican Revolutionary Party (PRD), 40, 41, 48
Dunlop, John, 25

economic development, 177
  challenges of, 177
  purpose of, 177
elites, creation of informal sector and, 7–8
emigration, as survival technique, 109
entrepreneurs, informal sector and, 8
Evans, Peter, 14–15
export-free zones (EPZs), 48 n. 10, 137
  in Costa Rica, 52–53
  in Dominican Republic, 47
export-oriented development (EOD) model, 46, 70
exports. *See* trade

FAY. *See* Fundación Acción Ya (FAY)
FDD. *See* Dominican Development Foundation (FDD)
Fernández, Leonel, 43 n. 7, 51
Figueres, José (Don Pepe), 39, 40, 53 n. 13
Figueres Olsen, José María, 53 n. 13
flexibility, 125–26, 175
FONDOMICRO, 156, 156 n. 3
formal firms, commodity chains and, 125–26
Fundación Acción Ya (FAY), 157, 157 n. 6, 165 n. 21

garment industry, 131–39
gender discrimination, 98–99, 101, 111–12, 114, 171
globalization, 23, 147–51
Guzmán, Antonio, 48

Haiti, 37
Hart, Keith, 4
Hereaux, Ulises, 37
horizontal linkages, 128–29, 131–39
human capital, 97

IDSS. *See* Instituto Dominicano de Seguro Social (IDSS)
IMAS. *See* Institute for Social Assistance (IMAS)
import-substitution industrialization (ISI), 30
  in Costa Rica, 43–44, 46
  in Dominican Republic, 44, 46, 57
  labor absorption and, 66

income segmentation, 93–99, 171
industrialization, 61
  labor absorption and, 2
  role of state in, 6, 43–46
informal economy, 8 n. 5
  capital accumulation and, 9
  defined, 3–4, 8–9, 11–12, 63–64
  economic actors in, 93–94
  future of, 176–79
  heterogeneity of, 158–62
  idea measure of, 65–66
  job allocation in, 100–101
  operationalization of, 63–66
  origins of, 4–5
  as partial proletarianization process, 1–2
  research methodology for, 24–27
  role of states in, 7–8
  social networks and, 150–51
  state and, 7–8, 13–15
  state regulations and, 7–12
  structuralist approach to, 9
  surplus labor and, 62–63
informal firms
  commodity chains and, 125–26
  crafts linkages and, 145–47
  garment sector linkages, 131–39
  shoemaking industry linkages and, 139–45
informalization, 81–82
informal microenterprises, 154. *See also* microenterprises
  development policies for, 155–58
  globalization and, 147–51
informal producers. *See* microentrepreneurs
informal sector
  creation of, 7–8
  defined, 5
  entrepreneurs and, 8
  policy approaches to, 155
Institute for Social Assistance (IMAS), 157–58
Instituto Dominicano de Seguro Social (IDSS), 50, 78–79
integrated linkages, 127–29
International Labor Office (ILO), 5, 64
International Monetary Fund (IMF), 47–48, 49

job allocation, 100–101, 171
job creation, export-oriented model of development and, 70
Jorge Blanco, Salvador, 48–49

labor
  formal employment of, 2
  history of, 1–2
labor absorption, 170
  in Costa Rica during import-substitution period, 67–69
  in Dominican Republic during import-substitution period, 67–69
  import-substitution industrialization (ISI) and, 66
  industrialization and, 2
labor markets
  deregulation of Latin American, 18
  deregulation policies for, 174–76
  effects of legislation on, 17–18
  evolution of, in San José in 1980s, 73–75
  evolution of, in Santo Domingo in 1980s, 71–73
  regulation of, 15–16, 175
  regulatory regimes and, 98
  state deregulation of, 174–76
labor market segmentation
  defined, 87–88
  functional logics of, 88
  historical logics of, 88–89
  state regulation and, 113–16
  survey design for, 91–93
  theories of, 88
labor mobility
  in San José, 102–6
  in Santo Domingo, 106–13
labor regulations
  class structure and, 9–10
  effect of, on linkages, 136
  types of, 18–19
labor standards, 17
Latin America
  access to social services in, 178 n. 8
  class structure in, 10
  labor markets in, 18
  neoliberalism in, 57–58
  predatory versus developmental states in, 14–15
  role of state in, 6
  urban economies in, 5
lending programs, NGO, 160–61
linkages, 9
  cooperatives and, 127
  in crafts industry, 145–47
  in garment industry, 131–39

Index

(linkages, *continued*)
  horizontal, 128
  in informal microenterprises, 147–51
  integrated, 127–28
  in shoemaking industry, 139–45
  vertical, 128

maquilas, 52–53, 52 n. 12, 137
marginality, 4
marketing cooperatives, 166
markets. *See* labor markets
mercantilist states, 7–8
microenterprises, 64–65
  informal, 147–51, 154, 155–58
microentrepreneurs, developing social capital of, 164–67
migrant remittances, 47–48, 48 n. 11
mobility, labor market, 101–2
  in San José, 102–6
  in Santo Domingo, 106–13
Monge Alvarez, Luis Alberto, 53

NAFTA. *See* North American Free Trade Agreement (NAFTA)
National Association of Craftsmen (ANDA), 164–65
National Liberation Party (PLN), 39, 40, 44–45
National Program for the Micro and Small Enterprise (PRONAMYPE), 157
neoinformality, 6
neoliberalism, 57–58
neopatrimonial regimes, 36–37, 36 n. 4
neo-utilitarian arguments, to state intervention, 8
networks, social, 9, 139–45
NGOs. *See* nongovernment organizations (NGOs)
nongovernment organizations (NGOs), 155
  in Costa Rica, 156–57
  lending programs of, 160–61
North American Free Trade Agreement (NAFTA), 57, 74 n. 10

Ochomongo, battle of, 37
Oficina Nacional de Planificación (ONAPLAN), 77
open unemployment, 75
organized labor. *See* unions
Otavalo, Ecuador, 127

Partido Revolucionario Dominicano. *See* Dominican Revolutionary Party (PRD)
paternalistic regulations, 19
Penn World Tables, 33 n. 33
Pérez Sáinz, Juan Pablo, 5–6, 126–27
peripheral states, 13
Peru, as mercantilist state, 14
Picado Michalski, Teodoro, 38
PLN. *See* National Liberation Party (PLN)
Popular Vanguard Party (PVP), 38
Portes, Alejandro, 7, 94, 172–73
  class typology in Latin America by, 10
  definition of informal economy, 8–9
  role of state in analysis by, 13–14
  role of state in informal economy, 10–11
poverty
  data for Costa Rica, 54–55
  informal economy and, 167
  labor market deregulation and, 174–76
PRD. *See* Dominican Revolutionary Party (PRD)
PREALC. *See* Programa Regional de Empleo para América Latina y el Caribe (PREALC)
Prebisch, Raúl, 5
predatory states, 14
production
  organization of, 125–27
  types of linkages for, 127–31
Programa Regional de Empleo para América Latina y el Caribe (PREALC), 5
proletarianization, 1–2, 7, 61
PRONAMYPE. *See* National Program for the Micro and Small Enterprise (PRONAMYPE)
protective regulations, 19
Puente Alto, Honduras, 149
PVP. *See* Popular Vanguard Party (PVP)

Reagan, Ronald, 47–48
regulatory regimes, 169–70, 173
  classifications, 20–24
  labor market structure and, 98
Reid Cabral, Donald, 41
remittances, migrant, 47, 48 n. 11
repressive regulations, 19

sanes, 110
San José, Costa Rica, 62. *See also* Costa Rica; Santo Domingo, Dominican Republic
  income segmentation in, 93–99

informal economy in, 22–23, 94–96
informal workers in, 111
labor market mobility in, 102–6
labor markets in, 170
labor market structure in, 114–16
labor market trends of 1980s in, 73–75
open unemployment in, 75
underemployment in, 79–80
San Pedro Sacatepequez, Guatemala, 149
Santo Domingo, Dominican Republic, 62.
    See also Dominican Republic; San José, Costa Rica
    income segmentation in, 93–99
    informal economy in, 22, 94–96, 171
    informal workers in, 111
    labor market mobility in, 106–13
    labor markets in, 170
    labor market structure in, 114–16
    labor market trends of 1980s in, 71–73
    open unemployment in, 75
    underemployment in, 77–78
segmentation. *See also* labor market segmentation
    income, 93–99
    job allocation, 100–101
    labor market mobility and, 101–2
self-employment, 64–65
    programs for, 163–64
severance payments, 107, 107 n. 11
shoemaking industry, 139–45
social citizenship, 153–54, 167, 178–79
social networks, 9
    informal economy and, 150–51
    shoemaking industry and, 139–45
social security systems
    access to, 178 n. 8
    in Costa Rica, 80–81
    in Dominican Republic, 50, 78–79
Standing, Guy, 18–19
state, the
    defined, 12–13
    historical analysis of institutions of, 14
    informal economy and, 7–8, 13–15, 164–65
    as institutional actor, 12–13

peripheral, 13
predatory versus developmental, 14–15
reproduction of labor force and, 15–20
role of, 6, 6 n. 3, 7
state employment, 76–77, 76 n. 12
state intervention, neo-utilitarian arguments to, 8
state regulations
    informal economy and, 7–12, 9
    labor market segmentation and, 113–16
structural approach, to informal economy, 9, 13–14
surplus labor, informal economy and, 62–63
survival techniques, 109

textile industry. *See* garment industry
Tokman, Victor E., 18
tourism, 145
    in Dominican Republic, 47
trade. *See also* export-free zones (EPZs)
    Costa Rica and, 52–53
    Dominican Republic and, 47–48
trade unions. *See* unions
Trujillo Molina, Rafael Leonidas, 40, 45, 68
TURCASA, 165, 165 n. 20

Ulate Blanco, Otilio, 39
Ulate-Figueres Pact, 39
underemployment
    in Dominican Republic, 81
    in San José, 79–80
    in Santo Domingo, 77–78
unemployment, 75
unions
    in Costa Rica, 21, 58–59
    in Dominican Republic, 21
United States
    Caribbean Basin Initiative, 48
    Dominican migration policies, 48 n. 11

Vanguardia Popular Party. *See* Popular Vanguard Party (PVP)
vertical linkages, 128–29

wage determination, 97